YANKEE SHIPS IN CHINA SEAS

As we use a glass to examine the form of things so we must study the past to understand the present.

CONFUCIUS

HOUQUA (1769-1843), THE SENIOR HONG MERCHANT AT CANTON
Portrait by George Chinnery

YANKEE SHIPS
IN
CHINA SEAS

*Adventures of Pioneer Americans
in the Troubled Far East*

BY

DANIEL M. HENDERSON

Essay Index Reprint Series

BOOKS FOR LIBRARIES PRESS
FREEPORT, NEW YORK

INTERNATIONAL STANDARD BOOK NUMBER:
0-8369-1950-5

LIBRARY OF CONGRESS CATALOG CARD NUMBER:
76-128258

PRINTED IN THE UNITED STATES OF AMERICA

To the

Young Men and Women of America

and China

Who Worked, Fought, and Died

in

World War II

That the Open Door, the Square Deal,

the Free Voice,

and Friendly Cooperation

Might Prevail

Among the Countries of the

Pacific

CONTENTS

BOOK TWO

THE SHIP OF STATE IN THE FAR EAST

ILLUSTRATIONS

FOREWORD

THE AUTHOR IS a story-teller who discovers his themes and characters in history. His imagination provides the epic of an expedition, and by patient research he assembles the characters, events, and incidents that go to make up the procession from pioneer days to the present.

Fiction has no place in this book. After discovering a character essential to his planned narrative, he consulted biographies, memoirs, and family papers to give a faithful and live portrayal. He has listened for heart-beats, opened his senses to spice, looked for Yankee and Oriental tricks and practices, and probed for character.

Business enterprises, life in shipyards and at sea, missionary adventures, and social and family life in the Far East have been covered.

An important part of the story, the author considers, is his sketching of the successful challenge made by our first ships to the monopoly of the British East India Company and his account of the growth of the great American commission houses, especially Russell and Company, the Yankee commercial octopus of the Far East.

Those who have read the author's recently-published book *From the Volga to the Yukon,* will see that while this is an entirely independent volume, it is yet a companion book in that it covers a vast trek.

Crowded with men adventurers within and without the law, *Yankee Ships in China Seas* has its gentler side. The work of the Church appears; the dramatic story of the poet Camoens is told; Chinese philosophy and art are noted, and women have their place. The scope of women characters is wide and varied, from the devoted young wife risking sickness and attack among savagely superstitious people to the grand if gory person Madame Ching, ruler of pirate hordes.

The book deals chiefly with Chinese history before the birth of its Republic, but as an example of the significance of history we point to the chapter about Commissioner Humphrey Marshall and the Taiping

xiii

Rebellion. This revolt foreshadowed the modern revolution that changed China into a progressive Republic.

Whatever repellent pictures of Chinese life appear in the story should not be considered as representing life in China today. They may instead be taken as a basis from contrasting life under the decadent Manchu rulers with life after the coming of Sun Yat-sen.

There is no political motive behind the book, except to show by the human narrative the linking of China with the United States and to intimate that the developed American policy of an Open Door in China, and a square deal for her among the powers, is a wise course for the future.

BOOK ONE

China Ho!

OPIUM CLIPPERS

Where are the opium ships—gulls of the Indian seas?
Where are the clippers that mated the gale?
Ships of the baleful flower, stealing from Singapore,
Mocking the brigs of war slow on their trail?

Where is the Waterwitch? *Where does the* Kelpie *flit?*
Where scuds the Falcon—*under what stars?*
Where is the Antelope—*who, when the pirates swarmed,*
Sailed with the yellow thieves hung to her spars?

Where are the men of iron, filling the topsail yards
While yet the ocean seethes from the typhoon—
Skippers who held their ships dearer than dancing girls
In Shanghai taverns or dives of Rangoon?

Where went the Ariel? *Where sails the* Wild Dayrell?
Where is the beauty that knew not it sinned?
Search for the rainbow that painted the stormy mist—
"Where flies the spindrift? Where went the wind?"

DANIEL HENDERSON
in *Frontiers*

CHAPTER I

A Soldier of the Revolution Takes to the Sea

Captain Green spoke. "Mr. Mate, are you all ready?"

"All ready, sir."

"Then heave ahead!"

"Aye, aye, sir. Man the windlass!"

Experienced sailors, roaring a chantey, and green hands joined in a stumbling ring around the capstan. The windlass turned. The chain cable came up and clanked on deck, and the ship went forward to meet the taut chain.

Then the first officer sent the crew aloft.

"Let fall and sheet home topsail and top gallant sail."

The ship *Empress of China* was setting out from New York via the Canaries and Capetown for Canton, China. The year was 1784. The War for Independence had been won, and this ship was going out to bring in some of the first fruits of it. British frigates were no longer a barrier on the Atlantic Coast of America. The freed colonists had renewed their taste for tea, but now, being independent, they wanted it brought to them in their own vessels, and were eager for their skippers to try out the temper of the British in the Far East, whose East India Company monopolized the tea trade.

New York, center of West Indian shipping, wanted to be first in the East Indian and China trade. Aware of proposed Oriental ventures in Boston, Salem, Philadelphia, and Baltimore, her merchants had hurried to take shares in the enterprise of shipper Daniel Parker, who wanted to bring to America the first cargo of tea direct from Canton.

The Philadelphia financier, Robert Morris, friend of George Washington and backer of the Revolution, was joining the Manhattan merchants. He was one of those who invested a total of

3

$120,000 in the Oriental enterprise and he would soon send his own ships to the Far East.

Captain John Green, Jr., commander of the *Empress,* was a man of note among the skippers of the Chesapeake. He had met the British in the Atlantic, and could be depended on in the Far East to do business with or evade them, as the occasion required.

There had been a grave conference in the South Street office of Daniel Parker as to who should be selected as supercargo for the voyage. The profits of the venture would depend on how shrewdly the chosen man sold the outgoing cargo and purchased the home-coming tea.

Merchant Parker had a candidate—Major Samuel Shaw of Boston, who had been a member of the staff of General Knox and at times attached to the staff of Commander-in-Chief George Washington. A gallant soldier, Shaw had been efficient in an executive capacity and carried as treasured trophies highly commendatory letters from Washington and Knox.

Robert Morris, who while entertaining Washington had met Major Shaw, supported Parker's recommendation.

Shaw had come out of the meeting of welcoming New Yorkers with a feeling of guilt. He had been stationed near Manhattan during the war, and had written home that its citizens were a mixed and greedy lot. But today they were giving him an opportunity his beloved town of Boston had not come forward with, and at his request, had also accepted his comrade-in-arms Thomas Randall.

Sailing a proud ship on a glorious venture, the pair of New Englanders wished that they could boast of a splendid cargo instead of a hold full of the herb ginseng. It was awkward to explain, especially to the refined ladies of Boston, the reason why it was calculated that ginseng would sell well in China. Those fat, luxurious mandarins—captains of East Indiamen had said—were as fond as Solomon of wives and concubines, and were always adding a new little Peach Bloom or Lotus Flower to their carnal collection. They needed the invigorating, rejuvenating herb ginseng.

4

Escorted out of the harbor by the share-holders, cheered by the townspeople, saluted by the Grand Battery, the *Empress of China* had left the bustling Old City Dock, and was sailing across the Atlantic to take the course of the China-bound British East Indiamen.

Supercargo Shaw and his comrade Randall would have been pleased if they could have read what a newspaper of the rival port of Baltimore—no doubt with some consideration for Captain Green, Baltimorean—had printed about their voyage.

". . . The Captain and crew, with several young American adventurers, were all happy and cheerful, in good health and high spirits; and with a becoming decency, elated on being considered the first instruments, in the hands of Providence, who have undertaken to extend the commerce of the United States of America to that distant, and to us unexplored country."

The newspaper, however, had made a slight error. The far eastern coasts had been explored long before by colonial Americans whose business was buccaneering instead of trade.

It is a mischievous thing to do, but the sea historian, noting the compliments made in this editorial, must need say that the sailors were pioneers only in the fact that their visit to the Far East was an honest one. Long before, there had been other men from America, although unscrupulous ones, who had made the journey.

The first Americans to visit the Orient were men from Massachusetts, Rhode Island, and New York who sailed as pirates during King William's War, 1689-97. Leaving their routes in the Atlantic, these sailors crossed the equator, sailed down the African coast, doubled the Cape of Good Hope, and navigated the Indian Ocean.

Returning to their native ports with their plunder, they astonished the townsmen by their rich foreign attire—"a broad crimson sash across the left shoulder, a laced cap, fancy jacket, white knickerbockers, a heavy gold chain, and no less than three or four richly-mounted pistols in a gaudy belt."

They had good Saxon names, these pirates—Captain Want, William Mews, Thomas Tew, Captain Mission. They brought the first Oriental goods to the United States, sharing the honor with Captain Kidd, who in 1699 brought in with other things "40 bails of East India goods."

The *Empress* touched at the Canaries, then followed the route of the big East Indiamen.

The Indian Ocean ... the weather almost unbearably hot. The pitch oozed from the seams of the deck. The sun overhead seemed to be trying to burn up the ship that dared to sail that brassy expanse of water. The air remained mercilessly clear and calm and day after day the sun beat down. The coppery clouds on the horizon were tantalizingly impotent. The ship, caught in cross currents, spun round and round.

The going was rough off Java Head. Against a head wind and an adverse tide a ship must often beat for several days till she made the great headlands of western Java and anchored in Angier Roads; but when the winds were brisk and blew from aft, ten knots were often made.

Used to the waters off the New England coast, or Cape Hatteras, the American skipper watched calmly the "mountain waves" come curving and frothing down upon the vessel. His ship was built to withstand this weight of water, and though the thud of the wave was as heavy as if the vessel had struck a reef, the men clung to their places on deck and shook off the spattering spray as spaniels shake off the rain; but they were glad when the cry "Land!" called them to watch the majestic outlines of Java Head rise out of the storm-gray waters.

The feared Straits of Sunda opened, and the ship, alert to repel pirates, passed close to the dense green forests hemming the water. The fact that the log of the *Empress* is clean of pirate attacks in these waters is no indication that other ships whose logs we will explore would be similarly fortunate.

The Malays, their fierceness fired by white crews from Europe who had scooped Malay boatmen out of the water to sell as slaves, or had made raids ashore and ravished the tribesmen's wives and daughters, would exact vengeance from white men's ships until the cannon of frigates cowed the rajahs and proa-men.

6

WHAMPOA REACH
By a Chinese artist about 1855

A CHINESE FORT ON PEARL RIVER
By a Chinese artist of the 19th Century

VIEW OF THE PRAYA GRANDE AT MACAO
By a Chinese artist about 1840

THE GARDENS OF HOUQUA
By a Chinese artist of the early 19th century

Glad to be greeted with offerings of bananas and pineapples instead of guns and krisses, Shaw and Randall made friends with the native boatmen and wrote home that one great hazard of the voyage had been passed in safety.

Harriet Low, who many years later went to Macao to visit her uncle in the Chinese trade, came this way in the ship *Sumatra,* which also anchored in Sunda Straits. The daring young lady kept a lively diary, published later by her daughter Katharine Hilliard under the title "My Mother's Journal."

No prude was Harriet, and when boats came out, and naked Malays stood up in them to offer foodstuffs to the voyagers, she did not retreat.

"I suppose," she wrote to her sister at home, "you will like to know what I thought of a Malay, and how my modesty could stand such a shock as seeing a man unclad, but I agree with Bishop Heber in thinking their color serves as a covering. They seem like a different race of beings."

When sailing up the Java shore, the crew of the *Empress* had sighted two vessels, and had hoisted the American ensign, after which the vessels showed the French colors. The Yankees, grateful to the French for having assured American independence, gladly dropped anchor beside them.

One was the *Triton,* whose armament had been reduced for this commercial mission to sixteen light cannon. She carried 184 men. The other was the *Fabius,* without guns, carrying 36 men.

Going aboard the *Triton,* Shaw, Randall, and Green were graciously received by the commander, M. d'Ordelin, a chevalier of St. Louis.

There being no official East India Company in France, the king had lent these warships to a company of merchants, with d'Ordelin in charge. He informed Major Shaw, who had been one of the organizers of the Society of the Cincinnati, that the French monarch had granted permission to the Marquis de Lafayette to join the order and accept its honors. The Americans were equally delighted to meet the captain of the *Fabius,* M. Cordez, for he had served with the Count de Grasse's fleet in the Chesapeake.

7

Lacking port facilities, needing charts, Captain Green of the *Empress* felt it a gift of good fortune to fall in with the amiable French officers and to be invited to voyage to Canton in their company.

Jonathan and Jacques, dining and wining together, toasted each other's country for the victory over King George, mourning together that the British had entrenched themselves at the expense of other countries in the East Indies. Grant the Englishmen that the sun never sets on their dominion, it was high time, Shaw said, for the Oriental sun to shine on the sails of Yankees coming to take cargoes directly to American ports, free of British charges.

Setting sail, d'Ordelin, proud of his seamanship, challenged Captain Green to an adventure. The usual route from that point was through the Straits of Banca, but the French commander said that a countryman M. Gaspar, had found and navigated a strait more to the eastward. Captain Green said, "Lead on." The first sounding showed only five and a half instead of the expected twelve fathoms, but a second sounding discovered the deeper channel marked on M. Gaspar's chart and the passage was made safely.

Leaving Gaspar Island behind them with its medley of frogs and cooing pigeons, the ships made a trail of foam on the phosphorescent waters of the China Sea.

The blue and white trail was ending. Breezes blew them across a smooth sea. The lookout sighted the Lima Isles, close to Macao. Chinese junks were sighted, and soon the *Empress* came to anchor in Macao.

CHAPTER II

Curious Business at the Port of Canton

MACAO, THE PORTUGUESE-CHINESE city where Occident and Orient meet; the town whose harbor resembles the exquisite Bay of Naples . . . weary of the sea, the fascinated Yankees hired sedan chairs and traveled up past the blue, green, red, and yellow houses which, seen across the bulwarks of the ship, had been so attractive.

The garden courts of the old typhoon-beaten houses, and the

latticed verandas with their green and blossomy vines, were both an invitation and a heartache to the homesick travelers.

No white man intent on transacting business with Chinese merchants stayed long at Macao. It was rather a place for recreation after one had finished his trading at the port of Canton, and so Shaw was soon inquiring as to how to get to Whampoa—the "Yellow Anchorage" of Canton.

Cleared by the moustached Portuguese custom house guard who stood beside his four-gun battery in the middle of the pier, Shaw employed a chattering moon-faced youth as pilot. Promptly the guide fastened the sampan, containing his wife and infant, to the *Empress of China*. Very proud in his suit of fine grass-cloth, the coolie assumed authority as sailing-master, and started the *Empress* on her way, with the little boat bobbing in her wake.

Where the shores of two islands came close, forming the fortress Bogue or Tiger's Head, the *Empress* passed, and came into the river proper.

What a chattering rose on the houseboats as the ship with its foreign devils went by! It was as if travelers in a tropical forest had disturbed flocks of macaws and parakeeets.

Following a tortuous path through fish-stakes driven into the bed of the river, the gondola passed between large elaborately-ornamented trading junks of a kind glimpsed off the coasts of India and Siam, and Shaw began to realize that the Chinese are as much of a seafaring race as the British, Portuguese, or Americans. It was remarkable that these junks had matting or bamboo sails, were equipped with wooden anchors, and were moored to the wharf at both ends with grass cables.

From such journeys, observed the later traveler, Osmond Tiffany, Jr., "the Chinese sailor becomes morally convinced, from the authority of old navigators, and from his own clear, unerring judgment, that the Celestial Empire, is favored of heaven, the centre of the earth, which is itself flat and square, not at all the round orange that lying barbarians have tried to make him believe it is; that the English are savages from a little island in one of the four corners of the earth; and that America, if he ever heard of such a spot, is about as large as Macao."

9

"There!" The Yankees were catching sight of flags of foreign nations flying above nesting ships—flags that seemed like sunset streaks against the misty sky. With ardor and pride they raised the circled stars of the flag of the New Republic among the ancient emblems.

Salutes were being fired. Whether or not the newcomers were sincerely welcomed, the courtesies of the sea were being observed.

The *Empress* found herself in company with dozens of ships from ports in Europe, whose custom was to come in the autumn and give their canvas the advantage of the southwest winds. Most of them would wait at their Canton anchorage until spring, and would have the northeast winds to fill their sails.

Spick and span were the shipmasters who came to greet the Yankees. They wore white hats of light cork, white linen clothes, and clean canvas shoes, and their garb was quickly adopted by the newcomers.

Free to go ashore, Shaw and Randall were envied by the grumbling crews, who for the sake of good relations were forced to live aboard their vessel under the scorching sun. The sailors' evening pleasures awaited them in the floating bagnios and gambling boats anchored near them. Devout elders of the crew, who had experiences with the tawny Circes of the West Indies, warned green young sailors to shut their eyes and ears to the call of the Flower Boats, but many a curious youngster was carried along by avid companions.

They were stormed at once at Whampoa by three waves of native solicitors: the compradores who wished to supply fresh provisions; the washerwomen whose tub was the filthy river; and the quack-doctors who hoped that the crew was succumbing to the fever-breeding air from the mud banks.

The puzzled harbor-mandarins called the Americans the New People; and when a factory was assigned to them at Canton, and the newly-created American banner flew above it, the Chinese admired the colorful quadrangle of stripes and the circle of stars in a blue field in the corner, and named it the "Flowery Flag." Then, because all foreigners were devils to the celestials, they called the Americans, the "Flowery Flag Devils."

It was in the day of Major Shaw as it was afterwards in the time of Commander Norman of the British ship *Martello Tower*. The calendar changes but the ways of women do not alter. Norman's experience with a pert young washer-woman was the experience of all officers arriving at Whampoa.

Saucy and self-possessed, she appeared in the door of the stateroom, and pidgin talk began:

"What you wantee?"

"I wash gal, sar; how you?"

"Welly, thank you; what name you?"

"Mine Missy Teapot."

"How much chargee?"

"Four da hun'." ($4 a hundred)

"You make good starchee?"

"Oh sar! You tinkee me foolo? Me washa closy plenty maysun sips (merchant ships). Me washa closy alla plopa!"

"Very well," said the officer, "here is the bag. Bring closy back starchee alla plopa. Chin-chin, Miss Teapot!"

"Chin-chin sar."

It was fascinating to see among these varied river craft the long, sharp beautiful mandarin boats—the revenue cutters of China—armed with a long gun in the bow and swivel guns along the sides. Like the galleys of the ancient world, they were manned by rowers, under whose rhythmic strokes the boats moved swiftly. The big red eye painted on the bow was blind to justice. Shielded by the matting thrown over a pole that ran from stem to stern, the mandarin owner loafed in his chair, chewing betel, and looking for chances to plunder the people of river and shore under pretext of collecting taxes. Yankees who were to follow Shaw would have engagements with these mandarins and galleys.

Towering pagodas, darkened by weather and moldering with age, rose before the absorbed Yankees. Two of them lifted from high locations, and their nine octagonal stories dominated the landscape. Erected during the thirteenth and fourteenth centuries, their builders believed them powerful in suppressing demons, and that the higher they were, the mightier the effect. But they had not prevented the coming of the Portuguese, Dutch, and English "devils"—and now the American "devils" were passing them with impunity.

But even though Whampoa, the anchorage of Canton, had been achieved, Canton city itself was the goal. The Americans were impatient to meet the merchants, get on with their work, and turn the season to profit.

Hiring a new pilot, they followed him to a sort of large boat which was worked by rowers on a platform in front, while at the stern the master plied a heavy scull. Between them the passengers sat in a neat, ornamented apartment. Glass sashes shielded them from the wind and green blinds shut out the blinding sun.

From inside the craft issued a pungent odor. Investigating, the passengers discovered that sticks of sandalwood were being burnt at a shrine in which were little gilded images decorated with colored paper. Faced by the costly demands of their religion that they keep offerings of food before the tablets of their ancestors, the boatmen had been forced through poverty to substitute paper tokens.

Every man aboard the thronging junks and sampans was a weather prophet, and foreigners could tell if the weather was to be fair or stormy by the way the boats spread over the river in good weather and huddled together along the shore when a gale threatened. Most absorbing of all sights was the river alive with Chinese humanity.

Our young men from the Occident, used to Western standards of decency, were abashed by the human life of the river. The shores and sampans seemed to be spawning places rather than a region where children are individually born and bred. Three generations often lived in a junk or sampan, the little clan having multiplied in a time so short as to be incredible to white people.

Teeming was the word for these people of poverty who lived along the river and knew no other home than a sampan from birth to death. Teeming also were the meadows one glimpsed, for thousands of industrious natives, men and women, could be seen harvesting the crops regardless of the blaze of the sun. Other groups, less priviliged than the field laborers, searched the shores for shellfish and reptiles to feed on. In the struggle of the multitudes for existence, any creature or plant out of which nourishment could be squeezed was valued.

The Emperor of China had granted a monopoly of the foreign trade of China, carried on at the one open port of Canton to a group of wealthy, responsible merchants called the Co-Hong. Licensed by the emperor to be the guarantors of foreign merchants, these brokers, called hong merchants looked for honesty in their clients, and matched it with trustworthiness. The dean of the hong had paid $200,000 for his privileges.

With amused interest, the Yankee partners studied the names of hong merchants from among whom they must select a customs agent. The names they bore were official titles. When a customer addressed Mr. Mouqua, Mr. Pinqua, or Mr. Houqua, he might be addressing Mr. Mutual Advantage, Mr. Good Profits, or Mr. Harmonious Relations. The same system of naming applies to the goods in which the firm dealt. The peculiar Chinese name of a firm's brand of tea might mean Cheerful Prospects.

The merchant Pinqua had been recommended, and Shaw and Randall found the way to his hong or factory. They went down a narrow street, crossed a stone bridge, took a few turns, and came to a heavy gate ornamented with brilliant figures and adorned by great lanterns. From a little table at the entrance where the gatekeeper sat keeping count of the entering coolies and their chests of tea, to the interior section where tea chests covered a half-acre, the hong offered a pageant of the tea industry which the Yankees grasped keenly.

There were long aisles of tea chests, and immense scales for weighing tea; and where the light came into the fullest, tables were placed for the superintendents. In another part of the hong, foreign commission merchants were being shown a newly-arrived shipment of tea.

The tea inspector or taster was busy at his fragrant trade. Coolie-attendants, opening containers, brought to his table samples selected from the various chests. The newcomers watched him take a handful, smell it repeatedly, chew some of it, and then write his verdict in a huge folio; so devoted he had been to the smelling, that bits of the flowery pekoe, souchong, or hyson clung to the tip of his nose.

13

Clapping his hands with the mystery of an elderly Aladdin, Pinqua summoned Chinese boys who came quickly with tea and almond cakes. While they ate they chatted, the interpreter being an excellent one.

It was humiliating for scholarly Samuel Shaw, who prided himself on his elegant writing and correct speech, to have to resort to "pidgin English" to get along with the Chinese merchants. How ridiculous to do business with the natives using such talk as "How muchee" and "Me sellee."

Yet he soon learned that it was either this baby-talk or sign language. In its fear of the foreigners, the Government had decreed that no Chinese should teach his language to a foreigner. The "pidgin" chatter was the merchant's way of getting around the edict.

Having studied in "the Athens of America," Shaw had felt himself equal to any occasion. Now, however, he had met more than his match in the merchant Pinqua, who spoke, not to exhibit knowledge but to pass on the wisdom of the past. The Major took to heart certain rules of conduct set forth by the hong-merchant from the teachings of Confucius.

"Why," he said afterwards to the equally-impressed Randall, "it was as simple as Mother Goose's 'The House That Jack Built' and yet how profound!"

"The ancients," said Pinqua, "wishing to illustrate illustrious virtue throughout the Empire, first ordered well their own states.

"Wishing to order well their own states, they first regulated their families.

"Wishing to regulate their families, they first cultivated their persons.

"Wishing to cultivate their persons, they first cultivated their hearts.

"Wishing to rectify their hearts, they first sought to be sincere in their thoughts.

"Wishing to be sincere in their thoughts, they first extended to the utmost their knowledge. Such extension of knowledge lay in the investigations of things."

It appeared to Major Shaw that the Chinese, in repelling foreign ideas, had turned their backs on the teachings of the great sage but he and his successors were to meet a number of tradition-steeped mandarins who were yet hospitable to ideas from the western world. Pinqua was one of these; in fact, all of the hong merchants were keenly progressive and world-minded.

Of one of these portly hong-merchants, Synchong, Master Ward of the *Minerva* wrote: "... a close-fisted old miser, gets drunk every day but performs his contracts and whatever you can bind him to."

Yes, Pinqua said when they began to talk business, he would be happy to take care of the business of the *Empress of China,* and to obtain for its shipmaster every possible privilege.

First there must be the ceremony of "Cumsha and Measurement" which would be performed at the Whampoa anchorage by the Hoppo himself. "The Hoppo," he explained, "is the Government's highest official—appointed by his Celestial Majesty as superintendent of the foreign trade of Canton."

Arrangements concluded, the Americans went back to the ship to await the coming of the great customs official. Captain Green made the ship spick and span, and bade his steward to provide the kind of refreshments that would most highly please the great mandarin. With a new flag flying, and the crew dressed in their best clothes—they watched the river traffic for the Hoppo's party.

He came with gongs sounding, the river craft scattering before his prow as ducks before a pelican. Out of the hubbub of the stream his huge ten-oared barge drew alongside the *Empress.* The great banner of the Chinese Dragon, streaming above the brilliant pennants of the barge, greeted the flag of the New People.

Heading a gorgeous procession, he came aboard wearing a purple silk spencer lined with costly fur to shield him from the chill of the river. Underneath it he wore a robe of gaily embroidered blue crepe trimmed with glossy sea otter fur—perhaps part of the cargo the crew of Captain Cook brought from the Alaskan coast. He strode in yellow leggings.

Shaw and Randall had rehearsed their greetings, and the linguist loaned them by Pinqua was at their side.

"Hail, hail!" they cried. "Does the honorable great man enjoy

15

happiness?" May nothing becloud your family's majesty. How many worthy young gentlemen (sons) have you?"

From the pleased Hoppo came a stream of gracious ejaculations, ending with "How may I presume to receive your honorable reception? Are the personages in the new ship well?"

These salutations exchanged, the high customs official got down to business. His attendants, scattering, ran a measuring tape from stern to stem, and took the ship's breadth amidships.

The partners hid their concern as fee after fee were added to the original measurement. One hundred percent more for "cumsha"; fifty percent more for the Hoppo; ten percent to the Superintendent of the Treasury; ten percent to cover transport of duty to Peking and weighing in Government scales; seven percent to cover differences in weights between Peking and Canton—a grand sum of well over $3000.

Pinqua having guaranteed payment of this sum, the Hoppo permitted the crew to open the cargoes and begin to discharge the cargo into the sampans that would carry it to the hong.

Down into the cabin for refreshments went the Hoppo and the victims, the sage Pinqua and his servants having suggested the delicacies the port official would relish. For all the feasting, however, it could be detected that the mandarin was unsatisfied. Seeing what was expected, Captain Green brought forth a Salem ship's clock. The delighted official stowed the gift up a capacious sleeve and departed majestically.

British East India Company officials stationed at Canton faced a new problem in trade diplomacy when the *Empress of China* arrived. They did not expect formidable competition from the Yankees. The Company had powerfully intrenched itself in the important ports of the Far East.

They hoped that Supercargo Shaw, who was strangely stiff for a supposedly liberal Bostonian, had studied the ancient and honorable history of their company.

Shaw *had* studied it and, desiring success for Americans in the Far East, was hoping that it was ancient and honorable enough to be weakened.

Here was a company that was really the monarch of Great

Britain in India and China. In 1600, the ministers of the declining Elizabeth had permitted a group of merchants to incorporate under this name to bring spices, dyes, tea, coffee, and jewels from India and the East Indies.

To obtain cargoes, the Company must control princes and ports; to conquer where needed, it must transport regiments. Though nominally subject to the crown and the British parliament, the monopoly became the most powerful influence in the empire, creating opportunities for adventure and wealth for both the nobility and the common people.

Joseph Child, head of the East India Company, in the reign of Charles II, gave that monarch, for the Company, a gift of ten thousand guineas, and though he had started life as a clerk in a London counting-room, Child, thereafter, became an associate of royalty.

When Clive committed suicide in 1774, he had made the Company the unofficial monarch of Bengal and other rich provinces. It ruled as the unofficial king of the Far East until its operations and cargoes hurt the conscience of the larger company of English people whose violent protests against the monopoly would sway the Parliament.

It is scarcely to be wondered at that the officials of this proud and mighty company were somewhat cool to the two unimportant Yankee officers who had come to China in company with the despised French.

Arriving in China with a chip on his shoulders against the British, Shaw had taken offense when Mr. Browne, the chief official of the British East India Company slighted him at Macao.

He was still resentful when the officials of the Company welcomed him and his American friends at Canton. Though he accepted their formal invitation to dine with them, he went rigidly.

The Chief of the East India Company for India and China had the rank of Baronet. He came to Canton in October from India and stayed until April, following the course of the monsoons. The China offices were allowed 100,000 pounds sterling annually for expenses, and the Chief's compensation, including emoluments, was 25,000 pounds.

Three supercargoes resided at Canton under the Chief, and there was a complete service of secretaries, chaplains, surgeons, tea-inspectors, writers, etc. After the families of these were admitted, they composed the British social life of Canton.

The Chief resided in the main British factory and the staff in a half-dozen factories in the rear of the compound. In the center of the front was the great hall, which opened on the terrace. It was a room so large that the entire community could be assembled at one time, leaving space for three times that number. At one end of the assembly room hung a grand full-length portrait of George IV, and at the other end, one of Ambassador, Lord Amherst. In the rear of the hall was the chapel, and a tower with clock and bells.

It was, he admitted, a privilege to be a guest in the dining-room of the Company, whose predominant feature was a long massive mahogany table set with heavy, highly-ornamented pieces. There was a nice blending of English and Chinese porcelains. Chandeliers, hanging like huge pears, lighted the delicacies of the silken Chinese hangings and screens.

The ceremonious British hosts could scarcely reconcile themselves to greeting former subjects of His Majesty as citizens of a free country, and the visitors could scarcely bring themselves to join in the toasts to the King. Shaw suspected that George IV, was looking down from his portrait and blaming him for the Revolution.

The leading official, explaining why Shaw had been neglected by them, said frankly that they did not like the French company he kept, an explanation that did not remove the chip from Shaw's shoulders.

On December 28, 1784, the last chest of tea was lifted aboard the *Empress of China,* and the courtesies of departure attended. Visiting Pinqua, they drank tea and exchanged felicitations.

Then came the obtaining of the clearance document, called "Grand Chop." (So many things were called "Chop" in China!) It warned all Chinese officials that the *Empress* had paid all duties, and that should bad winds and water drive her ashore in a Chinese province beyond the limits of Canton trading, she must be

THE LAUNCHING OF THE FAME FROM THE
CROWNINSHIELD WHARF, SALEM, 1802
From the painting by George Ropes

'HE MOUNT VERNON, 1799

ELIAS HASKET DERBY (1739-1799)
From a portrait by James Frothingham

allowed by the natives to continue on her voyage without delay or opposition.

The pilot came aboard; the topsails were set; a chantey went up from the crew at the windlass; the anchors came up dripping mud; the Chinese pilot took the wheel; the *Empress* went down the river nosing her way through junks and sampans. The comprador, sub-agent of Pinqua, returned a trifle of his earnings from the business of the ship by distributing "cumshas": to the officers and men, he gave presents of lichee nuts, oranges, and jars of ginger.

As his sampan carried him away, he paid a final, spectacular courtesy, by evoking the gods to bless the voyage. His holy petition was in the shape of a long bamboo pole with a big bunch of firecrackers at its end; setting these afire, he poked the blazing, crackling end towards the heavens, that the sleeping gods might awake to note and sanctify the departing ship.

Thomas Randall, as Shaw's partner, had prospered as Shaw had wished. The comrades chartered the ship *Pallas* at Canton and gave command of her to Captain John O'Donnell, an Englishman who had been engaged in the Indian trade. O'Donnell was to become a prosperous Baltimore skipper.

A profit of $30,727 was made on the first voyage of the *Empress of China* to Canton—it was more than twenty-five percent on the capital of $120,000 employed. Randall, in the *Pallas,* had teas worth $50,000 aboard, owned mutually with Shaw. This advertisement appeared in the *Independent Journal,* New York, May 25, 1785: "India goods, imported in the ship *Empress of China,* from Canton, for sale by Constable, Reeker & Co., consisting of Teas of all kinds. Chinaware, Silks, Muslins, and Nankeens."

Robert Morris, who acted as their sales agent for this cargo, offered to employ the pair of his agents at Canton for a term of several years; but they had become familiar with the privileges for making profits granted by the East India Company, and proposed terms that caused the financier to hesitate and withdraw. The partners were left free to explore other opportunities to engage in the China trade.

CHAPTER III

A Valiant Single-Sticker Comes in Second

OTHER VOYAGES CROWD in for the telling but, seeking to follow Albion's advice to maritime historians as to "crossing sailors' yarns with customs records" we will take them in order as they arrived at Canton.

The next ship that followed the *Empress of China* to the East Indies (the name the early Americans gave to all Asia) did not sail far enough to win the honor of flying the proud American flag in Canton harbor. Recent research has revealed the ship *United States* left Philadelphia on March 24, 1784, bound for the Orient. Leaving about a month after the *Empress of China,* she followed the same route around the Cape of Good Hope to Sumatra, where the routes separated, the *United States* voyaging to Pondicherry, the capital of all the French settlements in India.

The log of this ship was written by Thomas Redman, ship's surgeon, who recorded that the Commandant at Pondicherry "received us with the greatest demonstrations of pleasure and satisfaction. . . ."

The romance of trading with Far Eastern peoples was reaching as far up the coast as the Kennebec River in Maine, and was changing fishermen and lumberman into East India sailors. In building and sailing ships for the journey around Cape Horn and across the Pacific, Kennebec men held their own with the best of the men of Boston and Salem.

The port of Bath was alive with ship construction, and newly-built warehouses and shops began to come down the streets to meet the thin thickets of masts rising along the waterfront. Kennebec shipwrights had no enthusiasm for the Maryland custom of building fancy French-modeled clippers. "Big sturdy vessels for big cargoes," was their slogan.

In South Carolina, the shipping business was still coastwise, but crops of cotton and rice were being raised that found their way to northern ports for transshipment to foreign ports. And though the South did not vie with the North in those days for the commerce of the Far East, it already had a bond with East India through its rice crop, for in 1696 Charles Dubois, treasurer of the East India Company, had sent a money-bag full of East India rice to his friend Marsh, a planter in South Carolina. Ten years after this gift arrived, a Portuguese ship had brought to Charleston a considerable quantity of rice, along with a cargo of slaves; and with rice and slave labor thus joined, rice growing began in earnest. Later Vice-President Thomas Jefferson, preceding Johnny Appleseed as a seed distributor, presented to neighboring planters choice rice seeds brought to him from the Far East.

Philadelphia, torn between desires to push her trade west and to follow the New Yorkers into the China trade, did both.

It might have been expected that after Robert Morris had been placed in charge of the ships of the first American navy, his home town would become active in shipbuilding and ocean commerce; and so it was. The shipyards of Philadelphia began to turn out the largest and finest vessels produced in the quarter-century following the close of the war—the *Canton,* the *Ganges,* and the *China.* The last-named was a 1000-ton vessel—enormous and sensational.

Free-thinking Stephen Girard, the Franco-American merchant who had risen from cabin-boy to the captain of his own vessel, soon followed his neighbor Morris into the China trade, employing four splendid ships—the *Helvetia,* the *Montesquieu,* the *Rousseau,* and the *Voltaire.*

Baltimore shippers had needed only the news of the *Empress's* sailing to plunge into the East Indian trade. Foremost among them was the man from Donegal, William Patterson, father of the famous Betsy, wife of Jerome Bonaparte. The newly-opened Bank of Maryland had adventurous directors in Alexander Brown, John Carroll, William Patterson, and others, and a syndicate composed of its patrons gave shipbuilder Stodder an order for a ship of 600 tons, *Goliath*—the largest ship that had ever slid down the ways of a Maryland shipyard. On Lombard Street and around Locust Point, there was the same fever of interest that exhilarated merchants, clerks, and sailors around Manhattan's Old City Dock and the Derby wharf in Salem.

Mauritius, a besieged French base in the Indian Ocean, was preparing a welcome for two Baltimore ships loaded with flour from the Upper Patapsco mills of the Quakers Ellicott.

Canton, a water-front section of Baltimore, was getting its name as the point of the town's earliest connecton with the China trade. Captain John O'Donnell, whom Shaw and Randall employed to bring the *Pallas* from Canton to this country, had brought the ship to Baltimore. He became the toast of the town for bringing to its gracious circles rare teas, exquisite porcelains, silks, and fans direct from China. Out of the fortune he made he started an orchard of peaches—the kind that could be depended on to make the finest peach brandy—and named his pleasant estate after the port that was source of his wealth: Canton.

Baltimoreans sent out, under John O'Donnell, the first American ship to enter an Indian port—the *Chesapeake*. When she arrived at Calcutta, Lord Cornwallis, who though unfortunate as a British general in America, was successful and highly-esteemed as Governor-General in India, was consulted while inland as to how to receive the ship. He amiably decreed that American vessels visiting the East India Company's ports should be treated on the same terms as the most favored foreigners. The *Betsy* of Baltimore also enjoyed this Indian hospitality in the year of the *Chesapeake's* visit.

The proud Baltimoreans would have been glad to welcome to their port Maryland-born Captain Stewart Deane, whose amazing pioneering on the China run we now narrate, but that honor was reserved for the town of Albany, where his adventures began.

The second American vessel to anchor at Canton was the eighty-ton single-mast sloop *Experiment,* commanded by Captain Deane. That a vessel so little should dare the dangers of typhoons, treacherous tide, and Malayan and Chinese pirates, astonished both the Americans who cheered her going and the Chinese officials who watched her come to anchor.

Lief Ericsson in his longboat, Columbus in his caravel, and Magellan in his crude vessel had a later comrade in the little skipper of the *Experiment*. Her successful voyage was a sign to the maritime world of the Far East that an efficient new people, represented by mariners wonderfully at home on the sea, had entered the sharp competition for the trade of the Orient.

Deane had had salt in his nostrils since boyhood, because he lived in Somerset County, where the shores of the lower Chesapeake Bay take the winds and beat of the ocean. The Chesapeake with its many intriguing rivers was a splendid training-ground for a sailor.

"A nest of pirates," the blockading British admirals called the Chesapeake, and they itched to turn their guns on Baltimore, Annapolis, St. Michaels, and other bay ports from which came those white doves of ships that were yet as swift and rapacious as falcons.

At twenty-one, Deane had moved to Albany, and from this frontier town he marched against the British and Mohawks who invaded the Mohawk Valley. Later, with Hudson River coves for shelter, he commanded the privateers *Beaver* and *Nimrod* on prize-seeking voyages to the British West Indies.

He emerged from the Revolutionary period a wiry little man with a keen concern to be big in the forming new Republic. His height was just five feet six inches, and he was boyishly slight in build, but his spirit aimed at grand goals.

Robert Morris had owned the privateer *Nimrod* which Deane had commanded, and when the financier invested in the *Empress of China,* Deane decided to enter the Oriental trade. He superintended the building of the "queen of single-stickers" in the year the *Empress* sailed. The legend grew that he had built the *Experiment* in his own garden, at Albany, but it appears that the location of the shipyard was near the site of the Eagle Tavern.

On her initial voyage to New York she carried a cargo of salt; then Deane sailed the sloop to the Carolinas and to Madeira, and then he persuaded Messrs. Stewart and Jones, New York merchants, to send her on the China run. They formed a syndicate of eighteen merchants who invested $50,000 in the voyage, and loaded her with a cargo of tar, turpentine, Scotch snuff, Jamaica spirits, old Madeira wine, ginseng or "Gensang," and furs.

She was manned by eleven men, and carried as passenger William Stewart, part owner, "who adventured himself in the little vessel and returned in good health."

A wise choice was made in first mate John Whetten, who later became one of John Jacob Astor's captains and commanded some of New York's finest vessels. Of the two boys listed, one of them, "Prince," was a Negro.

Her owners had studied from English East Indiamen skippers the dangers of the course, and warned Deane in writing: "When you reach the Straights (Straits) of Sunda, it is recommended that you keep yourself always on your guard against the natives of Java and other islands. . . ."

To repel piratical Malay proas and Chinese junks, the *Experiment* was armed with six carriage and two swivel guns, small arms, boarding pikes, and other weapons.

On December 18, 1785, she cast loose from her moorings at Murray's dock on the corner of Wall and Front Streets on the East River, and started on her 13,000-mile voyage. Deane used an East India Company chart to and from the Indian Ocean.

When he anchored among the saluting ships at China, the sea captain there mistook the little ship for the tender of a large vessel, and inquired: "Where is the big ship?" The diminutive skipper stuck out his chest. "We are the big ship," he said. Unfortunately, he had arrived when there was keen bidding for the annual supply of tea that had come down the river. Twenty-three British ships from India, most of which had brought opium, and sixteen vessels from other countries were competing for the best teas, and the little capital at Captain Deane's command did not go far.

Deane bought for the *Experiment's* return voyage 300 chests of ordinary and 8 chests of best Hyson tea, and 100 chests of Souchong; 26 chests of China teacups and saucers; 5 chests of breakfast china; and 80 bales of nankeens. Among his prized trophies was a portrait of Houqua, leader of the co-hong.

Rolling homeward, the *Experiment* made a remarkably swift passage. Making 100 knots daily, she arrived in New York harbor four months and twelve days after leaving Canton.

The roof-tops and open spaces around the Battery were crowded when the intrepid single-sticker came into port. The crowds noted that Deane had carried over the discipline of privateering days into this commercial voyage. Over the water to the people on shore came the sound of military airs, broken by the boatswain's whistle. Then, as they listened and admired the pomp and circumstance of the little ship, her guns went off, and the· city heard itself saluted by thirteen rounds, one each for the stars in the *Experiment's* young flag.

The eager owners would have liked a little less pomp and considerably more profits, yet they acknowledged freely that Captain Deane's explanation was a just one:

"If the Chinese duty at Canton," he said, "had only required a sum in proportion to the size of my boat I would have made an advantageous voyage."

CHAPTER IV

Mr. Derby of Salem Answers a Far Call

THE VOYAGE FROM SALEM of Elias Hasket Derby's ship *Grand Turk* —first of a series of gallant ships of that name—was more than a trading journey to a remote and unknown coast; it was an epic of a little town's awakening to the call of the world.

Less glorious than his military kinfolk, Elias Hasket Derby is famous today when his gallant relatives are almost forgotten, because he was the first to link and establish Salem as a port trading with the markets of the Indian Ocean.

Long hailed as the pioneer of the East India trade, his glory is only slightly dimmed by the fact that Captain Hallet, of the 55-ton sloop *Harriet* of Hingham, Mass., had voyaged to the East Indies before him. Hallet sailed from Boston in December 1783, with a cargo of ginseng calculated to maintain the potency of roosterish mandarins, but at the Cape of Good Hope he met an East Indiaman, whose commander was willing to trade teas for the ginseng. Hallet made a profitable exchange and returned home without being able to give the curious town-people an account of the exotic harbors.

25

The *Grand Turk,* owned by Elias Hasket Derby and commanded by Jonathan Ingersoll, cleared from Salem eleven months after the *Harriet* sailed. Her cargo was diversified. She was the first of many similar ships sent to the Far East by Derby and is worthy of her fame.

Pent-up by the British blockade, the people of New England coast towns were hungering and thirsting for more than righteousness. Forced to "plain living and high thinking," they were avid for European furnishings and delicacies, and when it became known that as a result of the war our ships could sail direct to China and bring back teas and silks and dishes without paying tribute to King George, they eagerly supported their merchants in world-girdling enterprises.

In a somewhat ruthless way, Puritan families of New England had come to know the arts and crafts their ancestors had abandoned in Europe. Yankee privateers, sending their luxury-laden prizes into port, had created a hunger for beauty and comfort among the people used to simple living. The cargoes of the seized vessels were spread for sale on the wharves and counters and whetted appetites. Ship-architect Samuel McIntyre built grand new houses along fashionable streets to accommodate enthusiastically acquired curio cabinets, and Chippendale sofas draped with Singapore shawls.

The building of the *Grand Turk* had been a matter of sharing; when Robert Fels of Hanover Four Corners contracted to supply the ironwork for the vessel, he agreed with Derby to take payment in barrels of rum brought in by the latter's West Indian vessels, and in firkins of butter the merchant had traded for along the coast.

The attraction the enterprise had for the people of Salem and for the young men who composed her crew can best be understood from the words of Richard Cleveland:

"In the ordinary course of commercial education, in New England, boys are transferred from school to merchant's desk at the age of fourteen and fifteen. When I reached my fourteenth year it was my good fortune to be received into the counting-house of Elias Hasket Derby of Salem, a merchant who may justly be termed the father of American commerce to India. . . . He built several ships for the India trade immediately in the vicinity of the counting-house, which afforded me opportunity of becoming acquainted with the building, sparring, and rigging of ships. The conversations to which I listened relating to the countries then newly visited by Americans, and the excitement on the return of an adventurer from them and the great profits which were made, tended to stimulate the desire in me of visiting those countries, and of sharing more largely in the advantages they presented."

Many of the men who sailed with Ingersoll were amazingly young. They were, at sixteen, eighteen, or twenty-one years, veterans of the coastwise trade. Several of them who had shipped "through the hawse-hole," had been promoted to the rank of mate.

Loading the *Grand Turk* with tobacco, sugar, oil, tar, pork in barrels, flour and cheese—a cargo valued at $27,000—Derby entrusted to honest Shipmaster Jonathan Ingersoll ten thousand Spanish dollars with which to complete the cargo en route. Insurance rates being high, Derby insured the ship only as far as the Indian Ocean.

The owner's jurisdiction stopped at the water's edge, and the skipper then became commander both of the sailing and of the buying and selling.

The new boys came into their initiation of handling sails, though few of these Salem lads lacked experience climbing a mast.

The first duty of the green ones aboard ship was to learn the rigging—to climb to the masthead, to go up, up no matter how dizzy the clambering made them.

Whether wreathed in fog or under a bright clear sky, the rigging was their school. They must learn to know every mast, spar, sail, and rope.

This clouding canvas taking the impact of the wind and speeding the ship along was the sign of a master and men at the helm who knew perfectly the art and science of sail, and could change at once to the varying conditions of calm and storm.

At temperate and fruitful Capetown, the Americans remarked that the Table Mountain formation resembled the highlands of the Hudson. The English-ridden Dutch East India Company owned the soil and rented it to the settlers, who were mostly employees of the company. There was a large wooden pier at which vessels could easily fill their casks with fresh water.

There Ingersoll was kindly greeted by Captain Thompson, commander of an East Indiaman that was returning home from Canton.

Fortunately for the inexperienced Captain Ingersoll, who had found it hard to trade and was tempted to run over to the coast of Africa and take home a cargo of "black ivory," Captain Thompson was in a mood to dicker for the *Grand Turk's* cargo of rum. He had been allotted for his own use space in his ship accommodating sixty tons. This he had filled with tea chests, sateens and nankeens, the very goods Americans wanted.

Their talk over the Madeira ran like this:

"What would you say to this proposal?" Thompson said. "I can spare you, out of my own property, 200 chests of Hyson tea. You can recognize by the Chinese merchant's hong mark that it is fine quality. You may also have some cases of sateens and nankeens—I understand that American ladies are weary of wearing domestics."

"What price?"

"The price will be $15,000, but I will take your cargo of rum in full payment."

Ingersoll felt that Thompson's offer was extremely liberal. Was there a catch in it?

"You wonder," Thompson said, "how I can afford to offer you so much for the rum. There is one provision. I know a thirsty market where the rum will command big prices. You can sail there conveniently. It is the island of St. Helena—a thousand miles or so off the southwest coast of Africa."

"Very well; I'll deliver the rum at St. Helena. The health of your monarch, and of yourself, Captain Thompson!"

"Good luck to the new Republic, and a good voyage to you, Captain Ingersoll."

Delivering the rum to the isolated island soon fated to imprison Napoleon Bonaparte, Ingersoll went thence to Port-au-Prince, traded with the French merchants of the West Indies, again loaded the *Grand Turk* with sugar and rum, chartered the vessel *Lark* to carry an additional cargo, and set sail for the port of New York. Anchoring at a South Street dock, he sold both cargoes at a good profit.

By smart trading on the high seas he had produced for Derby and the sharers a hundred percent profit on the venture, but as he sailed into Salem harbor the modest Yankee expressed the hope that he would be well received by Mr. Derby.

Though the owner had maintained an undisturbed countenance during the long absence of the *Grand Turk,* he was spending more and more time in his observatory, sweeping the horizon with his spyglass.

One morning he came downstairs with his spyglass under his arm and calmly caused a sensation in his counting-house.

"The *Grand Turk* is coming in. She has had a successful voyage."

These things had been told him by the arrangement of flags on board the incoming *Grand Turk,* for he had at the outset arranged with the skipper a private code of signals.

Down from their high stools jumped the clerks. Quills stuck in their ears, they rushed shouting into the lane and aroused the town.

"The *Grand Turk* is here! The venture was profitable. Let's give her brave men a hearty reception."

Cheered by the swarming people of Salem, the ship drew up to the Derby wharf and let down her sails, and between deck and wharf ran happy communications.

Owner Derby was well pleased. The only disappointed people in the crowd were those who had expected the crew to bring them Chinese silks, jade and porcelain. The ports of Table Bay and St. Helena were poor markets for fine exotic things. What a pity Captain Ingersoll had not gone on to China!

The sateen and nankeen fabrics comforted them, however. Within a few days there were splashes of Oriental color in the simple fashions and decorations of Salem.

Owner Derby, acquisitive fellow, did not permit the *Grand Turk* to rest long beside the Derby wharf.

He sent her out again in November, 1785. She was to go directly to Mauritius in the Indian Ocean, but he gave her captain permission to continue, if trade induced, to Batavia and Canton.

Captain Ingersoll, having decided to rest on his gains and laurels, was succeeded by Nathaniel West, who during the Revolution had sailed on board the oddly-named Salem privateer, *Oliver Cromwell.* This new adventure, extending to China, was to make Captain West a man of mark in Salem, and he was to live to be nearly a hundred years old, pointed out by Salem urchins as Salem's pioneer skipper in the China trade.

The voyage of the *Grand Turk* under West had not started auspiciously. When he arrived at Mauritius, he found the people there too poor to buy his goods. Unused to trading in such ports he was at a loss, for Owner Derby had mentioned China only as a last resource. Stimulus to risk a sail to China came from a French merchant, M. Chataignerais, who heard of the American's dilemma and came forth with an offer.

"Monsieur, I will charter two-thirds of the space in the *Grand Turk* to take goods to Canton, and then I will use the same space to carry teas to that port where the famous tea-party was— Boston!"

"But I still have my cargo, and can't charter two-thirds of the space."

"Monsieur, I advise you to sell your goods at whatever prices they will bring. I assure you that you will make up the profits in the China market. Keep your ginseng, and add to it things from the resources of this island—ebony wood, betel nuts, cloth, and gold thread. There is a demand in China for these commodities!"

The Frenchman inspired confidence, and West agreed.

What a welcome sight to see, anchored at Whampoa, two vessels flying the American flag. West recognized one of them as the *Empress of China,* on her second visit. The second one was the *Hope,* and she had brought out Major Shaw, of whom West had heard favorably from Ingersoll.

Consul Shaw was very cordial to the perplexed shipmaster

from Salem, and after guiding him in the business of obtaining a Chinese agent, taught him how to obey the Eight Regulations, which governed "foreign devils." These rules stipulated that while in Canton foreigners might not leave the factories except on the 8th, 18th and 28th days of the moon. On these fortunate days, they could go with their interpreter to visit the Flower Gardens and the Honam joss-house, but the company must be less than ten. They must deal only with the hong merchants, and not encourage smuggling by selling to "rascally natives, goods subject to duty." The rules also forbade aliens to bring women, guns, spears, or any kind of arms into the factories.

West sold his cargo to advantage, and obtained a satisfactory miscellaneous cargo of Chinese goods. When he lifted the warp of the *Grand Turk* at Whampoa, sailing in advance of the time for the northeastern monsoon, he made a good voyage across the China Sea, left Java Head astern, and took a southwest course down the Indian Ocean. On May 22, 1787, the *Grand Turk* reached her home port.

Her guns saluting, she came proudly into Salem harbor—the first New England ship to make a China voyage.

There were no disappointed townspeople now. Each seeker of Oriental goods had his wish fulfilled. The women were especially pleased by the packages of "Bandanna Hdkfs," the chests of muslin, and the "Chinaware Table Sets, and Tea and Coffee sets," which were on the manifest.

For every dollar of value the *Grand Turk* went out with, she brought back two. No wonder the Derby family in coming years built a succession of *Grand Turks*.

From this China venture of the *Grand Turk,* we derive an idea of the progress of marine insurance in early Manhattan. Lloyds in London had underwritten the business of American colonial shippers, and Elias Derby turned to Lloyds for insurance on his ships and cargoes going to the Orient. The London company had no foundation for faith in the unknown *Grand Turk* and her captain, and quoted Derby prohibitive rates.

Spurred by Owner Derby, marine underwriting in the Republic grew adventurous. He went to New York and persuaded insurance men to insure the *Grand Turk* from Salem to Mauritius and return. To obtain a $20,000 policy he agreed to pay nine per cent interest.

Months passed without bringing news of the *Grand Turk*. When at last an incoming vessel brought a letter from Captain West telling of delays and of the extended voyage to China, Derby worried because he had not taken out insurance to cover the extra distance. Hurrying back to Manhattan, he paid higher interest to obtain the needed coverage to Canton.

For all the reluctance of Lloyds to underwrite the first American ships, the success of Shaw, Derby, and others impressed British merchant bankers, and they began to back American voyages to the Far East.

With various exciting cargoes arriving from many far markets, Salem came to have the smell, color, and drama of the globe. By 1800 the street well-named Derby was the business thoroughfare of the town, busy with the traffic of the wharves. It was a delight to the simply-reared townspeople to stroll through this and adjoining lanes whose shops had the enticement of Oriental bazaars. Gorgeously-colored parrots screamed from cages hung in doorways, and inside the shop monkeys chattered. Storekeepers began to spread silks, muslins, and nankeens on their counters which entranced the ladies, and the hostesses of the town vied with each other in buying exquisite plates and tea-cups from some ship that had just touched at the Derby or Crowninshield wharf from China.

At the height of the fashion in London for Chinese things, the poet James Cawthorn wrote:

"Of late, 'tis true quite sick of Rome and Greece,
We fetch our models from the wise Chinese.
European artists are too cold and chaste
For Mand'rin only is a man of taste."

The same desire for Chinese furniture and objects of virtu came to America with the returning tea clippers. One of the illustrations in this book is that of a fan of paper and mother-of-pearl. On it is painted a picture of the ship *Empress of China,* presented to Captain John Green in Canton in 1784. Consul Carrington brought back a sensational bamboo extension chair, two plaster figures of a mandarin and his lady, and several pieces of lacquer and porcelain. Consul Benjamin Chew Wilcocks brought to Philadelphia a gold and lacquered screen.

Warren Delano, partner of Russell and Company, brought back to Boston in his ship *Memnon* a bed of carved wood and ivory, two big bronze bells, a Ming mirror, and pieces of porcelain, lacquer, and jade.

Dutch supercargo Andreas Everhardus van Braan Houckgeest, who settled in Philadelphia and built a villa "China Retreat," filled his residence with Chinese curios. Among them were a portrait on glass, a lacquered stand, Chinese armchairs, and an ivory fan.

The Chinese potters were quick to seize upon the newly-opened American market. As early as 1800 Chinese exporters of porcelain produced a bowl showing a view of the foreign factories at Canton. An early piece brought to America was decorated with the new United States seal; another voyager brought home a toddy jar upon which was painted a picture of George Washington, whom the Chinese admired because he had defeated the British. The artists in porcelain were also quick to decorate a platter with the emblem of the order of Cincinnati, the society which Major Shaw had helped form.

Ship chandlers' shops, packed with all the supplies needed for a voyage, were filled with lithe young men, and close by the quiet instrument makers, whose sign was a quadrant, were busy selling to whiskered shipmasters the devices of navigation. In their lofts, sailmakers, their fingers shielded by curious thimbles, stitched at great white sheets of canvas.

These activities were the multiplied results of the voyages financed by a score of ship owners who had followed Elias Hasket Derby's lead. Especially active were Joseph Peabody, William Gray, Benjamin Pickman, and the Crowninshield men, who from grandfather to the youngest of the six grandsons, made their mark in Salem commerce and politics. The Crowninshield Wharf, with its fringe of tall masts, was a sender of homely goods and a receiver of exotic cargoes equal in extent and fascination to the more renowned Derby dock.

The Crowninshields had their own brand of originality and directness. The graceful *Belisarius,* a ship of 26½ tons built by Enos Brigg for George Crowninshield, was a predecessor in slender build and swift lines to the famous Baltimore clipper *Ann McKim.* They might despise each other, the Salem men and the Baltimore crowd, but they had the same taste, ambitions, and enterprise.

The Crowninshield boys loved the *Belisarius.* All of them were registered as part owners of her. She was used in the pepper trade, and in 1800 eluded a blockading English frigate. There were sixteen guns aboard of her, but it was her speed that made her safe.

These antipodean projects gave Salem historians good cause to boast truly that the town's ships traded "with more different peoples in Asia, Africa, South America, and the islands of the sea than the ships of all other American ports put together."

A Salem worthy as venturous as any East Indian shipper was William Gray. In 1805 he owned more ships than any man in the United States. Noteworthy also was Captain Joseph Peabody. He sent his vessels on thirty-eight voyages to Calcutta and thirty-two to Sumatra. Peabody's ship, the 287-ton *Sumatra,* made five voyages to China, and her owner paid to the Government in imports $587,000 on these voyages. Of the 7000 sailors Peabody employed, he promoted thirty-five, who had entered his employ as boys, to the rank of shipmaster.

Beloved was the Salem ship *George,* owned by Captain Peabody and named after his third son. Known as the "Salem Frigate," and manned by a crew in which there was scarcely a man over twenty-one, for twenty-two years she plied between Salem and Calcutta. It never paid to challenge her to a race or to bet on her defeat, for her sailing qualities plus those of her captain and crew were a victorious combination.

More than any other vessel of her time, the *George* was a training-school for the East Indian run. Forty-five of the young men who sailed on her became shipmasters, twenty became chief mates, and six became second mates.

Coming from the Cape of Good Hope in forty-one days, she made what was claimed to be "the quickest passage from the Cape to a North Atlantic port ever made under canvas."

She was chased by a slave-pirate, caught in terrible gales, and so driven and beaten by a hurricane that only one man stayed on deck, and he was lashed to the helm.

CHAPTER V

Major Shaw among Ladies of the East Indies

THREE YEARS HAD passed since Shaw and Randall had arrived at Canton. The pair had obtained a firm footing in the trade and were helpful guides to newly-arriving shipmasters from America.

The tea season was over. Randall having sailed with a cargo of choice teas, Shaw had time on his hands. He wished to visit the ports of the British and Dutch in the East Indies, and there is evidence that the visits would be more than social ones. Planning to promote an American East India Company, he meant to study the ground. The British were careless or contemptuous, and took his word for it that he was going merely for recreation. They gave him cordial letters of introduction into high circles.

He sailed on the independent British ship *Argyle,* with Captain Robert Martin Fowle. His fellow passengers aboard this opium ship were a Greek, an Armenian, and a few Englishmen. Before he landed at Calcutta he had broken down the reserve of the English travelers.

Mr. Turnbull, principal owner of the *Argyle,* living at Calcutta, had studied law in New Jersey and said that his brother had served in the Pennsylvania artillery. He welcomed Shaw and brought to greet him Benjamin Joy of Boston, an old acquaintance of Shaw's. The former was employed as a clerk in the British service, as was young George Scott, also of Boston. Shaw had to admit to himself that the British in Calcutta showed no prejudice against Americans.

Watching the commerce of the harbor of Singapore, Major

Shaw became absorbed in the little native open boats coming into port. They came, he was told, from islands more than a thousand miles south of Singapore, and passed several Dutch ports on the way because the English gave them freedom while they were in the harbor, whereas the Dutch officials severely restrained them.

The whole family had come along to enjoy the trading. At first sight these one-masters might have been called bird-boats, because cockatoos, parrots, and parakeets were perched along the sides, fastened by short strings. An important part of the cargo was sandalwood, and below deck were spices and pearl shells. These goods they exchanged for iron, nails, thread, and pieces of colorful Manchester cotton. When the northeast monsoon began to blow, they would give their sail to it, and go home from island to island, trading as they went. They, as well as the big East Indiamen, composed the trade of the East Indies.

Conforming to the peculiar social life of the British in the Far East, Shaw dined with gracious families at three o'clock and then rode with them to the race course. There were callers between eight and nine-thirty, and supper at ten.

He explained the late supper hour by saying that European ladies in India soon lose the bloom and freshness of their complexions, and "their appearance is not a little improved by the light of the candles, and by the extreme neatness, and if I may be allowed the expression, the *purity* of their dress, which consists usually of the finest muslin."

What a modest young man was this who hesitated to use the word purity in connection with a woman's apparel; what an exceedingly daring young man was he to mention the next intimate detail: "In the care of their persons they cannot be exceeded, and perhaps are scarcely equalled, by any in the world; few of them bathe less than twice, and some in the warmest season, as often as three times, during the twenty-four hours . . ."

He continued his shy yet acute observations when he called on the Dutch settlement of Hollanders up the river. Taken to call on Baron Van Haugwitz .and his lady, he played whist with them, but the hostess instead of the cards was engrossing.

"Madam la Baronne," he commented, "is a beautiful *brunette,* and has most bewitching eyes."

The Dutch Madame Wouldern, he found, was a *"belle-blanche"* with engaging features and a charming complexion in which the lily and rose are happily blended. She is twenty-five years old, but having had no children, preserves the freshness of eighteen."

Of the Dutch ladies of Batavia in general he said classically:

"In the arrangement of their hair, they are inexpressibly neat; without cushion, gauze, lace, or any other superstructure, it is put up with a few diamond pins, in such a manner as to give a lively idea of that simplex *Munditis* which of old was so pleasing to the elegant Horace."

It can be detected in Shaw's notes that armored as he seemed to be against the attractions of women, he could have succumbed.

Studying the intimacies of married life, he wrote: "There is an article in their manners not less peculiar than this of their dress. Whether in private or public, the ladies sit next to their husbands, and, on rising from the table, each makes a courtesy to her good man, and gives him a kiss."

But the Dutch wives did not receive the critic's full approval. He states than during the evening, while part of the ladies danced, "the others amused themselves with chewing betel and areca. This is said to be very wholesome in hot countries, and a great preservative to the teeth and gums. It is kept in gold boxes, and a little female slave attends with a gilt, and sometimes a silver jar, into which the lady spits as occasion requires."

Enticed yet repelled the fastidious Bostonian lamented: "It were to be wished that the use of this article could be confined to the toilet, for notwithstanding its salutary effects, it is certain that the finest mouth, when imbued with its juice, loses that charm which would otherwise render it irresistible."

As to the women of Malacca, he found them shocking. "They are extremely vulgar, and fond of frolicking to an extreme. At their dancing parties they drink vast quantities of beer, wine, and gin; chew betel and areca the greater part of the time; eat a hot supper; and then go dancing again, and seldom leave the house (of entertainment) till three or four o'clock in the morning. This mode of conduct renders them libertine to such a degree as to banish from the minds of their male companions every idea of respect or delicacy—I had almost said decency—towards them." The wives of Malacca, he complained, did not value their virtue highly enough to shun notorious women. He had accepted it as a weakness of the male tribe that some skippers on their voyages should have the company of the ladies afterwards called "China Coasters," but he felt strongly that wives should not receive these women when they came ashore.

Reporting the presence of skippers' mistresses in respectable houses, he said: "Yet the *filles-de-joie* of the captains of ships from India to Canton, who leave them here until they return, were not excluded. On the contrary, they board with respectable families, where they are the companions of the mistress of the house; and I was not a little surprised, on visiting two ladies of the first rank in the settlement, the forenoon of the wedding, to find one of these creatures, a mixture of Malay and India-Portuguese, passing the day with them, tete-a-tete."

Some of the East India Company's officers suspected Shaw of coming to spy out British trade methods and refused to honor the letter of introduction he presented; on the other hand, other Company officers received him warmly.

There was an odd Englishman whose free mode of living shocked the Bostonian. In Mr. Johnson, who had a country-seat, Raspugly, six miles from Calcutta's limits, he met a man of wealth living in the style of a native prince. The romantic characters in Kipling and Maugham are not more colorful and dramatic than Johnson who, having been employed at the courts of native princes, had become an master of Indian politics and intrigue.

Expecting to meet the women of the family, Shaw was mystified at first by their absence, but he soon found that this gentleman lived after the manner of a native prince, keeping a seraglio and secluding his women in separate apartments in a screened garden.

The reserved Shaw in his journals gives free expression to his observations of women he met in the Far East. In this he was true to his sex. The fact that he had little to say about women in China was merely because he lacked the opportunity of meeting them. American women had not yet come there. European women were admitted only to Macao, and the English ladies had little use for the aggressive Yankees. As for the Chinese women, they remained a mystery. Members of the MaCartney embassy while at Peking were persuaded not to climb the summit from which a view might be had of the Emperor's gardens in which his wives and concubines basked, even though the hill was two or three miles away.

Looking for beauty among the girls he saw along the shores his vessel passed, the traveler was baffled by the costumes of the women, whose forms were concealed from the neck down by loose dresses, with wide trousers from the waist down to the small of the leg, and with feet and ankles swathed in bandages.

Staunton, scribe of the MaCartney embassy, wrote of the lack of beauty in the women of the fields in a way that revealed a desire for further study. Reading it, one wonders what "accident" provided members of the embassy with the opportunity to observe some beautiful young Chinese girls.

"Those of a more elegant form," the polite writer stated, "were probably not employed in these rude labours. A custom which is said to subsist in China, must render beauty rare in the lower classes of life. It is assured, that the young maidens distinguished by their faces and their figure, are taken or purchased from their parents at the age of fourteen, for the use of the powerful and the opulent.

"Accident has thrown a few of these within view of the gentlemen of the Embassy, who considered them, from the fairness and delicacy of their complexions, and the beauty and regularity of their features, as entitled to admiration . . ."

Staunton, who was something of a Pepys in his gossip about intimate things, discovered and reported that "though the ladies reckon corpulence a beauty in a man, they consider it a palpable blemish in their own sex, and aim at preserving slimness and delicacy of shape. They suffer their nails to grow, but reduce their eyebrows to an arched line."

CHAPTER VI

Victim of Ambition

THROUGH DAYS OF merciless sun, and nights beautiful under the Southern Cross and a canopy of liquid stars, with the ship's bow stirring up the sea's phosphorescent asters, Shaw returned refreshed to Macao, and thereafter was kindlier in thought toward the British officials through whose influence he had been so kindly received in India.

Captain Robinson, commander of the British ship which brought him back to Macao, would take no payment for the passage, but the Yankee, not to be outdone in courtesy, gave him "an elegant traveling-case, and a portable kitchen, which the season before, cost $164."

A new tea season was on its way and American ships were arriving thick as gulls at Whampoa. Shaw observed that bigger and bigger American ships were being built, and he noted especially that the 1000-ton ship *Alliance,* which was one of the four frigates Congress had built for war purposes in 1778, had come into the hands of his former employer, financier Robert Morris, and was now at Canton awaiting a load of tea. He wondered why the Administration had sold her when there was need of frigates to protect American merchant ships from Malayan and Chinese corsairs, and he asked himself also by what kind of a deal Morris, who had charge of the Government's ships, had gotten possession of her.

A change had come over the selfless Shaw who had served with personal sacrifice the cause of the Revolution. Mingling since then with men whose chief aim was to amass fortunes and build great mansions on the finest streets of the home town, he was driven by the same ambitions, and was in a fever to become wealthy and powerful, though he did not possess the traits that make for such success.

There were two classes of men among our pioneers of the China run: the first class was composed of men of self-reliance like Amasa Delano, Richard Cleveland, and Samuel Shaw, who decided for themselves what they would do, and failed or half-failed through unsound business judgment, or through inability to work well with other men.

The other class were men like Astor, Russell, Olyphant, Cushing, and Warren Delano who, while self-reliant also, were early examples of the American genius for organization. The contrast between the two classes will present itself in later pages showing Robert Bennet Forbes's entrance into the great firm of Russell and Co., formed by men who started their careers much the same as Shaw.

His ambitions excited by the coming of the big ships, Shaw planned that the firm of Shaw and Randall should own one and that the larger profits obtained through a larger cargo should be used to build a fleet. Having come out to compete individually with the ships of the British East India Company, he had decided that the future success of Americans in Far Eastern trade would be "through national companies and with large ships." The East India Company he had spied upon had become his model, and Randall and he had already given a commission to Eli Hayden, supercargo of the brigatine *Columbia,* to act for them in making a contract for the first big vessel. When it was built, Shaw intended to use it as a means of interesting financiers in the organization of the American East India Company.

He was doomed to failure, and under the pressure of circumstances, according to the unaccusing evidence in Amasa Delano's journal, blinked at conscience and adopted the methods of a Yankee horse-trader in his haste to secure a dwindling fortune. We now examine the circumstances that put a question mark over a portion of Shaw's admirable career.

The shipbuilding plan was to engage William and John Hacket, of Salisbury, Massachusetts, who had won fame through the building of the splendid frigate *Alliance,* to construct a vessel along the lines of the British East Indiamen *Worcester,* which at the time of the arrangement with Eli Hayden was at Canton.

Whatever happened afterwards there was no intention by Shaw

or Randall to countenance shortcomings when the specifications were drawn up to submit to the skilled and reputable Hacket brothers. The shipbuilders were informed:

"This ship is designed for the India trade, where ships from all nations meet and where probably the best ships the world can produce may be seen. It is the expectation of Messrs. Shaw and Randall that they can produce from America such a ship as will bear the inspection of the most critical eye, both as to construction and workmanship."

The jury of readers should bear this statement in mind when considering what was done during the building of the ship.

Randall having contracted for the new ship, Shaw sailed for home January 28, 1789, on the *George Washington*, to superintend the construction of the grand vessel. In a port of the Dutch East Indies he met Randall in the ship which the partners had re-named in honor of their sponsor, John Jay.

Shaw was usually unemotional in writing his journal, but of this meeting he recorded:

"After a long separation, the sensations of friends so near to each other, on such a long-wished and unexpected meeting, may better be imagined than described . . ."

Pledging themselves to meet in America and pursue their fortunes together, they parted.

The *George Washington*, on the voyage home from the East Indies kept occasional company with Gouverneur and Kemble's ship *America*, the varied cargo of which contained an oddity that created much excitement while loading and landing. The skipper of the *America* was pioneering in bringing a Bengal elephant home to America, the first elephant of the endless procession of docile beasts that were to march as circus exhibits through the towns and villages of the United States.

The huge beast had appeared quite willing to make the voyage, and had been patient and accommodating when slung and raised by a windlass. Her Yankee crew, with a gift for improvising verses for familiar capstan chanteys, might well have sung in their merry-go-round as the elephant came over the side:

"Here is a Yankee ship, and golly, what a cargo!
    Hauling in the cargo, boys, gives us jolly work.
Heave away your capstan, an elephant of Bengal
    Comes aboard, my hearties, and trumpets, 'Ho, New York!'"

The important Shaw and Randall ship *Massachusetts* was launched in September, 1789. It was a late date for an owner who wished to load her with China tea that season and Shaw was worried.

The people of Massachusetts, knowing nothing of an owner's worries, made the launching the occasion for a holiday and flocked to the town of Quincy, where the vessel was to take to the water. The owner forgot his troubles for a time when the officers of five visiting French ships of war, and of the British frigate *Penelope,* resting amiably in Boston harbor, came aboard and praised the model in which beauty and utility were so well blended.

The Hacket builders, watching the satisfactory launching, were being complimented also. Were they uneasy as they watched young Amasa Delano, the sharp-eyed son of a rival shipbuilder, going about his work as second officer aboard the ship, and were they conjecturing as to whether his innocent air concealed the fact that he had discovered some defect in what was going into the ship?

Shaw chose Job Prince to command the ship, and appointed Josiah Robert of the West Indian trade as first officer. Applicant Amasa Delano had before then been selected as navigator and second officer.

Amasa, a Duxbury lad, was a fourth cousin of Warren Delano and his brother Frederick, who was the grandfather of Franklin Delano Roosevelt. Amasa at sixteen had served aboard a privateersman in the West Indies, and when ashore had worked in his father's yard as a ship carpenter. When the *Massachusetts* was put into commission, his was the honor of hoisting her colors.

Immensely proud was Amasa to have won the honor of a berth on the *Massachusetts*. "A station on board of her," he wrote afterwards to a relative, "was an object of consequence . . . she was the largest merchant ship built at that time in the United

States . . . Parties of people of every rank of society frequently came on board of her to gratify their curiosity and express their admiration . . . so much public attention has probably never been excited for any ship built here since."

Our third officer had too much to do to pay particular attention to the groups of citizens owner Shaw was showing through the ship. If he recognized among Shaw's guests the girl Hannah Phillips, the daughter of the prominent merchant, it was not a thing to make a note of. However, when it came to construction matters, Amasa had eyes to see and a quill to record.

A young man who has been brought up in a shipyard has an eye for what is going on. A sharp judge of timber, he knows when sound, well-seasoned wood is going into the hull. Amasa Delano stumbled into a dreadful dilemma when he discovered that the white oak which the carpenters were using for the underplanking had been cut green, as had also the pine planking; the spare masts and yards were also made of unseasoned timber.

Feeling an urge to inform his employer, Major Shaw, Amasa restrained himself, having a delicacy about complaining about noted shipbuilders who were competitors of his own shipbuilding father. And then, it was plain that Shaw was hurrying them to get the ship launched in time for the next tea season. A fortune was at stake. It was understood that certain Chinese hong merchants had invested in the ship, and they were said to be very exacting. If they lost money they might ruin the man who had caused the loss.

This thing was certain—to tear out the green timber and replace it with seasoned wood would cause serious delay, and probably result in a loss of the big profits on the season's business. Among canny superiors, Amasa became canny, and held his tongue.

Amasa is seemingly outspoken in his journal, but when it came to placing responsibility for the green wood that went into the *Massachusetts* he avoids giving his opinion. According to him, all the men who took part in the shipbuilding were of good character and training. Eli Hayden, who made the contract with the Hacket Brothers, was a merchant of integrity; William Hacket, who drew the plans and superintended the construction, was a distinguished designer who if bad at spelling was good at

44

his craft. Daniel Briggs, builder under Hacket, was an excellent carpenter and mechanic, and so were the four Briggs brothers who worked along with Daniel.

For all of this merit Amasa Delano sets forth suddenly the great fault in the ship.

"The ship," Amasa said, "was as well built as any ship could be under the circumstances. The timber was cut, and used immediately while perfectly green. It was white oak, and would have been very durable had it been docked, or properly seasoned. . . . Green wood should never be used in a vessel, especially above the navel timber heads. It will not last half as long in low latitudes [for which the ship was designed] as that which is docked or properly seasoned."

When the ship's hold was opened at Canton, another discovery of rottenness in the wood was to cause a sensation among her crew.

In the spring of 1790, the *Massachusetts* sailed to the salute of cannon and the roar of crowds. It was a proud occasion for a proud State, and only one or two persons ashore or on board had cause to worry about a mast that might change the celebration to a disastrous experience.

The music of bells; the rhythm of the masts and sails; the song of the wind in the rigging . . . the homely sounds from the forecastle . . . the ritual of the wheel where orders were given as emergencies arose: "Full and By"; "North West by West"; "Keep her off a point"; "Luff a little"; "Ease her"; and—when a wave rose—"Meet her!" with the helmsman repeating Navigator Amasa's order.

To the Cape of Good Hope . . . across the equator to the Indian Ocean . . . good sailing along the coast of Java with the southwest monsoon at her stern and spray showering the figurehead . . . the safe harbor of Batavia, with little islands shielding a ship from the winds. However, for Thomas French, midshipman, this Dutch port was a fatal harbor—he fell from the mainyard and was instantly killed. They buried him ashore "with decency and honor, with minute guns from the ship."

It was also an unfortunate port for owner Shaw with his vaulting ambitions to become a rival of the British East India Company in trading in these harbors. The Dutch market he had counted upon for exchanges of cargo had gone wrong. The Dutch, seldom generous toward aliens, were as active as the British in discouraging trade with Yankee ships. Shaw had counted on selling his cargo at Batavia. It would be worthless in China. Bitterly disappointed, he sent a letter of complaint to the President of the United States.

After she had left Batavia for Canton, a typhoon bedeviled the *Massachusetts*.

The breeze freshened and the skies grew ominous.

The officer of the deck, after a sharp scanning of the sky, shouted sharp orders through his trumpet, but the tearing wind split the mainsail, foretop sail, and the foretopmast staysail.

The sea was rolling now. The *Massachusetts* plunged through a fury of white froth.

The ship met the typhoon sturdily, as if eager to show the good workmanship that had gone into her. Would the masts hold? If the storm broke them, then the opening of the hold to bring out new ones would disclose a disgusting, disastrous secret.

Night passed and gray dawn appeared; again night passed and dawn came. Such was the grayness of mist and water that the lookout could seldom see farther than fifty yards ahead.

As a panther worries its prey, the wind worried the ship. Striking broadsides, it forced her to heel forty-fifty-sixty degrees. Then, shifting, it joined with the forty-foot waves to drop her into a valley of the angry sea, so that the crashing waves struck her with an exploding sound, and shook her violently from stem to stern.

Green hands looked to veteran sailors to read in their faces whether they thought she would pull through. Assured as to the ship's power to recover from these incessant shocks, the new sailors watched anxiously as the officers coped with the danger of her drifting on to one of those numerous shoals or reefs that were cemeteries of typhoon-driven ships.

The navigator had given her plenty of sea room, but the wind and the tide were always conspiring to drive her ashore. The lead when first cast showed twenty-five fathoms, but the next time it showed twenty-two and then twenty.

Desperate measures were tried. The drenched, weary men, fighting their way through a surge that threatened to carry them overboard, bent new topsails, while those below watched to see if these sails would be torn by the wind. Fortunately, the wind and the sea broke their conspiracy.

Suddenly a torrential rain seemed to press back the wind and level the sea. The wind shifted, and blew from another quarter, and filled the topsails without ripping them. The vessel wore around and sailed out to sea.

With the change of wind the mist lifted, and the coast of danger—a steep bluff on a rocky coast—was plainly in sight.

The *Massachusetts* had come out of the typhoon tight in spite of the terrific shocks. Whatever might afterwards be disclosed as to the spare masts, the Yankee shipbuilder had not failed in good workmanship. There was an abundance of good wood in the vital parts of the vessel, and the shipbuilders had kept up to their high mark in workmanship. Amasa made note after the storm: ". . . owing to the ship's being an excellent sea boat, we weathered the gale and suffered only trifling damage compared with what the other ships did."

Fortune was still adverse when Shaw arrived at Canton. There was satisfaction in bringing the beautiful *Massachusetts* out of the terrible storm to anchor among the international fleet and to hear her praised by foreign skippers as a masterpiece of ship design; but it was crushing to find that prices were low for the bigger cargo the vessel accommodated. Shaw's dependence on Randall's business judgment had not been well placed at this time, because, as Amasa Delano made note, "Captain Randall had been at Canton the previous season, and had contracted more debt than was owing before, and that was considerably large."

The cargo Shaw brought in was unsalable, and the amount of specie he carried amounted to only $15,000.

The scandal of the spare masts of the *Massachusetts* as discovered at Canton is set forth plainly by another member of the crew.

We insert here an extract from the sea journal of Seaman John Bartlett of Boston, Mass., who was one of the crew of the *Massa-*

chusetts on her voyage to China. John Bartlett is a true person who wrote an authentic manuscript—it is now in the possession of the Peabody Museum of Salem. Bartlett died some years before Amasa Delano published his journal of the same voyage, but his description of the rottenness found in the hold of the ship corresponds word for word with the account in Amasa Delano's journal. Probably remembering what he had copied, Amasa wrote in his preface: "The responsibility of everything in the book, where credit is not given, is entirely my own."

Here is the Bartlett narrative as to what was found in the hold:

"On her arrival at Batavia, and also at Canton, the Commanders of foreign vessels came aboard to examine her model . . . But when her lower hold was opened at Canton, for the first time since she left Boston, she was rotten. She was loaded principally with green masts and spars, taken on board in the winter, directly out of the water, with ice and mud on them. The lower deck hatches were caulked down in Boston and when opened at Canton the air was so foul that a lighted candle was put out by it almost as soon as by water. We had four or five hundred barrels of beef in the lower hold placed in broken stowage and when the fresh air was admitted so that men could live under the hatches, the beef was found almost boiled. The hoops were rotted and fallen off and the inside of the ship was covered with blue mould an inch thick."

An unpleasant description, and an unpleasant record of recklessness as to honor and safety. But where the blame rests is a mystery.

Captain Job Prince, writing to the builders Hacket after the voyage, stated that when they built a new ship he would have some suggestions to make. No doubt one of them would be— "honest timbers!"

Deeply in debt to the suavely demanding hong merchants, Shaw and Randall must pay them off and get rid of the ruining burden of high interest charges, and yet it was doubtful whether they could manage to buy a cargo that would produce a profit in America. Then there was the question of how the *Massachusetts* would hold up under another tearing, pounding typhoon.

To clear himself of debt and start all over again on his grand scheme of an American East India Company, Shaw's best resource was the ship itself. If he could sell it at a profit he could build another big ship and use it to induce financiers to invest. He must erase from his mind the hopes of the people of his State who had celebrated the launching at Quincy, and must write convincingly to his sweetheart Hannah Phillips and her father.

Fortunately, the destructive typhoon had created a dearth of capacious vessels and there were bidders for the *Massachusetts*. The Danish East India Company needed a ship to replace one ruined by the typhoon, and paid him $65,000 for her. The purchasers had full confidence in the ship that had withstood the typhoon. Amasa Delano's comment about the *Massachusetts* when she was sold adds to the confusion:—"So parted we with as noble a ship as ever swam the sea."

The best opportunity to use what money remained to Shaw was to rent a ship and buy a cargo from the European market. He took passage to stifling Bombay, chartered a Danish ship, sailed to Ostend, sold the cargo, and boarded a ship for the United States, having decided to take time out from fortune-making to marry Hannah Phillips. He must tell her that the honeymoon must be brief, but he was sure that she would be sensible and agree. The girls of New England ports who married seafaring men expected short honeymoons and long separations.

He had selected a substantial and sensible family to marry into. Hannah's father, William Phillips, was related to ministers, but his instincts had been to establish a mercantile house. He had achieved his ambition by wedding the daughter of his employer, Edward Bromfield, and by marrying the business.

When energetic Samuel Shaw first found time to court Hannah, who had been taking music lessons while he was studying Latin, her father, for his commercial merits and public works, had acquired the title Honorable, and was one that Shaw could approve as a father-in-law. The Honorable Phillips in turn approved of Samuel, who had helped the Virginian George Washington make a success of the War of Independence.

It was an excellent match. Major Shaw in courting, impressively ornamented his conversation with quotations from Addison

49

and Pope. Hannah proudly told her friends that gentlemen of the literary arts had bestowed on Samuel the honorary degree of Master of Arts, and that he had been elected a Fellow of the American Academy of Arts and Sciences.

Plato, Addison, and Pope had been succeeded in Samuel Shaw's conversation by quotations from Confucius and other sages, and by comparisons of Chinese standards of education with those of New England. Hannah was curious to know how girls were educated in China, and Shaw was ready with answers:

"Parents would not think of placing their daughters, of any age, under the instruction of male teachers, and due to the limitations on female education, good schoolmistresses are lacking; so the mother becomes the educator. Boys study the classics in the hope of passing examinations for government employment; but girls have only family interests to look forward to, and are taught to perfect themselves in the home arts. The study of literature is open to them, however, and I am informed that in the history of Chinese literature there are many authoresses of distinction. As early as a century after Christ, a woman writer, Pan Hwuipan, wrote a book entitled *Female Precepts* which is read and followed to this day. Her idea as to female virtue was that a woman must be modestly grave and inviolably chaste. It was not required that she be extraordinarily intelligent, but she must be unassuming and decorous."

From travels in India and his observations of social life in those feverish climates, from the teeming life on the river leading to Canton and the beauty and wickedness of Macao, Samuel Shaw brought back rich intellectual cargoes, and the Phillips' and their circle listened hungrily, and began to dream of the days when it would be safe for them to travel to the Far East.

How charming it was to be informed by Hannah's lover that the Chinese themselves were a wandering race, whose clumsy junks had greeted Vasca da Gama when he rounded the Cape of Good Hope. How marvelous it was that Chinese snuff bottles had been found in the tombs of Egypt. And what Oriental learning was his to be able to quote the inscriptions on those ancient snuff bottles: "The almond blushes for ten miles around," and "The bright moon shines amidst the firs."

THE HERCULES OF SALEM, EDWARD WEST, CAPTAIN, 1809

THE HOPE, OPERATED BY BROWN AND IVES OUT OF
PROVIDENCE, R. I. About 1800

Peabody Museum, Salem

THE BRIG GRAND TURK, WM. AUSTIN, COMMANDER, 1815
From the painting by Anton Roux

Questioned as to the family duties of a Chinese woman, Shaw was not at a loss.

"Her chief concern is obedience to her husband and to his parents. She must be submissive to his brothers and sisters, and be agreeable with her sisters-in-law. If her husband has other wives, she must show no jealousy. If the family is poor, she must be content with her lot, and if it is wealthy, she must not be haughty or extravagant. Along with these amiable arts, she must know how to avenge the murder of a relative. As to sorcerers and witches, she must avoid them. In preparing for maternity, and in child-bearing, she must depend on midwives—it would be a great indelicacy even to consider being ministered to by a male doctor.

"To teach children, to maintain etiquette, to rear silkworms and work the cloth, to serve food, and prepare the sacrifices to the gods—these are the duties of the Chinese woman."

The Phillips family, from which was to come Phillips Brooks, drank in this edification about Oriental life and, being religiously inclined, rejoiced when the Major said that reading and writing were permitted to women and that when devoted missionaries went to China with the Gospel, translators might easily distribute Christian tracts among them.

They were married on August 21, 1792. The wedding was a brilliant one, and the honeymoon was intellectually blissful. But the persistent business devil was whipping the bridegroom, and he took care not to miss the China season. Buying a ship in New York, he sailed in February, 1793.

Hannah had forebodings, but he pictured for her a fine mansion built out of the China trade, and assured her that in eighteen months she would see him again.

He left with her a large Bible—a gift from Richard Freeman, the friendly English supercargo who had first welcomed him at Canton. In it he had inscribed a devout passage stating that in his thirty-ninth year there had been added to his relations of son, brother, friend, citizen, that of husband. Adjoined was a prayer that he might rejoice in God's goodness: "Whether longer or

51

shorter, may I be satisfied with life, and cheerfully submit to the dispensations of Thy providence."

From Bombay to Canton the ship battled with typhoons, and was long delayed in arriving at Macao. During the voyage Shaw became ill. The buffetings by the storms and the lack of delicate fare inflamed the illness, and James Dodge, the ship surgeon, could do little to relieve it. When the ship arrived at Canton, Shaw took to his bed.

The East India Company's ablest physician attended him. Human need and suffering had driven out the thought of old battles and new competition.

The partners, conferring as to how to defeat this dreadfully menacing adversary, decided to seek medical aid at home. On March 17, 1794—less than four months after Shaw had arrived—they sailed in the *Washington* for the United States.

At a harbor on the homeward voyage they fell in with the British man-of-war *Lion* with the surgeon to the embassy of Lord MaCartney aboard. With grave sympathy, he and the surgeon to a British ship on the Hindostan run came to the bedside, but they found the disease beyond medical aid.

Dodge, in his journal, tells of the way Shaw died: "Not long before his death, as I was standing by him, he took hold of my hand and pressed it affectionately to his breast, he then sighed heavily, and casting his eyes on the miniature of his wife that hung at the foot of the berth, sighed again, and said, 'God's will be done.' I found it impossible to suppress a tear, which fell over my cheek upon his hand, which when he saw he said, 'My dear friend, you know I am dying; speak comfort to me.' From this time he sunk rapidly. He took an affectionate leave of all his friends."

When the ship of mourning arrived at Sandy Hook, Thomas Randall wrote Hannah Shaw about her husband's death. No intimation had come to her that he was ill, and she had begun to expect his return. Instead she received an abrupt and self-centered note from Randall which said: "With a heart deeply distressed I take the pen to inform you of the death of my beloved and esteemed friend, Mr. Samuel Shaw, who died on board the ship *Washington* near the Cape of Good Hope, on Friday afternoon,

3 o'clock, on the 30th of May last . . . My friend died with a calm strength of mind, and expressed his solicitude for his remaining friends to the last . . . Permit me to join my grief to yours."

CHAPTER VII

Salem Sniffs Pepper

THE SPICE ISLANDS . . .

Columbus sought them. They lured da Gama and Magellan and drew Drake across the Pacific. The Portuguese, subjects then of Spain, found and exploited them.

The English were not far behind. In 1591 James Lancaster led the first English fleet to the Spice Islands, and the word he brought home of the profits of the spice trade led to the formation of the British East India Company.

The Dutch had stopped the Portuguese monopoly and seized the spice trade and their forwardness was envied by the narrator of the Lancaster voyage. Writing of two Dutch ships he said: "These two ships had been at Patania (in Malaysia), where they laded pepper, and at the Moluccas, where they had cloves, and upon the coast of China, where they bought silke, both raw and twisted; so that their lading was very rich."

Thirteen years after the Lancaster voyage, Henry Middleton led English ships to the Moluccas for spices, but was forced to stand by and watch the Dutch, who profited where others explored, drive out the rightful claimants, the Portuguese.

The discovery of the Spice Isles by an American skipper was far less adventurous, as we shall see when we follow the Salem discoverer of the shores of pepper—Shipmaster Jonathan Carnes.

In 1793 Captain Carnes learned at Bencoolen that the red-berried shrub grew wild on the northwestern coast of Sumatra. Arriving home, he confided his secret to shipper Jonathan Peele, who deemed the opportunities for profit big enough to build a schooner solely for the pepper trade.

She was the 130-ton *Rajah*. Commander Carnes set out in 1795 with ten men. To keep her destination a secret from other hawk-eyed merchants, Peele took out clearance papers showing that her destination was an Indian port. She carried two pipes of brandy, fifty-eight cases of gin, and twelve tons of iron, tobacco, and smoken salmon. The cargo of pepper she brought back after eighteen silent months was sold at a profit of seven hundred per cent.

"Rival merchants," stated the Reverend George Bachelor, an early Salem scribe writing about the period of pepper rivalry, "sometimes drove the work of preparation night and day, when virgin markets had favors to be won, and ships which set out for unknown ports were watched when they slipped their cables and sailed away by night, and dogged for months on the high seas, in the hopes of discovering a secret, well kept by the owner and his crew."

Jealous shipowners tried to find out the source of the pepper, but the *Rajah's* crew kept the secret. All the merchants could discover was that Carnes had touched first at Bencoolen, and when they saw his ship being fitted out for another voyage, they sent several vessels to that port. He eluded them, however, and they were forced to trade for other goods; but finally Peele and Carnes shared the secret, and so Salem came to control for the New World market the pepper production of Sumatra.

Commander Benjamin Crowninshield, in 1796 and 1797, made two voyages to the Far East in the ship *America.*

On her first voyage, the *America,* manned by mere boys, touched at Madras and exchanged raisins and rope for a load of pepper. On her second voyage, she anchored off several East African ports and at Aden in Arabia. It is an example of the license the owner granted the master as to cargo that, while the *America* sailed to obtain a load of pepper, she came home instead with gum arabic, dye woods, sienna, goatskins, and frankincense.

With many a Salem shipowner and skipper, anything that was in demand in any port anywhere was a cargo, be it animal, mineral, or vegetable. Slaves, coolies, rum, and opium were carried as well as pepper, ginseng, flour, teas, dishes, and Bibles.

As for the shipboard habit of strong drink, there were tales to tell. One of these, told by Charles E. Trow, relates to the China trade:

A certain Captain L——— had shipped a first mate who when on shore indulged freely. The captain belonged to the temperance school, and when anchored in a Chinese port was shocked to see the first mate come aboard "drunk as a lord."

The mate's duty was to keep the log, but the captain made the entries this day, and added to his note: "The mate drunk all day."

When the ship sailed the next day the sobered mate resumed his duties, and was shocked to discover what the master had written.

"Cap'n," he said, "why did you write that in the log?"

"It was true, wasn't it?"

"Well, 'lowing 'twas, it was a bad thing to say about me."

"It was true, wasn't it?"

"Yes, but what will the owners say if they see it? 'Twill hurt me with them."

But the captain gave the mate no satisfaction.

The next day the mate made the usual entries in the log as to the course of the ship, and the state of the winds and tides. Then he wrote: "The captain sober all day."

The captain stormed:—"What did you mean, you rascal, by writing in the log that I was sober all day?"

"It was true, wasn't it, Cap'n?"

"You know I never drink liquor, and am always sober, and of course it was true."

When the owners read the log they saw no comments as to drunkenness or sobriety.

With these human weaknesses, there was much of moral strength and artistic worth in Salem, and these qualities revealed themselves especially in mathematician Nathaniel Bowditch and architect Samuel McIntyre, whose good works endure.

A boy in a ship chandler's shop, Nathaniel Bowditch listened intently to the talk of shipmasters who came in to purchase outfits for their vessels. They complained that the standard English book on navigation did not adequately cover the shores and harbors American ships sailed to. The lad remembered these things.

When he was fourteen, an elder brother told Nat that a school-master was showing pupils a way of working out mathematical problems by letters. Nathaniel was excited, and he asked the master to show him the book of algebra. The teacher lent him the rare volume, and the boy copied its entire contents and solved every problem. Then he got hold of a book, "Philosophical Transactions of the Royal Society of London," and copied it also, while studying Latin to understand its scientific terms.

In 1795, at twenty-two, he made his first voyage to study navigation, and visited Manila via Lisbon and Madeira. He made a sun dial, composed an almanac, and charted Salem harbor. Then he corrected and brought out "The Practical Navigator," which was founded on the thirteenth English edition of J. H. Moore's work of the same name. After bringing out several editions to which he contributed enormously the book became "The New American Practical Navigator." Adopted in London, it became the international authority.

Fascinated by people as well as by stars and instruments, Bowditch studied the peoples of the Philippines, and brought back an informing account of them:

A few hundred Europeans lived there, but the islands were mainly inhabited by Negroes, Malays, Mestizos, and Creoles. The blacks were the original inhabitants.

The Malays, or Indians, had emigrated from parts of Borneo and the Celebes; they were proud of their ancestry, and fond of dress and show. They were addicted to gambling, were prone to lead the soft life, and had good taste in music and painting. When challenged, they could be active and industrious.

The Mestizos were the descendants of Spaniards by Indian or Chinese women. Too proud to consider themselves Indians, they affected the manners of the pure-blooded Spaniards; but they wasted their money and time in law-suits, firing cannon, fireworks, gambling, and parades.

The bland, ubiquitous Chinese had established themselves in Manila before the Spaniards and Portuguese came to those waters. They were active in business, attentive to details, given to wiles and bribery to obtain their ends, and sensual in enjoying their gains. Marrying native women, they appeared to have no scruples about leaving the wives and children behind when they had amassed enough riches to return to their homeland.

Nathaniel Bowditch, the self-taught scientist, was given the highest scholastic honors, and lived a pleasant and vastly useful life. When he died the very Marine Society of Salem that had helped his immigrant father out of its charity fund wrote of him: ". . . no monument will be needed to keep his memory among men, but as long as ships sail, the needle points to the north, and the stars go through their wanted course in the heavens, the name of Dr. Bowditch will be revered as one who helped his fellow men in time of need, who was and is to them a guide over the pathless ocean, and who forwarded the great interest of mankind."

Another Salem celebrity as worthy of honor in his way as was Bowditch, was Samuel McIntyre, a ship carpenter, who, by self instruction and the study of architectural books brought from abroad by sympathetic skippers, created the Salem style of architecture that is today the chief attraction of tourists. He transmuted the fortunes merchants made in the West and East Indian trades into structurally simple houses whose doorways, cornices, gateposts, and other embellishments were in the exquisite taste that evokes reverence in every generation.

CHAPTER VIII

Amazing Oriental Ventures of John Jacob Astor

JOHN JACOB ASTOR, the steerage passenger . . . the baker's boy . . . the toy seller . . . the modest importer of musical instruments . . . the helper to a benign Jewish fur-trader . . . the penetrator of the lands of the Louisiana Purchase . . . the settler in the Pacific Northwest . . . the international financier.

With all these trades and achievements, John Jacob Astor was also a leader in the China trade; indeed, his ventures in Oregon and British Columbia had as their goal the trading of North Pacific furs for the teas of China.

For the intimate account we give of Astor's career, we depend on Joseph A. Scoville (pseudonym, Walter Barrett, Clerk). In his work, "The Old Merchants of New York," Scoville declared: "These facts concerning the renowned John Jacob Astor are true ... no man would enjoy their publication more than Mr. Astor, himself, were he now alive."

When he was nearly twenty-one, John Jacob Astor came to New York via Baltimore in the steerage, living upon a diet of salt pork and tea biscuits. From his birthplace in Waldorf, near Heidelberg, he had made his way at sixteen to London, where he worked for an elder brother who was employed in a piano and flute factory. Young Jacob soon set his mind on America, and took with him aboard the ship a few flutes which he hoped to sell in German circles there. On the first day of his arrival in New York he obtained lodgings with George Deiterich, who kept a bakery at Frankfort and Pearl Streets.

It was the custom of the bakers of those days to send their apprentices out to peddle "the luxuries of the oven," and young Jacob was hired by Deiterich and given the job of peddling cakes, cookies, and tea rusks. The apprentices were required to shout their wares, and Jacob's first lesson in English was the uttering of American street cries. He always spoke broken English, and his written scrawls were always outrageous in their grammar and spelling. His sister, Mrs. Ehninger, whom Jacob looked down on later because she had married a distiller of cordials, could not understand why he should be condescending toward her husband. She protested, "Yakob was noting put a paker poy und sold pread and kak!"

One day, observing Indians crowding into a lane called Bayard Street, he followed them curiously. They had journeyed from the northern outskirts of Manhattan and from the wilds of Long Island to visit their friend Hayman Levy, a peddler who first had come to trade with them.

The front of Levy's store was adorned with animal skins, from beaver to bear, and the place had the fascinating aspect of a barbaric trading-post. The enthralled Jacob asked the trader if he could work for him, and Levy said yes.

Standing at the fur-dealer's elbow, Jacob began to learn the

Indian language. He found out that the Indian name for Long Island was *Sewanhacky* (Land of Shells), and that they meant New York town when they said *Laapawacking* (the Place of Stringing Wampum Beads). He learned also that one of the secret of Levy's success with the Indians was his willingness to deal with them in terms of their peculiar currency—wampum.

At the trader's rough-hewn counter Jacob found out that wampum was made of selected, lustrous parts of large sea-shells. Fond of decoration, the Indians used it for necklaces, or for ornamenting their robes and moccasins. Three black beads of wampum had the value of an English penny, and six beads of white wampum had the same worth. With wampum as currency, Hayman Levy bartered for northern beaver and coast beaver; for raccoons, marten, deer leather and bearskins. Watching him, Jacob learned how to detect choice pelts among inferior ones, and he came to know which skins were a bargain at four shillings and which would be worth paying ten shillings.

Fur-trader Levy having become an important employer of Manhattan's young men, Jacob worked alongside a youth named Nick. The generous employer backed Nick by giving him a single hogshead of rum with which to trade with the Indians; and so began the business of the important merchant Nicholas Low.

Jacob also wanted to be in business for himself, and Hayman Levy gave him similar encouragement. On January 10, 1789— just five years after he landed on a New York wharf—Jacob issued this advertisement:

J. JACOB ASTOR

at No. 81 Queen Street,
Next door but one to the Friend's Meeting house,
has for sale an assortment of
Pianofortes of the Newest Construction
made by the best makers in London, which he will sell on
reasonable terms

HE GIVES CASH FOR ALL KINDS OF FUR

and has for sale a quantity of Canada Beaver and Beaver Coating,
Raccoon Skins, and Raccoon Blankets, Muskrat Skin, &c. &c.

Starting out independently, Jacob bought and peddled skins, and bartered cheap jewelry, birds, etc., from his peddler's pack. Then, taking Peter Smith as his partner, he set up business in a wooden shanty at 362 Pearl Street. Soon afterwards he discovered that a shrewd and comely New York girl was watching his progress sympathetically. She listened intently to his farreaching plans without making fun of his broken English. This girl, the poor but well-connected Sarah Todd, was ready to unite with him, and marry him she did. Though her dowry was only $300, he told her that her prudence and good judgment would be worth a fortune to him.

They began wedded life at the store, and she took charge of it while Smith and her husband traveled. She encouraged Jacob to go farther up toward Canada, where the rare and valuable pelts could be procured. From Schenectady to Utica he ventured, and made plans for future trading along the border when the long-delaying British should conform to the peace treaty and give up their military posts.

Meanwhile, in the depot in Pearl Street, Sarah sorted out Jacob's shipments of beaver, muskrat, rabbit, and squirrel. These common furs had a ready market at home, but unusual furs from the north were not appreciated by the restricted fashion leaders of Manhattan. Jacob and Sarah decided to pack them away in casks in their cellar, with a view to shipping them to the great fur market of London, where they could be exchanged for flutes and pianos.

When Jacob returned from one of his trips to the Indian tribes about Utica, Sarah charted the new course for him. He should sail to London and dispose of the furs himself, since no agent could get as much profit out of the voyage as could Jacob. He sailed on the next outgoing vessel and sold the furs at a satisfactory price.

Pleasing as was this transaction, there was an even happier fortune in store for him. His lucky fate handed him a free ticket into the lucrative Chinese trade.

Wandering about London, he visited the East India House and learned that its governor had been born in Germany. Remembering that in boyhood he had a friend of the same name as the official, he called on the latter, and was received with open arms.

At parting, the governor gave Jacob a secret list of the prices the British East India Company paid to Canton for teas and silks, and also gave him a permit on parchment granting any shipmaster the right to trade freely at any of the company's exclusive ports.

Up to this time, while Astor had taken note that British shipowners were gathering furs in the Pacific Northwest and selling them at Canton, he had never dreamed of entering the Pacific trade; but when he showed the two papers to his wife, they decided to test the tickets to fortune.

Seeking out James Livermore, he urged the merchant to send a ship to Canton, and in return for the use of Jacob's permit, give him half the profits.

Livermore signed an agreement providing that Astor should have half the profits of a cargo of ginseng, lead, and scrap iron he was sending to China. The ginseng, costing 20 cents a pound in New York, brought $3.50 a pound there, and the metal also was sold at an immense profit. The tea cargo bought for the return voyage sold for $1.00 more in New York than the price paid for it at Canton.

One day a wagon filled with barrels stopped in front of Astor's store. The casks were heavy, and Mrs. Astor went out to inquire what they contained.

"They contain the fruits of our East India pass," Astor said, and opened one that she might see that it was filled with silver coins. There was $55,000 in the barrels—the Astor share of the voyage.

Repossessing himself of the valuable ship pass, Astor decided to invest the profits received from Livermore in a ship he himself would load for a voyage to Canton. Going among the shipyards located below Grand Street on the East River, he ordered a ship from the Scottish-American shipbuilder, Henry Eckford. Jacob knew that the men of the Clyde were splendid ship builders.

At the Eckford yard, at the foot of Clinton Street, admiring crowds gathered to watch the building of Astor's 427-ton ship— well-named the *Beaver*.

Knowing that the Boston ships had gone safely around the Horn, up into the North Pacific for a cargo of furs, and across to

China, Jacob decided he could send the *Beaver* that way without much risk.

With Captain Whetten in command, and the later renowned captain Augustus De Peyster before the mast, the *Beaver* sailed down through the turbulent waters of Cape Hatteras and navigated the uncertainties of Cape Horn. Then she made her way up past the forbidden Spanish coast of California to the friendlier ports of British Columbia. Making a good exchange of his iron, trinkets, and ribbons for the glossy brown skins of the sea-otter—then the most valuable of skins—Whetten set out across the Pacific, stopping for supplies at the Sandwich Islands and taking on a load of fragrant wood. Whetten found the hong merchants at Canton as enthusiastic about the scented wood as the furs.

"It is sandalwood," they said. "Our people use the fragrant wood as sticks to burn before the family altars. It is worth $500 a ton in this market."

Astor indeed had the Midas touch.

In New York during the Jefferson embargo of 1808, 666 vessels lay idle, but one was busy. The active one was John Jacob Astor's *Beaver*.

While the competitors of Astor in New York were merely protesting against the embargo, Astor was mysteriously closemouthed. The reason for his placidity was soon revealed.

It was suddenly announced that the President of the United States had granted permission to Astor to send his ship *Beaver* on a voyage to Canton for the purpose of returning to China a distinguished mandarin who had become stranded in the United States.

The announcement amazed New Yorkers. Who was the great mandarin? Had anyone seen him in Astor's company? Why hadn't Manhattan's citizens engaged in the China trade been given the opportunity to entertain the Oriental personage at a public banquet? What must be the feelings of a high mandarin of China to be kept hidden from polite society by the uncouth Astor?

After such outbursts and secret complaints, the merchants began to smell a coolie in the woodpile. It was recalled that, a month before, Astor offered to make contracts with other merchants to bring home goods from Canton, even though the embargo was in force.

A rival of Astor's put the result of his sharp investigations into a letter to President Jefferson. It had been truly discovered that the supposedly Chinese official was no mandarin. He was not even a member of the group of merchants at Canton known as the Co-hong, but instead was a coolie who had slipped out of his country and become a New York wharf rat. Astor had found him, dressed him in Chinese silks and taken him privately into the cabin of the *Beaver*.

With the object of obtaining a valuable tea cargo when all other ships in the China trade were kept at home, the tricky Astor, the writer complained, had deceived the Administration by pretending that a mandarin of great influence wished to sail at once to the Celestial Empire.

Secretary of State Madison was suspected by the Manhattan merchants of playing the game of his close friend, Mr. Astor. His interest in the matter was ascertained because he gave Astor copies of the letters that had been sent to the President.

The newspaper, *Commercial Advertiser,* took up the cudgels for the protestors. It referred editorially to the strange permission granted by President Jefferson at a time when all other vessels were forbidden to sail. It pointed out: "The ship *Beaver* is one of the most valuable, the number of its men exposed to peril the greatest in any merchant's service, and the voyage not to the West Indies, but to the antipodes."

This attack brought from the fur trader his first and only defense—and a weak and evasive one it was, though evidently conceived by an employed scribe.

"If whoever wrote that article will give me his name," he stated in a letter dated August 15, 1808, "and if he is not prejudiced against any act of the administration, not influenced from envy arising from jealousy, he shall receive a statement of facts relative to the transaction in question, which will relieve him from the anxiety under which he appears to labor for the honor of the Government, and the reputation of all concerned. He shall be convinced that the Government has not been surprised by misrepresentations in granting permission, and that the reputation of those concerned cannot be in the slightest degree affected.

Your humble servant,

John Jacob Astor"

"Let us observe the progress of this affair," the *Commercial Advertiser* advised, and those who followed the advice found that the *Beaver* returned from the voyage with "two hundred thousand dollars more than she left with."

A colossal crash and sensational scandal was to occur a quarter-century later in the American tea market. Astor would be involved but would escape without financial ruin or moral blame.

We may as well narrate it here. The tea crash was caused in this way:

Thomas H. Smith of New York had begun business with a few thousand dollars. He became an importer of teas, and his business grew. The firm had built an immense tea-store in South Street, and its room extended through Water Street. Competitors admitted that Smith was "the greatest tea merchant of his day."

The operations of Smith were conducted in this fashion: At Canton, the Smith supercargo would load a ship with tea costing about 37 cents a pound, the duty exacted by the United States Government at that time being 75 cents a pound. With a tea cargo originally valued at $200,000 plus $400,000 for duty, and a profit of $100,000, the final worth of the cargo would be $700,000. The cargo would be sold to wholesale grocers, who would give their notes for $700,000 which could be very easily turned into money. As to the duty, the Government gave credit nine, twelve, or eighteen months, at the discretion of the Collector of Customs at the port, and Smith used the $400,000 owed to the Government for new cargoes and waited until the limit of time to pay the amount due Uncle Sam. The $400,000 due the Government permitted him to load two more ships with cargoes valued at $200,-000 each. Astor operated the same way, and was said at one time to owe the Government five million dollars duty. He had, however, sufficient resources for any emergency.

In 1826, the market having become overstocked with tea, the

64

Manhattan Collector of Customs grew worried about the millions the tea importers owed the Government, and when Smith, owing two million, tried to give bonds for an even larger amount, the Collector, distrusting the bondsmen he offered, shut down on him.

Tea cargoes of immense value were on the ocean consigned to Smith, and in desperation he plotted to bring them in at some other harbor. Going down to Perth Amboy, New Jersey, then scarcely known as a port, Smith talked to the Collector of Customs there, who assured Smith that he would take bonds for any amount. Thereupon, the tea trader built at unimportant Perth Amboy immense brick warehouses that later stood as a monument to his ingenuity and to the folly of the Collector.

Having thus provided a new port of entry for his teas, Smith sent out agents in pilot boats to divert his incoming ships from New York to Perth Amboy. His debt at the two ports rose to $3,000,000.

Down in Philadelphia, the large tea house of Thompson was getting into similar difficulties, and the Collector there, finding that Thompson had brought in an oversupply of tea, refused to take his bonds for incoming cargoes. The official arranged with Thompson to place his filled warehouses under Government control, the tea to be released in quantities as needed, and the duty on the amount taken out to be paid then and there. Thompson paid duty on a stated amount but enlarged the amount on the Government permit so that he took out ten times the amount without paying duty on the surplus. These teas he shipped to auctioneers John Hone & Sons, New York, and the auctioning of them flooded the New York market and precipitated the crash.

To protect themselves, Thomas W. Smith and John Jacob Astor entered the market and bought the Thompson teas at auction, planning to ship them to the Mediterranean market. Then the Government discovered Thompson's trick, and seized his tea stores in Philadelphia and Boston. The teas were sold just for the duty, and Smith and Astor bought them at this low price.

When the crash came, Smith made an assignment to Matthias Bruen, who set to work to effect a compromise with the Government for the $3,000,000 Smith owed. It was said that a payment of a million settled the entire debt.

Astor escaped ruin because he had shrewdly diversified his cargoes, so that the tea trade was just one of his ventures.

Tea remained queen, but variety had come into the China trade. For example, the Carnes brothers, merchants who had offices both in Paris and New York, were creating a demand for a diversity of Chinese goods.

Studying the Chinese, they discovered their skill as imitators, and decided to send to China samples of fancy articles popular in Paris. Sending a trusted clerk in the ship *Howard,* they achieved such success in obtaining a broad line of mattings that they invested in other voyages and induced New York merchants to help finance the enterprise.

Fans were the rage in Paris and, from samples submitted, the Chinese craftsmen produced at low cost fans of silk, ivory, mother-of-pearl, and peacock feathers. Pure attar of roses, worth twenty-five dollars an ounce in Paris, was excellently imitated at a cost of twelve cents an ounce. Lacquer ware, chessmen, fireworks, sweetmeats, and European silks were imitated. Gloriously colored shawls were imported and sold at high prices in the South American market.

This business in fancy goods flourished for a time, but at last high duties and high freight costs took the profit out of it. The continuing trade was composed of substantial lines—ornaments, furniture. and floor coverings.

CHAPTER IX

Captain Cleveland Braves Mutiny and Massacre

WE CONCERN OURSELVES now with ships that, like Astor's *Beaver,* sailed from the east coast of the United States, rounded Cape Horn, obtained furs among the menacing natives of the North Pacific, and sailed to exchange their peltry for tea in the welcoming China market.

Captain Richard Cleveland reversed the run in the face of

severe hardships and peril of wreck or massacre, and of him we particularly tell.

In 1787 the eager port of Boston sent out two little ships that were the first to circumnavigate the globe and to open the way for Oregon and Washington to be brought into the Union. They were the *Columbia,* Captain John Kendrick, 213 tons, and the *Lady Washington,* Captain Robert Gray, a 90-ton sloop.

The intrepid little vessels went staunchly around the Horn and up into the fogs of the North Pacific. They nosed their way into Nootka harbor, British Columbia, which had become a rendezvous for ships from Europe whose objectives also were to take furs to China and bring China teas to their native ports.

The rum-guzzling English, Danish, and Portuguese captains at Nootka Sound were boisterous in their welcome but deceptive in their information. However, the Boston merchants had put goods aboard that attracted the Indian chiefs, and from this keen rivalry of "King George's Men" and "Boston Men," Kendricks and Gray emerged with plenty of fine sea-otter furs.

In view of the increasing settlement of Alaska, it is worth noting that Kendrick gave the United States an early claim by purchasing from native chiefs large tracts of country along Nootka Sound. True, he obtained a tract eighteen miles square for two muskets, a boat's sail and a quantity of powder; but for all that he could boast to the British commander at Nootka Sound: "I buy my territories, while other nations stole theirs."

He had been instructed to send the *Lady Washington* to Canton after she had been loaded with pelts, and to send the *Columbia* to trade along the Pacific coast, but he obeyed his notion that it was wiser to send Gray in the *Columbia* to China. Gray's arrival there opened the American route to that coast by way of the now familiar islands of the Pacific.

The Massachusetts investors in the *Columbia* and the *Lady Washington* fidgeted and sweated three years before they received word of the fortune of their ships. Then happiness came in the arrival of the *Federalist* of New York, which brought news that she had anchored beside the *Columbia* at Whampoa.

After their long separation, the two vessels had joined and finally came together into Boston's harbor, immensely proud that their flags had been the first to carry the American colors completely around the world.

The Boston skippers were handicapped at first by their ignorance of the needs of the North Pacific natives. The fur-clad Indians had little use for the broadcloth and flannels the first vessels carried. A cargo of this kind was that of the 218-ton *Atahualpa,* which carried broadcloth, flannel, blankets, powder, muskets, watches, tools, beads, and looking-glasses.

When the *Hope* of Boston arrived in Northwestern waters with a cargo mostly of fabrics, her captain, James Ingraham, used Yankee resourcefulness to save his owners from loss. Finding that the chiefs wanted metals instead of cloths, he bade the blacksmith aboard set up his forge on deck and hammer out iron collars, rings, and bracelets. Ingraham sold one iron collar for three furs, and was able to sell the pelts at Canton for $25 each.

We take up now the heartening career of engaging Richard J. Cleveland, protégé of Elias Derby.

About 1807, when the embargo was starting at home, Richard Cleveland, twenty-three, bought at Havre the cutter-sloop *Caroline,* forty-three tons, and went trading in the Indian Ocean. When he arrived at the Cape of Good Hope, he got into grave trouble with the British governor by selling his cargo to a Frenchman at the Cape. Great Britain being at war with France, British officials seized the ship and cargo, and young Cleveland stood to lose his entire investment.

He acted with decision and sagacity: "I determined to write to Lord Maccartney (the Governor), and prove to him, by my contract for the sale of the cargo, the duties were not to be paid by me; and that . . . if the vessel and cargo were to be confiscated, I should be the sufferer, as it was doubtful if the merchant could make good the loss . . ."

And here we come to a delightful view of the simplicity of this American sailor:

"But how to write a suitable letter embarrassed me. I had no friend with whom to advise. I was entirely ignorant of the proper manner of addressing a nobleman, and at the same time was aware of the necessity of conforming to customary rules. In this dilemma I remembered to have seen, in an old magazine on board my vessel, some letters addressed to noblemen. These I sought as models, and they were a useful guide to me. After completing my letter in my best hand, I enclosed it in a neat envelope and showed it to the Admiral's secretary, who appeared to be friendly to me. He approved of it and advised my taking it myself to his lordship immediately.

"As the schoolboy approached his master after having played a truant, so did I approach Lord Maccartney on this occasion."

Though severe in his manner, the Earl gave the American hope, and finally our resourceful shipmaster sailed away from the Cape with $11,000 in his possession, ready to be invested in a ship and a voyage to the American Northwest for furs.

His intention had been to sail from Canton in February, when the weather would have been more favorable, but he had received news that competitive ships had sailed from Boston for the Northwest to bring furs to Canton, and he was eager to get a cargo of pelts and return before the "Boston men" reached China and glutted the market. Though warned by veteran navigators that the ship he had acquired for the new voyage could never make progress in the teeth of the violent northeast monsoon, still he went ahead with his plan.

The vessel would be forced to weather the northern end of Formosa, but his idea was that he could beat up the coast of China, keeping near the shore so that he could run in and come to anchor when wind and sea were so rough that he could not make headway.

Ebenezer Townsend, proprietor of the Tontine Coffee House in New York, was at Canton when Cleveland arrived with his project of sailing to the Northwest, and he added $3000 to Cleveland's investment of $11,000. Another Yankee advanced $3000, and Yougua, a silk merchant at Canton, invested $1000.

For a voyage so hard in a ship so light a good crew was needed, but Cleveland was forced to depend on the port's riffraff. Of the twenty-one persons in the vessel, only two were Americans. The rest, English, Irish, Swedes, and French "served," he said, "to complete a list of as accomplished villains as ever disgraced any country."

The starting day came. On the 10th of January, 1799, he weighed anchor at Whampoa and passed Macao. He sailed up the coast against the wind, but often at night found the ship about where she had been in the morning. All he had to go by were the directions given him by friendly fishermen along the shore. The vessel several times scraped sunken rocks.

After he had been two weeks out, the ship caught a "wholesail" breeze which he hoped would carry her around the north end of Formosa; but soon the wind shifted to its old quarter, the northeast. For two days he beat against it and then stood out to sea and tacked windward again. Carrying double-reefed sails in a high sea, the little sloop was mostly under water. The seas were so high that the watch on deck never escaped a complete drenching, and often the fire in the caboose was put out by a comber.

One day Cleveland saw the water breaking ahead but, thinking it was caused by a strong current setting to windward, he did not alter his course. The vessel thudded on a submerged shoal, but the next wave, while piling sand on the deck, carried her over. To avoid further hazard, he tried to find a harbor, and anchored at last among fishing junks in a calm bay.

The crew was rebelling. Twenty days out, the boatswain told Cleveland that the men would not work until he agreed that they need not perform unnecessary labors, and that they would be the judges as to which tasks were needed. Hating the first officer, they stipulated that he should not come beyond a line they would mark out.

The indications are that the leader of the mutineers was the same man of whom Cleveland wrote on his previous voyage:

"The first of my foremost hands is a great, surly, raw-boned ignorant Prussian, who is so timid aloft that the mate has frequently been obliged to do his duty there. I believe him to be more of a soldier than a sailor, though he has often assured me that he has been boatswain's mate of a Dutch Indiaman . . ."

Against the revolter, Cleveland mustered his faithful. His first mate was a Nantucket youth whom, on the earlier voyage, he had promoted from before the mast and instructed in navigation.

His second officer was also dependable. His bulwark among the men was George the cook, a freed Savannah Negro. Cheated out of his wages by a former employer, he had found Cleveland honest and kindly and stuck by him through this mutiny and through life.

At once Cleveland put locks on the harness casks and told the rebels that they must work to eat. Arming his supporters each with a musket and a brace of pistols, he ordered that the two 4-pounders on the quarterdeck be loaded with grapeshot and trained to sweep the decks.

The mutineers, armed only with handspikes and hatchets, stood at bay cursing the officers, but when Cleveland offered to put them ashore, thinking they would soon become tired of foraging for themselves, they agreed, considering that he could not sail without them and would be forced to make terms.

Days of parley between ship and shore followed, but Cleveland was determined not to take back the ringleader, and this mutineer detained those who were willing to give in. The master's character shows again in his terse account of how the matter ended:

"Having a light breeze from the westward, and a favorable current, I concluded to have no further altercation with them, and immediately hoisted in the boat and made sail, leaving on the island of Kemoy (350 miles northeast of Canton) six of my most able men. This was such a reduction of our number as would require unceasing vigilance and extraordinary caution to counteract, as the risk of being attacked by the Indians was, of course, increased in proportion to our diminished power of resistance."

The local mandarins sent the castaways to Canton, and their tale of the hardships of the voyage led Cleveland's friends to give him up for lost. But he at last sighted the north end of Formosa and after thirty-one days of battle with wind and sea rounded it, doing what his advisers had declared impossible at that season. Although the North Pacific was almost as violent as the waters off Formosa, he arrived in Alaskan waters without mishap.

There danger wore a new face. The diminished crew was confronted with the peril of massacre by the savage Thlingets who, if they had discovered what few men were aboard, would have attacked in overwhelming numbers.

To conceal this weakness from the Indians, the master put up stanchions all around the vessel and fastened to them a curtain of hides. Then, when the Thlingets came out to trade, he permitted only one canoe at a time to approach the vessel and made its boatmen come to the stern and do the trading there, where assailants could be most easily repelled. It was the more necessary to take these precautions because the ship, being small, went into inlets and bays larger ships could not enter, and in so venturing, the danger of attack from natives was increased.

It required courage to remain calm as one of the largest canoes, manned by thirty well-armed warriors, came close to the little vessel. From other shipmasters Cleveland had learned what an Indian victory over them would mean "death in its most horrid form, or still more horrid captivity among the rudest savages."

For the hardships and risks, he was well rewarded. He bought eight prime skins for each musket and collected 1900 sea-otter furs.

At one section of the coast, close to an Indian encampment, the vessel struck a sunken ledge and slanted so that it was impossible to stand on deck. If they had been discovered and attacked, the fifteen men would have had to take to the sixteen-foot boat and defend themselves against larger canoes. Their lives, the ship, and the rich cargo were at stake. Fortunately, the vessel righted herself when the tide rose, and the adventurers' Providence kept the Indians away.

Cleveland's relief at departing for Canton was expressed in these terms: "We put to sea, happy at having so fortunately completed our business, and doubly so at leaving this inhospitable coast. Indeed, the criminal who receives a pardon under the gallows could scarcely feel a greater degree of exultation."

He dropped anchor at Whampoa on September 15, 1799, and when his ship was recognized, his friends put out to express their sympathy for his apparent failure. Their doleful expressions changed when he told them that he had a fur cargo aboard worth $60,000. He sold the sea-otter skins for $26 apiece, and all concerned in the venture received large profits.

Bad luck was to follow him on later voyages, but no one called him a failure. A consoling friend, George Cabot of Boston, said to him, "You have cut a great deal of hay, but you have got it in very badly."

CHAPTER X

Amasa Delano Sees a Commodore Go Native

AMASA DELANO, LATE of the unfortunate ship *Massachusetts,* was marking time in China. Possessing skill as a shipwright, he found that the typhoon that had swirled about the *Massachusetts* had provided a job for him by damaging a Danish ship at Whampoa. Having heard of the skill of the Delano brothers as shipwrights, the Dutch supercargo Van Brann recommended Amasa for the work of repair. Amasa made his brother Samuel his foreman and employed idle members of the *Massachusetts'* crew.

British masters were amazed that a young man who had risen to second officer on the new American ship would be willing to come down to the plain job of ship carpentering, and it occurred to one of them that an officer who was both navigator and re-pairer was a good one to employ.

This perceptive British naval officer, Commodore McCluer, had been employed by the East India Company, in keeping with a policy to study the regions it served and to enlighten the world about them, to command an exploring expedition.

He spoke persuasively to Amasa:

"You will be useful to me as an officer, a navigator, or a ship repairer," he said, "and if you come with me aboard the *Panther,* you will receive the same pay and emoluments as my lieutenants and scientists. You will be subject only to my command, and as the purpose of my voyage is survey and discovery in New Guinea, New Holland, the Spice Islands, and elsewhere, the trip should be to your liking. I will do all I can to make the voyage pleasant for you."

Gladly accepting, Amasa went out to enjoy a two-year cruise. He took hazing good-naturedly and before long was getting along well with the Commodore's staff. His one enemy was the American boatswain, who resented having to knuckle under, and tried to maroon the newcomer.

The first important stop was the Sooloo Island group, which lay beyond Borneo. The Company's ships had had trouble with their Malay inhabitants, but Commodore McCluer was eager to exchange the calicoes, knives, scissors, perfumes, and opium in his holds for the islanders' sago, pearls, gold dust, turtle shells, camphor, beche-de-mer, and birds' nests, and he hoped to make peace.

Anchoring beyond the guns of the ramshackle fort, McCluer waited to see if the Malays would be cordial or hostile. The Sultan was in an affable mood and revealed it by sending his daughters aboard, much to the delight of the lascivious sailors. Far more free in their manners than the daughters of a Turkish sovereign, the ladies basked in the pretended or sincere admiration of the officers and crew.

Among the officers escorting them was a Moor who had formerly commanded an East Indiaman. He invited Amasa to go ashore with him, assuring him that he, the Moor, would be a good interpreter.

Recalling the trouble he had had with these Malays, McCluer warned Amasa against going, but Delano had youth's daring.

"Very well," said the Commodore, "if you are arrested, say you went ashore to meet a girl. Any Malay ruler will forgive you for women-hunger, just so long as you do not plunder his harem."

"That will be all right," Amasa said, "I am curious to see the Moor's daughter." Throwing a robe over his uniform, he followed the Moor.

His host had a dumpling of a wife and a smaller dumpling of a daughter. Amasa's romantic or amorous feelings were cooled at the sight of them. Two women neighbors insisted on coming in, and they were no more fetching. For their part, the quartet looked up to him with unconcealed admiration. The Yankee sailor was a prince!

Regaled by coffee, dates, raisins, and confections, Amasa answered endless questions about the customs, fashions, and house-

74

keeping of the women of New England. The oriental women laughed and tittered as the Moor translated what he said about American courtship, monogamy, and child-rearing. They made no attempts to conceal their thought that his handsome stranger had come from a ridiculous people.

The romantic adventure had been a dud, and Amasa told the Moor he must return to the ship; but the latter told him that it was not convenient to escort him through the dangerous lanes at that time. The host must take his station as a guard of the palace, but he would return soon after midnight.

Shortly after he departed, a startling thing drew Amasa to his feet, with his fingers slipping toward his sword hilt. Fifteen Malay warriors, with dread krisses gleaming in their sashes, burst in and surrounded him. He wished he understood enough of their language to say that he had come to meet a woman. It was fortunate that he did not say it, for he discovered afterwards that the Moor's daughter was married, and that her husband was one of the palace guard.

His host returned just as he was groping for an excuse, and explained with uproarious laughter that the men were his comrades and, like the two women visitors, were merely curious to see a man the English called a Yankee.

The guard went on duty again, the Moor with them. Again Amasa tried to leave, but more abruptly, the Moor told him to stay. It was long past midnight and the Yankee wanted to go to sleep, but the women visitors stayed on.

Then it happened. Suddenly a crowd stormed the locked door and set up a clamor. Amasa comforted himself with the thought that the Commodore would think that a riot had broken out and would land a party to rescue him. But the ships apparently were paying no heed.

Two shrill male voices rose above the mob and the American gathered that they rose from the husbands of the two Malay women who were in his company.

Motioning him to follow her, the wife went toward the stairs. The movement alarmed Amasa, who felt that virtue and safety lay in staying on the ground floor. But the merry wives of Sooloo pulled and pushed him up the stairs, and he ascended on a sea of cushiony bosoms.

The quartet stopped, not at a bed or divan, but at an upstairs window. The Moor's wife seized one of the visitors and hoisted her through the window, motioning Amasa to aid. Seizing her under the heaving hillocks as he would a pair of melons, he lowered her into the upreaching arms of her maddened spouse, and then repeated the blushful performance with the other laggard wife.

The Moor came home again in time to disperse the crowd, cowing them by saying the Yankee in his house was to be the guest of the Sultan, and remarking that they had insulted their sovereign by not offering for his comfort that night some pleasing young slave.

The guardsman's words were true. The Moor went with Amasa to the ship to report that the Sultan had invited the Commodore and his staff to visit his palace, and had graciously offered to let them meet the women of his seraglio. McCluer had the American to thank for paving the way to peace and for opening the door to the Sultan's mansion of bamboo.

An unconventional Mohammedan was this Sultan. He delighted in showing his numerous wives. The visitors were led through a bolted gate into a high-walled inclosure through the verdure of which a stream glinted. Out of the bordering tree-shaded houses came the wives and concubines, their faces uncovered and their eyes dancing. Much admiration was expressed among the white men as to the ability of the sixty-year-old Sultan to take care of three hundred wives and concubines.

Leaving with good feelings the luxurious Sultan of Sooloo, McCluer directed Navigator Delano to head for the Pelew Islands, where the Commodore had left a friend to look after British interests. On arriving there he found that his trust in this comrade had been misplaced. The man had killed a native in a quarrel over a woman, and King Abba's brother, Raa Kook, who wanted to depose Abba, cried out to the people that the king favored the white raper of their women and killer of their men.

King Abba died or was murdered, and Raa Kook, succeeding him, seized the muskets and powder McCluer had given Abba.

Commodore McCluer became dejected when he heard the news. In backing King Abba with guns, he had been preparing a flight from civilization. This remained his aim despite the revolution, and he sent gifts and messages of congratulations to Raa Kook and was greatly pleased to receive assurances of the chief's good will!

Suddenly he gave strange orders. "I am retiring from this expedition," he said to Amasa. "You will take the *Endeavour* to Macao, and I will follow in the *Panther*."

Up past the Philippines and Formosa, the surprised Delano navigated the *Endeavour,* and came to anchor in Macao Roads. The British there asked for news of McCluer, but Amasa said nothing.

From the land of the Puritans, Amasa had watched almost incredulously his admired commander's flight from duty.

When McCluer landed for a life of social uplift or sensual enjoyment on one of the Pelew Islands, he took with him, Amasa Delano learned afterwards, a Bombay female, born of European parents, and five or six male slaves from different eastern coasts. With these he resided in the islands for several months. Then he came to Macao and purchased a ship, returned to the Pelews, took a number of well-selected female slaves aboard, and left the islands forever.

Young women were abundant in the Pelews, and the chiefs of the tribes made no objection to the departure of the girls. A gift of guns or tools was considered ample exchange for a group of comely females. Commenting on the morals of the tribes, Amasa Delano said—"Previous to marriage, there seemed to be little restraint imposed on the sexes by public sentiment as it regards their conduct toward each other. It was considered an honor for any woman, married or single, to be in a state of pregnancy; and if she were unmarried it recommended her to a husband." After marriage, he said, the women were faithful to the solemn vows they made before the king or chief.

Having given Amasa Delano's Yankee view of McCluer's

escape from civilization, we balance it with the English side of the story as found in the journal of Staunton, Secretary to the Earl of MaCartney, Plenipotentiary to the Emperor of China.

"Captain McCluer," the perhaps white-washing Staunton noted, "was considered a diligent and capable observer. He had either visited formerly the Pelew Islands, or had formed an exalted idea of the climate, and of the disposition of the inhabitants . . . Captain McCluer determined to seek for that happiness in the Pelew Islands which he considered, no doubt, as less obtainable in a larger and more complicated, but perhaps more corrupt society . . .

"He was well received by the natives of the Pelew Islands, and honourable distinctions, with considerable authority amongst them, offered to him, which he declined, contenting himself with a moderate portion of land allotted to him; and was better pleased to benefit the country of his adoption, by the advice which his superior knowledge and experience might enable him to give, than to exercise any command among them."

Fate did not permit McCluer to continue his transformation. Amasa Delano received a letter from Bombay dated May 6, 1800. The writer was Samuel Snook, his former shipmate under McCluer, who told of the tragic end of the Commodore.

Poets and historians, engrossed with McCluer's social experiment, have overlooked this letter in Amasa Delano's journal.

"You must have heard ere this of the loss of Captain McClure (McCluer) in a vessel called the *Venus,* which he purchased at Macao . . . After obtaining the vessel, he returned again to the island, and by permission took away several female natives."

Officer Snook went on to tell how McCluer in the appropriately-named *Venus* sailed for Bencoolen, Sumatra, and after meeting Captain Pickett, commander of a Bombay frigate, sailed with his beauties to Bengal and there obtained the Government's permission to sail for Bombay. "It had been threatening weather a good while," the letter went on, "and McClure was advised to delay his departure a little, but he did not regard this advice and it is supposed he suffered in a gale, which happened soon after he parted with the pilot."

Having spent months in a tropical Eden, the sea had called to

McCluer again with determination, and he and his Bombay woman and Pelew female slaves never went ashore across a white beach to the indulgences of a palace under palm trees.

Concluding the strange episode, we wonder whether the two leather-bound volumes of *Staunton's Embassy* gave poet Alfred Tennyson his inspiration for *Locksley Hall,* in which he wrote of the tropics:

"There the passions, cramped no longer, shall have scope and breath-ing-space.
I shall take some savage woman, she shall rear my dusky race."

Paid off at Macao by the East India Company, Amasa tucked away the $14,000 he had earned and, glad to loaf for a while, began to look for an opportunity to invest it.

In Macao Roads, the squadron bearing Ambassador MaCartney was waiting, and Delano watched its proud departure for Peking and its rather inglorious return.

It was the powerful British East India Company that had urged the King to send the ambassador. Its shipmasters had brought back from Canton a report that the Chinese court had become curious about the nature of the English—whom the mandarins called red-heads or carrot-pates—because of the vast increase in shipping at that port and through alarm as to British victories in Bengal.

For this important mission to China, the Admiralty chose the sixty-four gun man-of-war *Lion* under Captain Erasmus Gower. The East India Company, in its turn, sent the commodious *Hindostan* to carry the minor persons of the embassy, the gifts, speci-mens of British manufacture, and goods for trading. There was a bit of English naval humor when the tender for the *Lion* was named *Jackal.*

MaCartney embarked from Portsmouth in September, 1792 and, after reaching Macao, sailed across the Yellow Sea, entered the Gulf of Peking, and, without violent opposition, anchored near Tiensing, the nearest harbor to the Forbidden City.

One of the diversions of the voyage was the game of distinguishing by their dress the nine ranks and distinctions of the mandarins who visited the ships at every port.

The military mandarin wore a red globe on his bonnet, which bore also a peacock plume, a gift from the Emperor for valor. His silk robe was embroidered with the four-clawed dragon, military emblem. He carried himself like a warrior, and bore the mark of wounds. His arms, from the use of the bow and arrow, were uncommonly muscular. Yet, for all his warlike appearance, his manners were pleasant and familiar.

The civic mandarin was a grave scholarly person who wore a blue globe on his bonnet to show that he was a man of learning and judgment. His robe was embroidered with the sign of his civic class—the Chinese pheasant.

Sailing up the Pei-ho River toward Peking on handsome government yachts, the ambassador wondered what was the legend in Chinese characters flaunted on the flags flying from the yachts. He was told by an interpreter that the words were "Ambassadors bearing tribute from the country of England." He could never change this conception of his mission.

As night came on, the visitors saw a typical Chinese scene of fascinating beauty. The banks of the river were illuminated with variegated lights from transparent red, white, and blue lanterns. The lights of the boats on the river—which by law hung one lantern on its mast for every person on board—blended with the general illumination. To the visitors it seemed that on this night in China they were sailing amidst clouds of titanic fireflies, but if one were inclined to indulge in poetry, the hum of the mosquitoes ended the mood.

En route, the ambassador had succeeded in making a compromise with the Chinese dignitaries who visited him. They had insisted that he kowtow seven times to the Emperor—but he said that his monarch was equally great, and that he would make one profound obeisance instead.

When the embassy arrived at Zhehol, the summer residence, the emperor immediately entered the tent and mounted his throne. Then the Chairman of the Board of Rites presented the British ambassador, who wore a richly-embroidered suit of velvet, adorned with the diamond badge and star of the Order of the Bath. He merely bent on one knee in presenting his credentials.

MaCartney and his suite stayed a week at Zhehol and attended the ceremonies of the emperor's birthday. They heard the Birthday Ode sung by innumerable voices, accompanied by solemn bells and varied music. The courtiers, in their state dresses, fell prostrate in unison at the refrain of every stanza of the ode: "Bow down your heads, all ye dwellers on earth; bow down your heads before the great Kien-long!" But the stubborn Englishmen only bowed.

Having given the Emperor the letter from the King of England —a sacred document contained in a jeweled box—MaCartney waited hopefully for the Emperor's answer.

When at last it was brought by a mandarin and translated for delivery to King George, its contents enraged the ambassador. The letter illuminates the Chinese attitude of superiority which the nations of Europe, followed by the United States, had to break down before they could do business with China.

"You, O King," the patronizing emperor wrote to King George, "live in a distant region, far beyond the borders of many oceans, but, desiring humbly to share the blessings of our civilization, you have sent an embassy respectfully bearing your letter. To show your devotion you have also sent offerings of your country's produce.

"Our dynasty's majestic virtue has reached every country under Heaven and kings of all nations have sent their tribute by land and sea. We possess all things; we are not interested in strange and costly objects and we have no use for your country's products. I have accepted your tribute offerings only because of the devotion which made you send them so far. . . ."

Amasa Delano heard his English friends say that the embassy had been successful in that it added considerably to Great Britain's knowledge of China, but he did not hear what the English statesmen were saying among themselves—that their diplomacy was wasted on a nation like the Chinese; that force must be applied.

The failure of these missions to open ports nearer to the tea lands was especially disappointing to the British merchants at Canton. The confinement of the European trade to Canton meant that they had to pay for the transport of tea from an immense distance, with a corresponding increase in price.

The incoming American firms could well sympathize with the British merchants in wishing for a shorter haul, for there were many difficulties in transporting the tea from the principal tea districts to the port of Canton. Mountain ranges had to be crossed; shallow rivers navigated, and the chests of tea—slung on poles and carried by men—had to be precariously transported by crowds of laborers who toiled under the whip and bamboo of the local magistrate.

After watching the spectacle of the frustrated British embassy, Amasa Delano suffered personal frustration in his investment of precious funds in an enterprise of Yankee skipper William Stewart.

There came to anchor in Macao Roads an American sealer *Eliza,* under Captain Stewart. Inquiring as to what American could guide him in the sale of his furs, Stewart was directed to Amasa.

Accepting the commission, Amasa advised Stewart to enter his ship at Macao and pay there the customs taxes the Hoppo at Canton would require, but Stewart pooh-poohed the idea of paying Canton taxes while his ship was far down the coast at Macao. Amasa urged him then to engage a Chinese pilot and sail the *Eliza* up the river to the Whampoa anchorage, but Stewart followed his own notions and engaged passage for Delano and himself in a Chinese junk sailing for Canton.

The Hoppo's police arrested Stewart and bade him pay what he owed the government for tonnage, anchorage and "cumshaw," threatening to seize his ship if he did not comply. Amasa's friend Van Brann interceded, and Stewart was let off with a fine of $500. However, the price for sealskins fell during the controversy and, though he had a cargo of 38,000 pelts, his net profit was little.

In need of an outgoing cargo, the discomfited Yankee accepted Van Brann's offer of a cargo of sugar to be delivered in Ostend, Holland—an offer made with the condition that Delano be given

THE AUXILIARY S. S. ANTELOPE
From a painting by F. H. Lane, 1855

THE NIGHTINGALE GETTING UNDER WEIGH OFF
THE BATTERY, NEW YORK

THE HOUQUA, N. B. PALMER, MASTER, 1851

THE FORMOSA, CHARLES H. ALLEN, JR., COMMANDER, 18

By a Chinese artist at Hong Kong

command of the ship. The three men became partners in the cargo, and Amasa invested his $14,000.

In the first rough sea the sluggish *Eliza* sprang a leak, which steadily grew worse. Thinking that she would be easy prey, a fleet of pirate proas approached her off Sumatra, but Amasa fired two six-pounders at the foremost proa and worked such havoc that the pirates abandoned the attack.

The cargo of sugar, wet by the sea water that leaked into the hold, was melting away, leaving a trail of sweetness that attracted innumerable fish.

Amasa saw his investment melting away too. "We must put into the Isle of France for repairs," he told Stewart. "Perhaps we can sell the sugar there."

The trouble with this plan was that ships owned by England, Spain, or Holland would be confiscated at the intended port, because the new French Republic was at war with these powers. To prevent this, Amasa's name as owner must be substituted for Van Brann's. Considering that the end justified the means, he let the port officials think the *Eliza* and her cargo were American-owned and told them that his purpose in coming into harbor was to put the ship into drydock. Of course, to make repairs, the cargo of sugar must be unloaded. When the sugar was out of the vessel and piled on the wharf, he found a customer for it and then sold the unseaworthy *Eliza*.

The partners then seized what seemed to be a good chance to recoup their fortunes. They bought the 1400-ton *Hector,* which the French captured from the Dutch East India Company.

Since the warehouses of the island were stuffed with cotton seized from enemy ships, they decided to load the *Hector* with cotton, sail her to Bombay, and there take a cargo for Canton.

The cost of the cargo and of changing the merchantman into a cotton ship was heavy, and they had to borrow a large sum of money. Four days out of the Isle of France, they sailed into a hurricane which damaged the *Hector's* spars and rigging, but Bombay was reached safely, and the cargo sold. The profits of the venture, however, depended on the cargo they would load for China. At Bombay, Amasa learned that the British fleet was engaged in home waters and that French privateers were blockading the harbor.

Afraid of seizure, the English merchants at Bombay dared not give the *Hector* a cargo. To make matters worse, a demand came from their creditors at the French isle that they pay what they owed—$20,000.

Mr. Dunlap, a calculating American merchant at Bombay, came forward with an offer to pay off the ship's debt, pick up freight, and sail her to Calcutta, and there obtain a cargo for America. He must, however, be paid big interest on his loan and receive a liberal share of the profits. The anxious partners were forced to agree.

Misfortune followed them to Calcutta. Coming into the harbor, Amasa followed a pilot boat; but a storm the night before had shifted the channel buoys, and when close to safe anchorage, bad luck struck again. The replacements and repairs cost $10,000.

Creditor Dunlap had arrived overland from Bombay, and the costly accident to the ship and the delay in finding a cargo at Calcutta infuriated him. With Dunlap threatening law proceedings, Stewart and Delano were forced to auction the *Hector*. She was sold for a price below the amount of Dunlap's claim, and he himself bought her. This seawater Shylock then demanded the difference between the selling price and the amount of his claim and brought suit against the partners.

With a debtor's prison actually looming for the two unfortunate men, they followed in a panic the procession of bankrupts who fled from Calcutta to the Danish settlement of Seramphore, from which they could not be brought back.

From this disgraceful plight Benjamin Joy, as a true American consul, rescued them. Pointing out to Dunlap that Delano and Stewart could delay the trial while the ship lay decaying and accumulating port charges, he persuaded him to give up the chase. The pair had freedom, but very little money in their pockets.

The American ship *Three Brothers,* Owner Jeremiah Stimson, was about to set sail from Calcutta to Philadelphia. The kindly Stimson offered Amasa a passage home. Crossing the Indian Ocean, he more than paid for his passage by repairs that relieved the owner of the need of incurring a big bill in a foreign harbor.

Amasa came home penniless into a rich community whose rows of carved and gabled mansions were trophies of successful voyages. Upon his record, it would be hard to persuade an owner to trust him as a master of a ship, but as a shipwright, any shipbuilder would employ him. At thirty-two, he began all over again as a master builder.

Hopeful in his humiliation, he four years later saw the China coast again. Brother Samuel and he formed a company to finance a three-year voyage, and they significantly named the ship *Perseverance*. She sailed in November, 1799, and came home at last with good profits for all concerned.

In middle age, Amasa settled down to a custom-house job, and with plenty of leisure in such a position, expanded and published his sea-journal. Without departing from the facts, we have dramatized some of the lighter incidents he mentions.

If an apology is needed because Amasa Delano did not retire wealthy, it will be found in the fact that he, along with Richard Cleveland and other shipmasters, suffered losses through wars and embargoes.

It was through the disastrous experiences of these preceding skippers that American shipowners began to design ships that would elude the blockading French and British navies, who were waiting to ruin a merchant-ship's voyage by seizure or delay. The solution came in building long, lean, deep-decked brigs and schooners with towering spars bearing veritable clouds of canvas.

Fast in a gale or when beating to windward with yards sharp up and sails down flat, they easily drew away from the frigates. Added to their fleetness was the advantage of what we today call camouflage, because with their full spread of canvas they resembled fog-clouds drifting on the horizon.

CHAPTER XI

Our Women Went Too

THE EARLY VOYAGING of Americans to the East Indies and to China was so masculine an adventure that for many years wives and sweethearts were seldom if ever taken. These men, hard on the surface, were gentle enough not to want to expose their women to the pestilences of India and Malay, the dangers of pirate attack and rape, or of arrest and execution by Chinese authorities who feared the propagation of "foreign devils."

True enough, captains of whaleships were different in this respect from commanders of merchant vessels. As whalers extended their voyages, and the period of absence stretched into years, some wives and sisters went along, and the cabin became a home aboard ship. Such repressive seagoing wives and sisters may not have been welcomed by sailors hoping to frolic with girls of the South Seas, but they won perhaps grudging praise by keeping the men's clothes in good order and by challenging the careless cook to prepare well-cooked and varied meals.

This chapter is mainly about women who sailed with the men going to the Far East, but first we give an example of a sailor who preferred to leave his women folks at home, and accept what the world offered as to women, civilized or barbaric.

Arriving at the harbor of Saignon, Indo-China, Captain John White, of the Salem brig *Franklin,* was invited by Pasqual, a Spanish trader, to visit his house.

"Pasqual's daughter, a coarse girl of 19, was seated in a corner weaving a sort of rough silk stuff of a yellowish color . . ."

Then the skipper saw:

". . . a blear-eyed old woman, furrowed and smoke-dried, whose blackened and lank jaws and gums, sans teeth, grinned horribly a ghastly smile. A few hoary elf-locks undulated on her palsied pate, whose vibrations, which at first view might have been mistaken for courtesy, were by no means in unison with the hag-like expression of her visage . . .

"We were reconducted to the veranda, where tea and confec-

86

tionery were presented us. A female figure, of ample proportions and a smiling countenance, was our Hebe. She was about 16 and a ward of our host . . . She was the most interesting object we had seen among these people, but our feelings of complacency were not a little deranged when, approaching us with her offering of tea and betel, we 'nosed her atmosphere.'

"She was dressed in black silk trousers and a tunic, or robe, which descended nearly to her ankles. Her hair, glossy with cocoanut oil, was tastefully gathered in a knot at the top of her head, which was encircled with a turban of black crepe. Her face and neck, guiltless of meretricious ornaments, were, however, decorated with variegated streaks, the accidental accumulation of extraneous matter which had come in contact with them. Her feet were naked and indurated, and the forefinger of each hand was armed with an opaque claw two inches in length."

We now come to a gentler person and scene, for though accounts of voyages by early American women are rare indeed, we have a clear and treasurable one in that of the before-mentioned Miss Low of Salem, a young woman who sailed from America to Macao in 1827.

Miss Low's uncle, James Low, was the representative in China of the firm of A. S. Low and Brother, of New York, whose house flag of yellow, red, and yellow horizontal bars with a white "L" in the center waved over some of the finest ships in the China trade. The Lows were related by family ties or trade with Samuel Russell, who was then intrenching himself in the trade of China, and both of these families were to entertain the young lady of twenty-three.

Wrenching herself "from the bosom of my family and those I love," Miss Low went aboard the ship *Sumatra* and sailed to Macao.

Out of the lonely ocean, she came to the Catholic-Buddhist atmosphere of Macao.

Miss Low, severely Protestant in her views, was a devotee of the simple New England service, and her glances during the long sermons at home had probably seen no other art than the lines of the pulpit, the curve of the window, or the staid sculpture in the churchyard. She was unprepared for a religion of symbolism and pageantry and was dismayed that her sedan-chair seemed to be part of a Catholic cavalcade.

Our Miss New England maintained her faith by having recourse to books of sermons, and she read to her patient uncle and aunt the sermons of Thatcher and Buckminster. On Sunday she dutifully went to the house of the Reverend Thomas Morrison, who was restricted by law in his preaching and missionary work. "There were only six people there, but the sermon was very good."

Aside from the images and pageantry, the girl found the old typhoon-beaten city delightful.

Inevitably she found her way to the most impressive natural feature of Macao—a high place on the western shore of the peninsula, from which could be seen the city, the harbor, the waterways, and the neighboring islands. The splendid house which crowded this site, and the beautiful landscaping of the hill had created its name, *Casa da horta,* or Garden House. First the abode of Portuguese grandees—who at last could not afford to maintain it—and later the residence of rich Englishmen, it was an attraction for all travelers. Torn by storms, the bowldered garden was a wild place that resisted the toil of gardeners. Its shining distinction was that here Camoens, poet-adventurer, sharing in the discoveries of his countrymen beyond the Cape of Good Hope, wrote his epic of the discovery—the famous *Lusiads.*

Keen to extend her knowledge, the girl enjoyed tracing the history of this Portuguese poet.

Born in Lisbon, Luiz Vas de Camoens was a contemporary of Cervantes, across the border. Failing to win the love of his adored Caterina de Ataide, who became the unattained Beatrice of his life, he joined the army and lost an eye in battle, yet sailed for service in India.

A born rebel and protestor, he found fault with the conduct of the Portuguese authorities at Goa, and with his clever pen satirized their rule. They were glad when he sailed for Macao in 1556. With no politics to disturb him there, he began writing his epic of conquest, *Os Lusiadas, The Lusitanians,* or *The Lusiads.*

Attended always by Antonio, his faithful Javanese, Camoens returned to Goa, was cast in prison, and became crazed by the news of the death of his beloved. In a poor state of mind, body, and purse, he returned to Lisbon, where he brought out *The Lusiads,* a publishing achievement accompanied by the frenzy of jealous poets—this jealousy being an enduring trait of a class that should be the most generous. In the convent of Santa Ana, Camoens found refuge from this malice.

When Camoens died in extreme poverty, Fra Jose Indio, a Carmelite monk, wrote on a flyleaf of a copy of *The Lusiads:*

"What thing more grievous than to see so great a genius lacking success! I saw him die in a hospital in Lisbon, without a sheet to cover him, after having triumphed in the Indies, and having sailed five thousand leagues by sea. What warning so great for those who, by night and day, weary themselves in study without profit, like the spider weaving the thread to catch small flies."

In view of Pearl Harbor, Camoens was a poor prophet as to the future Christian enlightenment of Japan, when he wrote:

"Pass not unmarked the islands in that sea,
Where nature claims the most celebrity,
Half-hidden, stretching in a lengthened line
In front of China, . . .
Japan abounds in mines of silver fine,
And shall enlightened be by holy faith divine."

The girl found that her singleness was as honey to bees in the male society of Macao. "You must know," she wrote, "that I am the only spinster in the place, and I am pulled about in every direction." The scarcity of white women—single or married—was so acute that they were obliged to take a different partner for each figure of the quadrille.

She sent her sister tantalizingly brief pictures of her beaux. There were several "clever youngsters," of whom she chose Mr. Howard as a type to depict, describing him as "shrewd, quick-witted, sensible, handsome, a fine singer and mimic." Curiously interesting to her was the long black beard flowing from under his chin; in addition he had black moustaches and side-whiskers. It was the English style, she said, but she added, with a vivid metaphor: "It seems like looking through a forest and discovering, at a distance, two stars, to look at his eyes."

One of the men who amused Miss Low was the gifted Irish artist George Chinnery, who lived in Macao by tolerance of the English authorities. He had been discovered engaged in the rebel movement of Lord George Fitzgerald, but had been permitted to live in India and China. When he joined the social set at Macao, he exhibited a self-portrait, showing himself leaving Calcutta. Under it were the words—"Too hot." His friends whispered that it was his way of saying that he had incurred too many debts there. He was welcomed at Macao for his talent for dramatics, and in the theatricals there played well the part of Mrs. Malaprop.

The omen of his wife's joining him caused Chinnery to escape from Macao to Canton where she could not follow him. When he stepped ashore at Canton he said: "What a kind Providence is this Chinese Government, that forbids the softer sex from coming here and bothering us."

The artist did well in Canton. Many a Yankee skipper brought home with him a portrait of some hong merchant painted by Chinnery.

During the first months of her visit she saw much of the high-minded English physician, Dr. Colledge. ("It is a shame that he is a bachelor!")

The Dr. Colledge to whom the Yankee girl refers was indeed attractive to an idealistic young woman. A physician in the employ of the East India Company, he opened at his own expense a dispensary in Macao which gave medical relief to many persons. Finding the number of his patients rapidly increasing, he obtained financial support to the extent of $6500 from the foreign residents and rented two houses for their accommodation. In four years he had healed or relieved 4000 patients. It became, however, such a drain on his own income that he was forced to close the hospital, for few of his swarming patients could pay except with gifts of fruit, firecrackers or written cards of gratitude which informed him that his goodness was as lofty as a hill, his virtue as deep as the sea, and his renown such that during a thousand ages it would not decay. But usually the writer added: "Your profound kindness it is impossible for me to requite."

Colledge was assisted in the dispensary by Dr. Bradford of Philadelphia and Dr. Cox of London.

It was on this foundation that Dr. Peter Parker afterwards built his Ophthalmic Hospital, which was supported by Dr. Colledge and by missionary Bridgman.

Used to simple gowns, the girl was dismayed by the grand fashions of the English ladies and the formality of the dinners. One letter discloses that she was making a dress with her own needle. To a quadrille party she wore "muslin trimmed with yellow satin over white satin." Confiding her plans for attending a formal dinner, she wrote:

"I shall rig myself in a white satin underdress, with a wrought muslin petticoat and a pink satin bodice to set neatly on my neat little form."

One dinner she attended was a stiff ceremony, with sixty persons at the long table. The plate and porcelain were magnificent—"every delicacy served in the most elegant style." Each guest brought his own Chinese servant, who stood behind his chair. These extras fell back to permit the regular servants to carry out the dishes and give them to the butlers. The sister in Salem, reading to her literary or sewing circle parts of the correspondence, must have borne down impressively on the statement that at the end of the many courses the lights of the dining-hall were extinguished and the table was dotted with "blue lights"—this being the term for dishes of burning brandy and salt.

Dancing . . . glees . . . theatricals—scenes from the Merchant of Venice, with the ladies and gentlemen making love on the moonlit veranda—were all enjoyed.

A daytime diversion was attendance at the racegrounds at the Barrier, the dividing-line between foreigners and natives. For the accommodation of the foreign ladies, the officials had built on the high walk a bamboo shelter, and they looked down on thrilling, well-matched horse-races thronged by an excited and motley swarm of Chinese, Lascars, and Portuguese. In the turbulent crowd the girl watched curiously the many Chinese women who carried their babies in bags on their backs.

Our engaging traveler, perhaps rebelling against British condescension, made this tart comment: "Mrs. F's husband, the host, insisted on telling people that his wife was the daughter of a baronet and was well-born and well-bred—which made him ridiculous."

Miss Low's ire at the lofty British had flamed. How dare that English author traveling in the United States ridicule the American people! She wrote indignantly to her sister asking for news of the impudent, obnoxious Mrs. Trollope.

Forbidden to visit Canton—where later she went, dangerously smuggled in and out of an American factory—our Salem girl questioned the genial hong merchant Mouqua, who visited her uncle at Macao.

He wore his winter dress of various shades of blue, surmounted by a blue cap that was strikingly peculiar in that its crown was scarlet, topped by a blue glass button.

"Why can not I go to Canton?" she asked Mouqua.

He answered laconically, "Too much man want to look."

Gideon Nye, Jr., American merchant at Canton, mentioned Miss Low and her aunt, Mrs. Low in a speech he made recalling his early career at Macao and Canton. We discover from it that Miss Low's surreptitious visit to Canton created a lot of trouble for the men who sponsored her going. His reminiscences support other statements as to the danger of bringing white women into Canton.

The native pilot from Macao, when approaching the Canton anchorage—Nye stated—was obliged to report the passengers and cargo truthfully—and especially to declare that no foreign women or other contraband were on board.

"There was a period," he went on, "when I saw neither woman or child at Canton for three years and two gentlemen at Canton had not seen such for seven years."

Speaking of the later period when the force of the British Navy made itself felt at Canton, he told her how Chief Baynes of the East India Company "persisted in keeping Lady Baynes and her companions (Mrs. and Miss Low, wife and niece of the then chief of Messrs. Russell and Company) here for six weeks."

The Baronet held to this course in spite of the action of the Viceroy at Canton, who to drive the women back to Macao stopped the trade of foreign ships with China for six weeks. After his defiance of Chinese law, white women did not enter Canton until the war of 1841-42 opened the way for them.

Just as foreign women were excluded from Canton, no Chinese woman was permitted in the company of a foreign male resident. But progress was made in this custom also, and Nye told of how afterwards six Chinese ladies of the Houqua family spent the day and took tiffin at the Nye warehouse, to meet an English lady who was his guest. The advance had continued when the Seward party visited China a quarter-century afterwards.

While the Seward group were staying at the Russell building at Shanghai, the comprador, who was security agent for the firm, brought his wives and daughters-in-law with him on his annual visit to the factory. The women had come to pay their respects to Mrs. Warden, wife of the manager of the Russell compound.

The Chinese ladies shook hands with the Americans in the way of the latter, but were very careful as to their finger-nails, which were as long as the fingers they grotesquely adorned. They were elegantly gowned, and profusely decked with jewels, but were very timid. As neither group understood each other's language, there was nothing to do but to study each other's fashions.

Curiously examining the furniture and ornaments of the Wardens' rooms, the Chinese ladies asked to see the upstairs; but the matter of getting them on their tiny feet up the stairs was a problem. The help of a man's arm was forbidden. The difficulty was met by the American women offering their arms. Olive Risley Seward wrote:

"As we assisted the women, or rather carried them in our arms, up and down the staircase, bright-eyed, gentle, and sweet-voiced indeed, but dwarfed, distorted, enslaved, their dependence was touching."

Did Miss Low fall in love? We gather from her journal that if asked she might have accepted Dr. Colledge. He, however, married another girl, and our young lady seriously considered

93

marrying another beau; but at last she refused him and wrote her sister that it was for the best.

This suitor was probably the one with whom she became entangled on a hill stroll, though the chain was only a ribbon. Walking with a "Mr. V." up a dangerous path by a cliff, the wind blew her long muslin gown and tripped her. Trying to support her, he caught his foot in the trimming and stumbled. They both barely escaped falling over the cliff. No more was heard of Mr. V. as an escort.

Toward the end of her visit our spinster was writing home: "There is no gentleman here that I can call upon, and even if there were, it would be a crime for me to go out unattended without a chaperon."

She was indeed in a scandalous city, but the only hint of high doings or low doings is in this passage:

"You have no idea how circumspect it is necessary to be in this place. This gossip concerns me only as it concerns the whole sex, but I intend to learn a lesson from another's experience. It is about a lady who has been staying in Macao for the last six months. Thank fortune, she has now gone! It really made me quite melancholy . . ."

More attractive than men were the creatures that sang to her from the aviaries: the birds of paradise; the gold and silver pheasants; and the slate-colored dagger-breasted pigeon, whose white breast has a spot resembling blood.

Something very serious must have happened to put the once-eager visitor in the mood she was in when she made plans to return home: "The men are a good-for-nothing set of rascals—all they care about is eating, drinking, and frolicking . . ."

Frolicking is a word that can cover many things.

Home she went to fall in love with and marry one of her own people, and to bear a daughter who years later wisely edited and published the very human—"My Mother's Journal."

A decade after Miss Low's visit, the European and American ladies in Macao were pleasantly agitated by the coming of Chaplain Fitch W. Taylor. We meet the Reverend Taylor in advance as his ship stops at Singapore; we pause to watch with him the tragic fate of an American girl pioneer.

At Singapore, Taylor met Mrs. Wood, the young wife of a missionary, and the daughter of the Johnstons of Morristown, New Jersey. Serious illness and death struck quickly there, and he was called upon to attend her funeral. In these quaint touching words, he tells of her brief career:

"She became pious at the age of fifteen—left the endearments of a refined society, home, and relatives, for the purpose of entering on the work of missions among a benighted people . . . I had learned to admire this lovely woman."

The chaplain gives us also a picture of Mrs. Davenport, wife of a Baptist missionary to Siam, who had come to Singapore to attend to the casting of a font of Siamese type for printing tracts. "They are from Virginia; and Mrs. Davenport is a sprightly young lady, who left her native land with her husband at the age of seventeen. She has accomplished a knowledge of the Siamese with great facility . . ."

Taylor met too, at Singapore, Mrs. Balastier, wife of the American consul, who had been cordially accepted into the English set. We gather from his restrained notes that Mrs. Balastier and her English friends were extremely gay and convivial. He did not attend a lively party she gave on the grounds that it would "compromise his proper dignity," but he was host along with the officers when "the civilities of shore were reciprocated by Commodore Read, by an entertainment given aboard the *Columbia*."

When he came to know the Consul's wife better, he was pleased to discover that she was something of an artist and collector, and delighted the chaplain with a gift of her paintings of fruits of the Malacca Straits.

The squadron of which Taylor was minister at last arrived at Macao, and the gracious chaplain became very popular among both English and American wives. He felt especially at home in the houses of two American missionaries, Brown and Shuck and, having known the two brothers of Mrs. Brown at Yale, he went into rhapsodies with her over the charm of his "elm-embowered" college town—that "exquisite specimen of *rus in urbe*."

Chaplain Taylor was more fortunate than many American

travelers in meeting ladies of refinement. A biological yearning appears between these scribbled lines of Thomas F. Ward, master of the Salem ship *Minerva*:

"You may perhaps see at the windows some handsome Ladies to regale your eyes after four or five months' passage."

These missionary wives, Taylor observed, were making approaches to the natives by studying their classics, painting Oriental landscapes, and collecting specimens of native arts and crafts. They sought wistfully to blend with their own civilization what was beautiful in pagan culture.

Mrs. Shuck, the first woman missionary to the Orient, a member of the American Baptist Mission to China, had developed, for instance, a taste for Chinese verse, and was engaged in translations. She gave Taylor a copy of one of them—a translation having the true Chinese feeling:

On Taking Leave of a Friend

"Ten years have elapsed since last we parted;
And no sooner have we met than we part again.
We bind ourselves by promises to renew this meeting,
But we shall never be so young as we are now.
The shadows of the passing cloud speedily vanish,
The falling leaf returns not to its branch;
Should I fly like the wild bird to seek you in the south,
In what part of yon blue mountain shall we meet?"

Among the differences Taylor noted between Anglo-Saxon customs and those of the Chinese were these:

The Chinaman will not contaminate his tea with cream and sugar;

The tea-cups are not put into saucers, but instead, the saucers are laid on the top of the cups, to keep in the aroma;

Precocious children are suppressed rather than encouraged; old men play like little boys, and little boys are as grave as judges;

A man dresses like a woman, and uses a fan more than a woman does;

Instead of leaving his knife or chopsticks on the table, he carries them away with him;

At ceremonious feasts, he eats the fruit first, and the soup last; He writes perpendicularly instead of vertically.

He whitens the edges of the soles of his shoes instead of blackening them.

When he is in extremely elegant company, he discards his shoes.

It was only remotely that the American women could touch the arts and thoughts of the Chinese. Prevented from meeting highborn Chinese women, all the inquirers could see were evidences in translated literature that distinguished women had lived, and that the Chinese for all their suppression of the average women appreciated and reverenced the few. The number of those esteemed, however, averaged one to a million women, and the reasons for their distinction were strange to the Western mind.

They were honored because they had committed suicide out of devotion to husband or parents, or through fear of shame; or when they were widowed, they mourned to the end of life; or they remained unmarried to serve their own parents, or, after the husband's death, to attend to his parents. Glorified by emperors and mankind, the main reason for esteeming them was their submission to the wishes and will of the men of China.

Among the renowned women were empresses, women of letters, artists, and because of the liberality of Chinese standards— courtesans. Most famous of the authoresses was Pan Chao, who lived about the time of St. Paul and wrote the deathless book, *Female Precepts.*

Life was easier with these American women of Macao than it was with the wives of missionaries who had gone ashore from American ships to settle at posts in India and Malaysia.

Chaplain Taylor publishes with admiration a letter from the father of one of these less fortunate wives. Reading it in the light of today, one wonders if life in a barbaric country was not more enjoyable than living with this tyrannical champion of the rights of the males. This is the epistle:

A Few Private Thoughts to Mary

". . . One principle *must*, of necessity, be acted on, and that is, *you must yield to the will of your husband,* whenever the point is made . . . God has constituted the man, as the stronger in mind and body, to have the government, and in proportion as you may be disposed to usurp the authority which belongs to him (the husband), you destroy the order of Providence and the harmony of the connubial state. Never, therefore, oppose the will of your husband. You may reason with, and persuade, but do not attempt to dictate to him. *'I will not'* are words which should never be found in a wife's vocabulary. Never use them to your husband . . .

"Your husband may die before you. In that case, remember that if I am living you should take no important step without my advice, however distant, if it can be avoided . . .

"Do not be impatient when sick. You are rather predisposed that way."

The patriarch, apparently wishful to be the father of a martyr, sought to nail her to the task:

". . . There is one thought that I would impress deeply on your mind, and that is that you have enlisted *for life;* and that, unless extraordinary occurrences of Providence shall otherwise indicate, you will never return to America—never, unless the Board here shall advise and require it . . . Assure me that all is right in motive with us all, and that God requires it, and I rejoice in the prospect of your living and dying on heathen ground. I should look on it as a last stigma were you to become tired of your vocation, and quit the service in which you have engaged. . . . Prepare your mind for the worst. You should not, however, doubt the faithfulness of God—that he will be with you always."

The deaths of white women noted by Chaplain Taylor were only a small part of the mournful record. The climate was fatal to many of the American and English women who accompanied their husbands into the treaty ports of China. In four years at Amoy, four wives died, and others were forced to quit the climate because of fever.

One of the first American women visitors to the Orient, Mrs. William Cook, wife of the U. S. Commissioner at Swatow, discovered at Whampoa that European and American residents had overcome objections to the presence of wives by living in boats on the river. Old ships had been converted into floating dwellings called "chops." The spars and rigging had been removed, and the cabin and stateroom altered into storerooms, pantries, bathrooms. They were anchored in the wide part of the river, and therefore escaped the malaria issuing from the marshes of Whampoa. The family apartments were in the center, and verandas screened by Venetian blinds were provided. The kitchen and servants' quarters were in the forecastle. Compared with the restricted space of the crowded sampans, these ship-homes were luxurious.

If there could be flowery, floating harlot-boats in Canton harbor, why shouldn't there be floating Sunday-schools? American missionaries started these. Hearing Chinese children singing American hymns, Mrs. Cook traced the singing to a "chop church" called "The Bethel," conducted by American missionaries and anchored nearby.

Visiting Hong-Kong, Mrs. Cook was cordially greeted by Lady Robinson, wife of the British governor, and by Mrs. Smith, spouse of the English bishop. As did Miss Low before her, Mrs. Cook resented the English references to the Americans' "nasal twang" and "Puritan sniffle" but found a British friend vastly helpful in teaching her how to manage a cheating coolie. Borne in a sedan chair, she suddenly became aware that the forward bearer had slackened his pace and was breathing hard. Alarmed for his health, in pantomime she told the apparently agonized coolie to put the chair down.

Her English companion, following in a second chair, told her that the sickness was an old trick—that the bearer was working on her sympathy and wanted to be paid on that spot and dismissed.

Descending on the cheating coolie, the English friend said:
"Fightee la (quick, directly) I tellee Massie of you and he no give you one cash (the smallest Chinese coin, equal to a farthing).

Takee up chair chop-chop (quick, quick) no can carry alla proper, no can catchee cash."

The threatened coolie took up the chair and bore it with ease.

To the sisterhood of American women who shared their husbands' dangers and discomforts in China belonged Harriet C. Webster, whom medical missionary Peter Parker met and married in Washington, D. C.

The bride's sister, Priscilla, long afterwards, gave her recollections of the wedding:

"In the meantime," she wrote, "sister Harriet was married, March 29, 1841, and I was the bridesmaid. This was the first wedding I had ever attended, and it naturally caused a good deal of excitement.

"Your grand-uncle Parker was then a young man, tall and fine-looking, a perfect blonde, contrasting well with your grand aunt Hattie's handsome black eyes and dark curls . . . she looked very lovely in a tulle veil, soft white muslin and lace, as she entered the parlor on the arm of Dr. Parker."

In his day-journal for November 6, 1842, the physician wrote: "At length the desire was realized of being permitted, with my dear wife, to reside in Canton . . . as we passed through the company's factory, the crowd began to collect to see the foreign lady. The hong coolies, who acted as policemen, drove them back, and we walked quickly through, without inconvenience or rudeness from the populace. Occasionally was heard, 'The doctor has come!' "

Parker might well have indulged in a more dramatic account, because the arrival of Mrs. Parker marked a great change in the customs of Canton. Never before had a white woman been allowed to stay in Canton. Several months passed before the wives of other foreigners dared join her.

Knowing the danger of mobbing or arrest, Dr. Parker had previously obtained the consent of the Emperor to bring his wife with him; but nevertheless he was in constant trepidation.

On the first evening of their residence, Mrs. Parker appeared on the terrace and created a sensation. People crowded the street below and adjacent China Street. They thronged the tops of houses and the boats on the river, watching with avid curiosity the first white woman they had ever seen. The chief comment overheard was on the arrangement of her hair.

Six weeks after the arrival of the bride a dangerous outbreak occurred.

"In an evil hour," Parker wrote, "our peace and quietness was disturbed from our promixity to the English, who, in the course of the late war, had rendered themselves particularly obnoxious to the Chinese. A quarrel with a Lascar became the occasion for the pent-up feeling to manifest itself in the burning of the English factory and the plunder of nearly a half-million dollars in specie.

"Hatty was early removed to Mingkwa's factory (in company with Mrs. Isaacson, an English lady who was visiting her), and was then moved to Whampoa." The wife returned after things had quieted down, when a guard of 1100 Chinese soldiers was placed around the foreign factories.

When another outbreak appeared imminent, Mrs. Parker was sent to Macao in the *Natchez,* to visit Mrs. Sword, "a pious and excellent lady from Philadelphia now residing at Macao." It is a pity that the flustered Dr. Parker did not find time to give an account of the captain of the old packet *Natchez* which had then completed her first trip to Canton. The master who took care of the gentle Mrs. Parker was none other than "Bully" Waterman, who drove ships and crews with notorious firmness. Escaping from the ordeal of the mob, the wife faced ordeal by fire that autumn when fire swept the city. "Canton was visited by a fearful conflagration, reducing more than a thousand dwellings to ashes," Parker wrote. "We were compelled to retreat from the approaching flames, fearing that we should never return to our house again; but divine goodness spared our habitation."

CHAPTER XII

Whales, Sea Snails, and Mortal Mermaids

THE SPOUTS OF the sperm whales were fountains marking the trail for early American skippers searching Pacific and oriental waters for whale oil. Soon after American freedom was proclaimed, the shore-clinging whalemen of New Bedford and Nantucket were building larger ships and making farther voyages.

The sea-snails referred to in our chapter title were *beche de mer,* a delicacy prized by the mandarins of China. The trade in them became a by-product of the sealing and whaling industries.

The mermaids we mention were the girls of the South Sea islands who, in accordance with a custom noted by the Spaniards, swam out in shoals to welcome the white men to their shores, and climbed aboard and scattered themselves about the ship in lavish greetings. We will see that when the scandal of it came back to New England towns, the wives did something about it.

What was whispered by homecoming seamen in the taverns became vehement talk among the wives of New England, and thereafter those who could persuade their husbands into taking them on the voyages went along. Such a helpmeet was Mrs. Wallis, whose husband gave his name to an island. She kept her own journal and wrote at Pleasant Island:

"The girls came on board for the vilest of purposes, but they said these were not accomplished as the sailors were afraid of the captain's woman."

These handsome unmoral women, the journals stated, were nearly naked, but wore a grass covering from the waist down. They kept their skin soft and smooth with cocoanut oil. Yankee wives who watched them over the ship's rail admitted that they were skilled in other things besides enticement—they tilled the ground, fished, and cooked in earthen pots which they had made.

There were other reasons beside the guardianship of morals for a wife to go along on a whaleship. Three or four years is a long time for a girl to be separated from her man. If her love for him was deep, she would want to nurse him if wounded or if stricken by pestilence. There was also her own love of adventure and travel. A ship following the spouts of whales across the seven seas was better than an academy for education. And what treasures for housekeeping a woman could obtain!

Whalers and sealers from New England flocked to the South Pacific at the beginning of the nineteenth century and were the first to link the interests of Australia and new South Wales, including New Zealand. The first Yankee ship arrived at Australia in 1792, and in the following eighteen years, forty-six American vessels dropped anchor there. The principal cargo they brought to the colonists and natives was rum.

The American whaler, who rounded the Horn in 1818 and discovered numerous spouts of the whale, led a procession of whaling ships which, for a time, made the ocean an American possession marked by American names. Unnamed isles were christened Bowditch, Coffin, Folger, Macy, and Starbuck, and kept these names until other countries renamed them while the United States slept.

Finally the whalers pushed their bows through shoals of glistening "whale feed" off the coast of China and Japan. The leader, the Nantucket ship *Columbus,* left other whale ships and skirted the north coast of Africa, crossed the Red Sea, and roved the Indian Ocean. She returned at last loaded with whale oil as proof that she had discovered the preferred feeding ground of the great whales.

The lusty New Bedford and Nantucket whaling crews left more than names to show that the isles were linked to America. The willing castaway David Whippy had several children by his Fiji princess, and many another American sailor left offspring in those island groups.

When it came to experience, the whaleships were the vessels to count on.

For instance, nine years after Pitcairn Island had been taken as refuge by the mutinous crew of the British ship *Bounty,* Captain Mayhew Folger chanced on it. Cruising for whales in the whaleship *Topaz,* he saw this island rising sleepily from the sea to a height of a thousand feet. On a plateau he noted signs of human life. His sea-journal contains the story of his visit to this village where white men lived with their Polynesian wives:

"Saturday February 6th 1808. At 2 A M saw Pitcairn's Island bearing South. Lay off and on till daylight. At 6 A M put off with two boats to explore the land and look for seals. On approaching the shore saw smoke on the land at which I was very much surprised as the island was said to be uninhabited. I discovered a boat paddling towards me with three men in her. They hailed me in the English language and asked who was the captain of the ship. They offered me gifts of cocoanuts and requested I would land, there being a white man on shore.

"I went ashore and found an Englishman named Alexander Smith [the later John Adams] the only person remaining out of nine that escaped on board the ship *Bounty*.

"Smith informed me that after putting Captain Bligh in the longboat and sending her adrift, Christian, their chief, proceeded with the ship to Otaheitia. There all the mutineers chose to stop except Christian, himself, and seven others, who took wives and also six men as servants, and immediately proceeded to Pitcairn's Island where they landed all the goods and chattels, ran the *Bounty* ashore and broke her up.

"This took place, as near as he (Smith) could recollect, in the year 1790: soon after which one of their party ran mad and drowned himself, another died of fever; and after they had remained about four years on the island, their men servants rose up and killed six of them, leaving only Smith alive, and he desperately wounded with a pistol ball in the neck. However, he and the widows of the deceased arose and put all the servants to death, which left him the only surviving man on the island with eight or nine women and several small children. He immediately went to work tilling the ground so that it produces plenty for them all, and he lives comfortably as commander-in-chief of Pitcairn's Island.

"All the children of the deceased mutineers speak tolerable English. Some of them are grown to the size of men and women, and to do them Justice I think them very humane and hospitable people; and whatever may have been the errors or crimes of Smith the mutineer in times back, he is at present a worthy man and may be useful to navigators who traverse this immense ocean . . ."

We have reserved from our earlier chapter about Elias Hasket Derby and his Salem rivals, the story of how competitor Joseph Peabody was the first American merchant to send a ship to load up *beche de mer,* the sea-snail, starfish, or sea-cucumber, whose gelatinous quality is liked by mandarins.

The venture of Peabody was suggested to him by Henry Archer, Jr., first officer of the Salem ship *China,* which Captain Hiram Putnam sailed to Far Eastern ports after loading her with copper obtained in Peru. On the homeward passage the *China* met skippers of whaleships gaming in the South Seas, and there Archer learned of the scarcely-known but profitable trade in sea-snails.

Owner Peabody gave his informant command of the *Glide,* 306 tons, which had already made thirteen trading voyages to ports all around the world. Archer sailed in 1829 for the Central Pacific and stayed several months among the clustered Fiji Islands, whose tribes ranged from the amiable to the ferocious and cannibalistic.

To the sailors who superintended the curing of the *beche de mer,* the work was obnoxious, and the temptation to escape and live among the island beauties was strong. Third mate William Endicott of the *Glide* gives us an idea of the disagreeable task of curing:

". . . I found the men curing fish as usual . . . some were scolding the natives for their laziness . . . others were dodging the smoke and steam from the pots, with an occasional oath, and trying to get a sniff of fresh air; while the men to the windward pots, though free from the other annoyances, were compelled to take a double share of mosquitoes."

Sticking to Yankee standards of economy, the officers of the *Glide* offered a man a chisel for his work. This offer of a tool made by the blacksmith from a hoop iron induced the Islander to sail fifteen or twenty miles to a reef and work six or eight hours knee-deep in water.

A detailed account of the method of gathering and marketing *beche de mer* is found in the journal of William D. Cary, of Nantucket, whose ship *Oeno* was wrecked on Turtle Island in the Pacific, April 5, 1825. Found in a fish-house near Siaconset, the log was published in the *Nantucket Journal* in 1887; then reprinted by the *Nantucket Inquirer and Mirror*.

"Mr. Driver (the first officer) on shore was continually crowded from morning till night with women and children bringing *beche de mer,* mats for bags, fruits, vegetables, and everything which they thought he would buy. The price of a musket was sixteen hogshead full of *beche de mer,* which it took them five or six days to get from the reefs. Some of it they got in two or three fathoms of water, diving for it and bringing up one or two at a time. That obtained in deep water is the most valuable kind to the Chinese. When first taken it is about a foot in length and from three to four inches wide. The under side or belly is flat, and the back rounding. When taken it is quite soft, and if not boiled, soon spoils. The entrails and water which come from the fish is of a bright purple and those employed in opening them get their hands so stained that it is impossible to wash it off. It is quite lifeless. We never found anything inside but this purple water and coarse sand and gravel. The back is covered with prickles from an inch to an inch and a half in length. When taken it is of a reddish cast intermingled with white, but when properly cured is entirely black.

"To procure, it the natives go out on the reef, let the canoe drift, with their eyes fixed on the bottom, and when they see one, dive and secure it. When cured the prickles become hard and brittle as glass. Captain Vandaford took one of this kind on board and weighed it green. It weighed five pounds, but when cured it only weighed three quarters of a pound. There are five or six different kinds of *beche de mer.* One kind is about a foot long and three inches in diameter, smooth, and of a reddish black color. The mouth is very small and round and has four or five teeth. It is not as soft as the prickly kind but is generally found with it in deep water."

The ship *Clay,* which Cary was helping to load, sailed for Manila with her cargo and returned when promised for another load. He sailed in the ship on her second voyage to Manila and made note:

"Our cargo was readily disposed of to Chinese merchants, who came off to see it weighed, after which the ship's hold was prepared to take a cargo of sugar."

CHAPTER XIII

Once In a While—a Warship

THEY MUST SHIFT for themselves, the American who went to China in the early days; they must learn how to get along with the Chinese authorities, and with commanders of foreign ships gathered in Chinese waters, without the support of an American warship to back up their claims for justice. Even the consuls appointed by the Government at Washington could only write home when American merchants or skippers complained to them, and there was no expectancy that in response a United States warship would come with her guns trained for action.

The truth was that our merchants and ship-masters had leaped beyond the processes of establishing the new Republic, and the Administrations and the Congress had not yet become persuaded that they should build a strong navy and spare a warship to sail to the Far East to cow the Chinese officials as the British were doing.

It was an exciting event to Americans, in the Far East, in 1800, when the United States warship *Congress* visited there to see to it that the privateers of France licensed by Napoleon stopped seizing American merchant vessels.

There was something to be said on both sides in the bitter competition for labor for ships sailing Oriental seas. Yankee skippers and crews let it be known that wages and living conditions were better aboard Yankee ships, and thus induced British seamen deserted the vessels of the East India Company. The result was that American skippers had to suffer the indignities of being boarded by British naval lieutenants seeking sailors.

In 1804, H. M. warships *Caroline* and *Grampus* searched American ships off the coast of China and took off several seamen, which the American consul Carrington, in his indignant protest, asserted were true Americans.

In 1807, the ship *Topaz* of Baltimore, which had succumbed to that port's habit of privateering, was seized at Whampoa by British warships and sent as a prize to Bombay, the accusation being that she had engaged in piracy off the coast of South America. In resisting arrest, her captain was shot.

In 1814, H. M. ship *Doris,* Captain O'Brien, captured at Macao the American brig *Rambler* of Boston, which under a letter of marque had previously seized the English ship *Arabella* of Calcutta. The *Doris* also seized the American ship *Hunter* off the Ladrone Islands and brought her as a prize to a China port.

The friendship that had developed between the Americans and the Chinese brought action by the Viceroy at Canton in defense of the Yankees. Summoning the representatives of the East India Company at Canton, the Viceroy commanded that the seizures by the *Doris* be stopped, with due compensation for the hong merchants who had gone security for the American ships she had captured.

The Company's officials protested that they had no control over His Majesty's warships, but the Viceroy refused to admit that they lacked authority.

"Someone must be held responsible for the offenses of your nation," he said. "The captains of the warships are at sea, but you are a body of British subjects who reside here and profit by commerce with the Chinese people. Since you are on the spot, and your naval captains distant and unreachable, you must bear the burden until your Government rectifies these injustices.

"I prohibit all Chinese linguists, boatmen, and laborers—to work at the British wharves and warehouses. I forbid the use of the Chinese language in your letters to the Emperor's officials. Any petitions you send to me for transmission to the Emperor will be returned unopened."

"These measures," the British supercargoes protested, "will kill our trade."

That appeared to be the object of the Viceroy.

One could print on two or three pages the record of the early visits of ships of the American Navy to the Far East. In 1815 Commander John Dandridge Henley, a Virginian, took the frigate *Congress* on a two-year cruise in eastern seas. His orders were to proceed to Canton, and then convoy all American ships through that haunt of pirates, the Straits of Sunda. While at Canton he was humiliated by his country's lack of prestige, for when he requested of the Viceroy the same privilege granted to the British of obtaining supplies for men-of-war, his request was ignored.

American merchants in Canton wished that Commander Henley had been given orders to use guns if necessary to teach the Canton mandarins to respect the United States; especially since a short time before Commander Maxwell, of H. H. ship *Alceste,* had taught the isolent offical a lesson.

Shortly after the *Alceste* had let down her anchor in the river, a port official, mistaking her for a merchant ship, rowed out to order her commander to return to Macao, the official port of entry, and there report his cargo so that custom duties could be collected.

"What do you mean?" asked Captain Maxwell after the interpreter had delivered the command.

The mandarin repeated the order.

"Are you aware, sir," exploded Maxwell, "that this is a ship of war, King George of England's frigate, the *Alceste?*"

The mandarin began to lose some of his assurance. "I merely wish to learn," he said, "what kind of goods you desire to dispose of."

"Goods to dispose of?" Maxwell thundered. "Powder and shot, sir, are the cargo of a British man-of-war. Did you see His Majesty's pendant flying at the masthead? If you did not, take a good look at it on your way to Canton. Tell the Viceroy you have seen a flag that has never yet been dishonored—and, please God, while it waves over my head, it never shall!"

The mandarin turned away, but suddenly Maxwell changed his fierce mood and rang the bell for cherry brandy.

Some days later, the needed document of free permission or

Grand Chop being still withheld, Maxwell sailed to the narrow entrance called the Bogue or Mouth.

There he found his way barred by seventeen war-junks, which fired one after the other at the frigate; however, none of the shots hit her, and Maxwell sailed to the very entrance. The wind having died away, and the tide having set in strongly, he was compelled to anchor there under the firing cannon.

Loading a thirty-two pounder, Maxwell himself aimed it so that the shot passed over the very center of the admiral's junk. The effect was ludicrous. The Chinese crews fell flat on their faces, and the admiral himself, after leaping high, fell prostrate. The cheering English sailors thought his head had been shot off, but he was safe enough to order, "Cease firing!"

Later, when the batteries fired at the *Alceste,* the English cannoneers demolished them; whereupon the Viceroy became civil, but announced that the British warship, sent by a tribute-paying monarch, had come up to Whampoa by his own express permission.

With the same naval might to support him, a Scotch commander soon afterwards showed his contempt for the Chinese.

A fleet of tea ships having arrived while the *Alceste* was at Canton, the Scot commanding one of them was greeted with disgusting gestures by Chinamen he passed. As they presented their backsides, he replied with oaths in broad Scotch, and then, as the gestures became more indecent, picked up a fowling-piece loaded with snipe-shot and peppered the offenders.

"There, you long-tailed rascals," he cried, "I'll give you a second edition of Captain Maxwell!" Aside from the trouble of picking the shot out of their hams, no harm was done.

Another American warship to visit those waters was the *Vincennes* commanded by William B. Finch. Sailing in 1830 and arriving at Canton, he asked Acting Consul C. N. Talbot and commission merchants J. P. Sturgis, Samuel Russell, J. R. Latimer, and W. H. Low, whether periodical visits by American warships were advisable to impress the Government with the importance of the United States and to cow the piratical tribes along the route and received the answer yes.

Two years later Commodore Downes arrived at Canton in the *Potomac* and reported that one of the opium receiving ships he saw at Lintin flew the American flag.

In 1838, Commander George C. Reed, stopped at Macao with the frigate *Columbia* and the ship *John Adams,* and in 1842 the historic *Constellation* and the ship *Boston,* under Commodore Lawrence Kearny, a commander of the old school, went to Macao. In the face of opposing merchants, Kearny announced that the Government of the United States did not sanction the smuggling of opium on the Chinese coast. He seized the opium runner *Ariel* and tried to capture the offending *Mazeppa.* His vigor pleased the Viceroy, who said of him: "He manages affairs with clear understanding, profound wisdom, and great justice."

CHAPTER XIV

Gantlet of Pirates

THE FIRST REPORTS of piratical attacks on American ships in Chinese waters came from Major Shaw, first American consul at Canton. He informed the State Department that Captain Metcalf, of the brig *Eleonora,* New York, had been attacked while approaching the China coast. Metcalf was taking to Canton a valuable cargo of furs obtained in the North Pacific. Fighting doggedly, he and his crew beat off the pirates, but the ship lost two officers in the battle.

Our best source of information about the dangers American as well as European ships ran was the recorded experience of Richard Glasspole, an officer of an East Indiaman. He tells of an unnamed American schooner which took part, with results fatal to her crew, in a blockade of the pirate fleet.

As in the case of the buccaneers of the West Indies, these Chinese pirates had not always been thugs and murderers. They were originally tribesmen who had rebelled against the oppression of the mandarins. Organizing themselves off the Cochin-China coast, they manned boats carrying thirty or forty men each, and drew to their fleets thousands of poor farmers and fishermen.

With these armies, the pirate leaders swept the coasts, blockaded the rivers, and even captured government war-junks, which they used to lead their shoals of boats.

The noted corsair Ching-yih or Ching commanded a confederacy of 800 war-junks manned by 70,000 to 80,000 thieves. His ambition increasing with his strength, he declared that he would hurl the Tartar dynasty from the throne of China; but instead, this man of mighty threats met an accidental death.

Having picked up at sea a poor fisherboy Paou, Ching at last promoted the youth to captain. The young man also, in a more intimate way, won favor with Mistress Ching, wife of the leader; and when this woman of force succeeded Ching as commander, she promoted Paou to admiral.

Among ambitious chiefs, however, he must show more than the gifts of a lover to hold his leadership, and he met the test by a herculean deed. There was on the seacoast a temple dedicated to the "Three Old Women," and in it was an image of them so heavy that a group of men could not move it from its base. Lifting the statue himself, he forced the superstitious crew to help him carry it aboard.

Instead of bringing misfortune, "Three Old Women" brought luck and victory.

It was when the ferocious pirates, after many battles at sea, had entered the Pearl River leading to Canton forts, that the Englishman Glasspole fell into their power.

He had left the East Indiaman *Marquis of Ely,* in a cutter with seven seamen, to go to Macao to procure a pilot. A squall came when the cutter was returning, and the pilot advised him to take shelter in a narrow channel. There they came amidst a fleet of what seemed to be fishing boats but which were pirate craft.

"About twenty savage looking villains," Glasspole wrote, "who were stowed at the bottom of a boat, leaped on board us. They were armed with a short sword in either hand, one of which they layed upon our necks, and pointed the other to our breasts, keeping their eyes fixed on their officer, waiting his signal to cut or desist.

Seeing we were incapable of making any resistance, the officer sheathed his sword, and the others immediately followed his example. They then dragged us into their boat, and carried us on board one of their junks, with the most savage demonstration of joy, and, as we supposed, to torture and put us to a cruel death."

When on board the junk they rifled the Englishmen and brought heavy chains to chain them to the deck.

"At this time, a boat came, and took me, with one of my men and the interpreter, on board the chief's vessel. I was then taken before the chief. He was seated on deck, in a large chair, dressed in purple silk, with a black turban on. He appeared to be about thirty years of age, a stout commanding-looking man. He took me by the coat and drew me close to him; then questioned the interpreter very strictly, asking who we were, and what was our business in that part of the country. I told him to say we were Englishmen in distress, having been four days at sea without provisions. This he would not credit, but said we were bad men, and that he would put all to death; and then ordered some men to put the interpreter to the torture until he confessed the truth. Upon this occasion, a ladrone, who had been once to England, and spoke a few words of English, came to the chief, and told him we were really Englishmen, and that we had plenty of money, adding that the buttons on my coat were gold. The chief then ordered us some coarse brown rice, of which we made a tolerable meal, having eaten nothing for nearly four days, except a few green oranges."

Using the pilot as interpreter, the chief told Glasspole that he must write to his captain to send a hundred thousand dollars for their ransom. If it was not sent within ten days, the English captives would be put to death.

Glasspole wrote the letter, and a small boat took it to Macao. Meanwhile, the ladrones stripped the officer's uniform of its gilt buttons, which they thought to be gold.

The corsair fleet sailed and joined that of Admiral Paou, and then Glasspole saw the immensity and power of the combined sea forces.

"At daylight the next morning, the fleet, amounting to above five hundred sail of different sizes, weighed, to proceed on their intended cruise up the rivers, to levy contributions on the towns and villages.

"The ladrones now prepared to attack a town with a formidable force, collected in row-boats from the different vessels. They sent a messenger to the town, demanding a tribute of ten thousand dollars annually, saying, if these terms were not complied with, they would land, destroy the town, and murder all the inhabitants: which they would certainly have done, had the town laid in a more advantageous situation for their purpose; but being placed out of the reach of their shot, they allowed them to come to terms. The inhabitants agreed to pay six thousand dollars, which they were to collect by the time of our return down the river. This finesse had the desired effect, for during our absence they mounted a few guns on a hill, which commanded the passage, and gave us in lieu of the dollars a warm salute on our return.

"October the 1st, the fleet weighed in the night, dropped by the tide up the river, and anchored very quietly before a town surrounded by a thick wood. Early in the morning the ladrones assembled in rowboats, and landed; then gave a shout, and rushed into the town, sword in hand. The inhabitants fled to the adjacent hills, in numbers apparently superior to the ladrones. We may easily imagine to ourselves the horror with which these miserable people must be seized, on being obliged to leave their homes, and everything dear to them. It was a most melancholy sight to see, women in tears, clasping their infants in their arms, and imploring mercy for them from those brutal robbers! The old and the sick, who were unable to fly, or to make resistance, were either made prisoners or most inhumanly butchered! The boats continued passing and repassing from the junks to the shore, in quick succession, laden with booty, and the men besmeared with blood! Two hundred and fifty women and several children were made prisoners, and sent on board different vessels.

"The pirates lived on their vessels. The after part of the ship was the quarters of the captain and his wives—he generally had five or six. Savage as were the corsairs, they were religiously strict in their rules as to women—no person was allowed to have a woman on board unless he was married to her in accordance with their laws. Each man stowed himself, his wife and family,

VIEW OF THE FOREIGN FACTORIES OR HONGS AT CANTON
From a Chinese laquered tray about 1825

E BURNING OF THE FOREIGN FACTORIES AT CANTON—1856
a Chinese artist

MISS HARRIET LOW
Painted at Macao in 1853 by George Chinnery

in a berth four feet square. The ship swarmed with rats, but this was pleasing to the crew, because they ate and enjoyed them. One of the delicacies served to the prisoners was caterpillars boiled with rice."

·The English officer appears to have been prized as a captive by the redoubtable Mistress Ching, for she frequently sprinkled him with garlic water, which was considered an effectual charm against shot.

That felicitous couple Mistress Ching and Admiral Paou had drawn up a communistic agreement, share and share alike. Any men who stole out of the general fund or concealed booty was put to death.

As to the ways of the pirates with women, one must judge for himself as to the delicacy of Mistress Ching when she decreed:

"No person shall debauch at his pleasure captive women, taken in the villages and open places, and brought on board a ship; he must first request the ship's purser for permission, and then go aside in the ship's hold. To use violence against any women, or to wed her, without permission, shall be punished with death."

A more violent story about women captives is told by the native Chinese historian, Yuen-tsze, who wrote about the same pirates and warfare.

"Mei-ying, the wife of Ke-choo-yang, was very beautiful, and a pirate being about to seize her by the head, she abused him exceedingly. The pirate bound her to the yard-arm; but on abusing him yet more, the pirate dragged her down and broke two of her teeth, which filled her mouth and jaws with blood. The pirate sprang up again to bind her. Ying allowed him to approach, but as soon as he came near her, she laid hold of his garments with her bleeding mouth, and threw both him and herself into the river, where they were drowned. The remaining captives of both sexes were after some months liberated, on having paid a ransom of fifteen thousand leang or ounces of silver."

The murdered wife Mei-ying became the heroine of a Chinese ballad, the poet declaring: "The spirit of the water, wandering up and down the waves, was astonished at the virtue of Ying."

To return to the long-suffering Glasspole: After several exchanges of letters, the chief reduced his demands to a ransom of ten thousand dollars, two large guns, and several casks of gunpowder, and then sailed the fleet up a narrow river to the town of Little Whampoa, where he prepared to attack several government vessels lying in the harbor.

Accustomed to life in the East, Glasspole was not greatly shocked when the chief proposed that if he and the quartermaster would man the great guns, and if the English sailors would join in the attack on the town, the pirate would accept the $3000 first offered as ransom money, and would pay besides $20 a head for every Chinaman's head they cut off in the attack.

"To these proposals," Glasspole confessed, "we cheerfully acceded, in hopes of facilitating our deliverance."

Preferring the killing of Chinese to living with pirates, the English tars therefore landed the next day, with about 3000 ruffians. Once in the fight, they fought as if they themselves belonged to the pirate horde.

One of the sailors did great execution with a little musket and was called the "foreign pirate."

Conquering the town, the ladrones loaded their boats with plunder and went out to the junks. Upon this, the inhabitants who had fled to the hills recaptured the town and slew 200 pirates, killing also one of the English sailors.

"The ladrones landed a second time," Glasspole wrote, "and drove the Chinese out of the town, then reduced it to ashes, and put all their prisoners to death, without regarding either age or sex! I must not omit to mention a most horrid (though ludicrous) circumstance which happened at this place. The ladrones were paid by their chief ten dollars for every Chinaman's head they produced. One of my men turning the corner of a street was met by a ladrone running furiously after a Chinese; he had a drawn sword in his hand, and two Chinamen's heads, which he had cut off, tied by their tails, and slung around his neck. I was witness myself to some of them producing five or six heads to obtain payments!"

Finally released, Glasspole and his men arrived on board the *Antelope,* after a captivity of eleven weeks and three days.

At this time the pirates were at the height of their power, but they fell to quarreling among themselves, and when a strong force of the emperor's ships had cooped them up in harbor, the powerful chief O-po-tae refused to obey Paou's commands, with the result that Paou lost many vessels and hundreds of men when he began to fight against a superior force. Fearing the vengeance of Mistress Ching and Paou, the rebellious chief offered to submit to the government and, being granted mercy, struck his free flag. He was appointed an imperial officer and changed his name to one meaning "The Lustre of Instruction."

Months later, the uneasy Mistress Ching said to Paou: "I am ten times stronger than O-po-tae, and if I submit, the Government will perhaps act toward me as they have done with him."

A rumor of the widow's intentions having reached Macao, a certain doctor named Chow came out to offer himself as negotiator, and later two mandarins brought the imperial promise of free pardon.

The corsair leaders, suspicious of treachery, were wary about entering the Canton stronghold, but the dauntless Mistress Ching said:

"Why should not I, a mean woman, go to the officers of government? If there be danger in it, I will take it on myself. My mind is made up—I will go to Canton!"

Paou gave in to her, but said that they would fix a time for her return, and that if she were not free to come back by that time, the pirate fleet would sail up to Canton and demand her release.

Thereupon the intrepid lady Ching set out, and with her went a number of the wives of the pirates, with their children.

It was policy for the Viceroy at Canton to forget the men, women, and children fiercely slaughtered by the thieves under the amiable Mistress Ching, and he received the lady kindly, and served tea to the women who attended her, and gave the children toys and confections, and pardoned the entire navy of cutthroats and beheaders. Then Mistress Ching went back and told Paou and his fellow chiefs that all was well, and they brought their vessels to Canton, and hauled down their independent flags, and hoisted the imperial banner. Every vessel was supplied with pork and wine, and the relieved mandarins and the carefree pirates who lately had poured gunpowder into their wine held a love feast.

There remained other pirate fleets to be put down. Paou and Mistress Ching gave themselves to this task and forced the corsair captain "Scourge of the Eastern Seas" to surrender. They also drove the dreadful corsair "Frog's Meal" to Manila. · The chief who complacently called himself "The Jewel of the Crew" lost his lustre and value.

Mistress Ching retired contentedly from public engagements, and the Viceroy of Canton, for bringing about this happy peace, received from the Emperor the supreme decoration: the two eyes of the peacock feathers.

For a time the rivers became quiet, and the people along the banks could plow their fields in peace. Saying prayers on top of the hills, they thanked their gods that this tranquillity had come. And also for a time there was peace on the ocean, and merchant vessels came and went without molestation, and the only thing that troubled the China seas were the fights of the "white barbarians"—the English frigates pursuing American merchant ships to get back their sailors and the American ship furiously resisting.

Out of the annals of Salem has come the most graphic account of the gauntlet of Malayan pirates our early ships run. The voyager was John White, Lieutenant, U. S. Navy, who on January 2, 1819, sailed from Boston for the China Sea in the ship *Franklin*.

Writing a day-to-day journal, the man from Salem when passing the island of Tristran d'Acuhuna, made a proud note about a preceding Salem mariner, Jonathan Lambert, who in 1811 took possession of that island and issued a proclamation inviting sailors of all nations to touch there for refreshment, paying what they could. Unfortunately for this sailor who would be king, he died by drowning two years after he had announced his monarchy, and his followers abandoned their miserable huts.

The *Franklin* passed the Cape of Good Hope and ran up her easting in the latitude of forty degrees south. On May 25, having crossed the Java Sea, White entered the Strait of Banka and met his adventure:

"We discovered three large proas in the offing, standing for us, and as it was nearly calm, with the assistance of their oars, soon approached sufficiently near for us to discover that they were full of men, and had each two banks of oars, with a barricade built across their forecastles, above a man's height, and projecting out several feet beyond the gunwale. . . ."

"From the center of this barricade projected a brass eighteen-pounder they had captured from some frigate they had over-whelmed. The leading boat was propelled by seventy-four oars, and the three proas had altogether 185 oars.

"As their intention was to attack us, preparations were made to repel them. It being nearly calm, they possessed a great advantage over us by means of their oars, in point of maneuvering, and kept their heads or barricades constantly presented towards us. They approached with a great appearance of resolution till nearly within range of our guns, when they began to slacken and kept aloof, probably for reconnoitering.

"With a view to ascertaining their distance from us, we gave them a shot from a six-pounder . . . immediately, as if electrified by this salute, every oar was set briskly to work, and they made directly for us."

White was afterwards told by a Dutch commandant that the pirates had captured a cargo of opium and were stupefied from the drug. This accounted to him for their strange course of attack; they were "tossing up the water with their oars, which moved without the least regularity, and assumed the appearance of the legs of a centipede in rapid motion."

A broadside from the *Franklin's* six-pounders stopped them, the shot striking around them like hail. Then a squall came down on the almost-becalmed ship, and her navigator immediately made all sail on her course. Coming within a short distance of the confused proas, White ordered another broadside with grape and double round.

The pirates retreated, but after the ship had passed they set out in swift pursuit, firing their eighteen-pounders continually. The Americans returned the fire until all their guns were dismounted, and then, knowing that they would be defenceless in case of an-other calm, put in at Minton, a Dutch harbor, while the proas lay off the entrance and waited for their prey. White, however, arranged with the captain of an English brig to sail in his company, and both ships left the harbor at night, and eluded the pirates.

The Dutch commandant, congratulating the Americans on their escape, said that the ferocious corsairs were excited both by opium, and by the juice of a root called "bang," which caused them to fight so desperately that even when badly wounded they would thrust with their spears and hurl javelins.

A similar adventure with a serious effect for the Salem ship attacked, and with a severe punishment for the pirates and their people, came to the ship *Friendship* in February, 1831.

Captain Charles M. Endicott, commanding the *Friendship*, had sailed to the coast of Sumatra to purchase a cargo of pepper. He made contracts with the rajahs and principal merchants of the island, and came to the port of Quallah-Battoo to complete the cargo.

One morning he went ashore to supervise the weighing of the pepper. He took with him second officer, John Barry of Salem, and four of the crew.

The custom was to load the pepper in large proas, which brought it out to the ships.

Captain Endicott observed that one of the proas which had left the shore was halted on the opposite shore, instead of being rowed directly to the ship. He suspected that the rowers were stealing pepper from the boat, and sent two of his men to watch their movements. Returning, they reported that they had seen nothing suspicious—that the boat had her usual complement of men.

When this proa arrived at the ship, however, her crew began to crowd aboard the *Friendship*. Knight, the first officer, who was in the gangway, grew suspicious and questioned them, but they told him they had come only to see the vessel. He ordered them into the boat again.

Then their treachery showed. Grabbing krisses concealed in the folds of their long sashes, they attacked Knight and his men, and when he turned to seize a boarding pike, he was stabbed in the back and killed. The crew, fighting back, were overwhelmed, and several of them were slashed to death. Jumping into the river, the survivors swam ashore.

Captain Endicott had watched helplessly. He realized now that the rajahs at Quallah-Battoo had conspired to replace hired assassins in the boat, and when the boat stopped on the far shore the exchange of crews had been made. Knowing that he and his men would soon be attacked, he hurried his party into the boat.

Then a surprising thing happened. Po Adam, one of the rajahs who had traded with Endicott, had been present at the weighing. He owned a fort and property at a place three miles away and had been friendly to Americans. At once he threw himself on their side.

Leaping into the boat, he cried: "Captain, you get in trouble. If Malay kill you, he kill Po Adam too."

Offering his cutlass to Barry, who was unarmed, Po Adam seized an oar and rowed desperately.

The Malays on land had postponed their attack on the shore party until they received a signal that the ship had been captured. When they saw the sashes of the thugs waving from the rigging —the planned signal—they pursued Endicott's boat in a large sampan, but they met their match. Instead of retreating, Endicott turned the boat and attacked the sampan. Barry, standing in the bow, plied his weapon so effectively that the Malay thugs gave up the pursuit. Under fire from the pirates aboard the *Friendship*, the Americans started on a thirty-five-mile row to the port of Muckie, and reached it safely. There they found anchored the ship *James Monroe* of New York, J. Porter, master; the brig *Governor Endicott* of Salem, H. H. Jenks, master; and the brig *Palmer* of Boston.

A resolute message was sent to the rajah at Quallah-Battoo, demanding that the vessel be returned. "Come and take her!" he replied.

Manned by thirty officers and men, the Americans put out from their ships to recover the vessel. Watching their steady approach, the pirates aboard the ship fled, taking with them specie and opium valued at $30,000.

The news of the attack stirred the people of the United States and excited the Congress. At last a disposition showed itself to support and protect merchant ships engaged in the Far Eastern trade.

Commodore Downes, of the frigate *Potomac,* then under orders to take his vessel to England and thence to the Pacific by a passage around Cape Horn, received new orders to proceed to Sumatra on a punitive expedition.

As he approached the pirate coast, the Commodore disguised his ship, giving her the semblance of an East Indiaman. The main-deck guns were hauled in, and the half port shut.

Arriving at Quallah-Battoo, Downes sent a force of 250 men under Lieutenant Shubrick ashore at night. At daybreak, Shubrick's party, concealed by wood and jungle, advanced on the town.

Several forts, bedded deep in the jungle, were attacked and captured. The rajah, who had been bold in attacking a few, turned coward now and sent a flag of truce to the frigate, informing the Commodore that many natives had been killed and begging abjectly that the assault should stop. Other rajahs from towns along the coast sent messengers begging for peace.

The expedition had accomplished its purpose. Downes told the rajahs that the damages he had inflicted were done as vengeance for the murder of the *Friendship's* men and warned them that if other American vessels were attacked, naval ships would blast their towns off the coast. He was warranted in the bombardment, and had taught the Malay chiefs to respect the American flag, but afterwards he was obliged to prepare a defense of his act, because the Department of State felt that he should have first notified the piratical rajahs that he was coming to punish them.

The *Eclipse* of Salem was similarly boarded and plundered by Malays, on the coast of Sumatra in 1838, and her captain Charles P. Wilkins was killed.

The reluctance of the State Department to permit naval officers to punish Malay murderers without giving warning of approach did not daunt Commodore George C. Read, commanding the frigate *Columbia,* when he heard in Eastern waters of the killing of Captain Wilkins.

At that time Read had been sent by the Navy Department on a circumnavigating cruise, and his ship had as consort the sloop of war *John Adams.* An alert American, J. Revely, Consular Agent for the United States at Penang, Prince of Wales' Island, addressed a startling letter to the *Penang Gazette,* and the letter was republished in *The Observer,* a newspaper in Colombo, the capital of Ceylon. Commodore Read, who was visiting Colombo, found printed in the newspaper this appeal to him:

"From a number of the *Penang Gazette,* of the 13th of October, we extract a description of the murder of the captain and some of the crew of the American ship *Eclipse,* by the natives of the west coast of Sumatra, published at the request of the Consular Agent of the United States, at Penang. Perhaps COMMODORE READ may be induced to bend his course, with the *Columbia* and the *John Adams,* now in our Roads to Sumatra, to avenge the death of his countrymen."

Commodore Read sailed at once to Muckie, and anchored close to the place where the *Friendship* had been attacked. Thereupon the friendly Po Adams came on board and offered his services. One of the murderers, he said, was at Kwala Batu, whose rajah possessed $2000 of the money stolen from the *Eclipse.* There were other murderers at Muckie and at Soo-soo, and the rajahs at those places kept the balance of the ship's funds.

Po Adams advised Commodore Read to send a party ashore to speak to the rajah at Kwala Batu, and to demand that the murderers there be surrendered. Suspicious of treachery among the Malays, Read studied Po Adams and decided that he could be trusted. He gave orders to Lieutenants Parmer and Pennock, and Lieutenant Baker of the Marines, to accompany Po Adams. One of the sailors who spoke the Malay language was taken along as an interpreter.

The boat landed about sunset and was met by a crowd of a hundred armed Malays, who snatched their krisses out of their sashes and waved them above their heads. Undaunted, the three officers leaped ashore and walked into the midst of this thicket of terrible blades. Po Adams, expostulating with the pressing crowd, led the way through a series of stockades to the bamboo palace of the rajah, a ruler of size and dignity who looked down on them from a bamboo throne.

The rajah withdrew with Po Adams into his adjacent council-chamber, while the Americans made sure that their pistols and cutlasses were ready. To their relief, the rajah behaved courteously to them when he returned to the throne-room. He did not deny that the crime had occurred, and he assured them that he would send his men to arrest the murderer.

The officers, with their backs to the Malays, made their way to the beach with great uneasiness, but the presence of Po Adam was a powerful shield, and they were not attacked.

Receiving his officers' report, Commodore Read was mystified as to how Po Adams could be so friendly with the rajah and his people and at the same time be a protector of American interests. Read decided to send a direct message to the rajah of the place, and this time Commander Thomas W. Wyman, of the *John Adams,* went ashore with Po Adams and an escort of six officers.

The rajah, upon his bamboo throne of state, welcomed them by rising and bending down to shake their hands. He led the visitors to the second-story veranda of his house, which was carpeted with matting strewn by Persian rugs. Meanwhile his retainers had gathered coconuts, which they opened with their krisses and handed to the Americans.

Then Captain Wyman got down to business, Po Adams and the sailor serving as interpreters.

Had the murderer been arrested?

No, the rajah had sent fifty men, but the rascal had eluded them.

Would the rajah return the $2000 that had been taken from the *Eclipse?*

The ruler replied that he had received not a dollar. It had been distributed among his people; he knew nothing about it and could do nothing about it.

Captain Wyman told the rajah that it would depend upon his action whether the United States would be friendly toward him, and that the murderer and the money must be returned to the *Columbia* by sundown of the next day.

Chaplain Taylor was in Wyman's party, and when he returned to the boat he fell behind the commander and came close to the edge of the jungle. Under a tree he passed were thirty or forty Malays and, having the sailor interpreter with him, he talked with them.

"Me belong to another king," the leader said. "Me no afraid to go board ship. Me want to make present of buffalo to Commodore and be friends."

The chaplain told the young man, who was the son-in-law of a rich rajah of an adjoining district, that he must come aboard and offer the buffalo himself; but agreed to visit this sub-chief in his fort.

They went through the jungle to an inclosure under a bower of tall bamboos, and there within the gate, tied by ropes to three or four trees, was a beautiful young wild buffalo. He was like, the chaplain said, "a sleek-limbed two-year-old heifer, petted and rendered a prize specimen for the city market." When approached the beast snorted, lowered his horns and rolled his big eyes; then bounded away as far as the ropes would allow him.

The wild buffalo was an appropriate sacrifice for the altar of amity, and the offer of the beast served to free the young chief from suspicion or punishment. He assured the chaplain that the rajah of Kwala Batu had received the $2000, and said that he would never take the murderer. "When you fire your guns at his fort," he said, "I want to come on your ship with my family and property."

"And what would you do if we destroyed the town?"

"I would return and gather my men around me. I would be the new rajah, friend to America."

Commodore Read, however, had not come to displace a rajah and put a new one in his stead. He devoted himself solely to the mission of punishment.

The chaplain asked Po Adam if he thought the rajah of Kwala Batu would meet Read's demands.

"Rajah is fool," he said. "He give up murderer—he give money —then he save pepper trade. What can rajah do with pepper—no ships come and buy? He no eat pepper. He give up murderer, he have plenty friends in America—they come and buy pepper. But he will not give up Makayu—he fool—he damn rascal—he buffalo!"

We gleam these things from the amusing conversation: the weakness and uncertainty of the rule of a Malay chief; the lack of unity among the many rajahs, and the dependence of these people on the American ships of the pepper trade.

The time had expired. All expectation of satisfactory action by the guilty rajah had been given up. Commander Read commanded his officers to weigh anchors and take a position nearer the town, where his guns might be brought to bear with the greatest effect on the forts and houses. The *John Adams* moved to a position close to the *Columbia*.

After having been anchored in that threatening position for several hours, with no signs from the shore that the ruler would meet the demands, the Commodore gave orders.

Three taps upon the drum . . . then the thrilling summons to quarters. The guns were cleared for action—the tompions out; the shot, grape, canister and wadding arranged; the matches made ready.

But still the order to fire did not come. An hour passed, and then the beat to quarters was again sounded. With the forts as target, the firing commenced; splintering and destroying the foliage which screened forts and houses. Another shot struck a group of Malays who had gathered in front of a cluster of bamboo houses. They were waving a white flag for protection.

For a half hour the cannonading continued, and then the order was given: "Cease firing."

The killing of Captain Wilkins had been avenged, largely at the expense of the civilian population.

As late as 1854, George Perkins, a partner of Russell & Company, was murdered by pirates on a passage from Canton to Macao. Returning from a voyage to the United States, he decided not to stop at the destination Hong Kong, and when ten or fifteen miles from there he hailed a Chinese boatman to carry him to Macao.

Attacks by river pirates at that time had been so many and

dreadful that foreign merchants had stopped traveling in Chinese fast-boats, but Perkins took the risk.

He did not arrive at Macao. The boat and crew were discovered and the crew were brought to trial by the English at Hong Kong. One of the Chinese boys on the boat turned State's evidence and testified that Perkins' throat had been cut while he trustfully slept.

As to following years, we have the word of a naval commander as to the boldness and ferocity of Chinese pirates, and the need of naval protection against them. This note by Executive Officer John Philip is in his journal of a cruise in the Far East, 1865-68:—

"Busy all day preparing to escort a number of American merchant vessels well outside of Hong Kong to protect them from pirates. It is so bad now that it is really dangerous for any merchantman to leave. No longer than last Saturday, just after we arrived, a merchant vessel got under way and had scarcely got outside the harbor when she was boarded by pirates and all hands on board were most brutally murdered—and in sight of one of the best English colonies."

The action of the American navy in protecting American ships in the waters about Hong Kong was severely commented upon by a newspaper in British Hong Kong.

On the river steamer *Kin-Shan,* plying the Pearl River, extraordinary precautions were taken to prevent the boat from being taken over by pirates, who had devised a way of shipping as passengers and then, en route, seizing the vessel, murdering the officers and travelers, and taking possession of the steamer.

The lower deck of the *Kin-Shan* was crowded with Chinese of the poorest class, and the entire lot were padlocked in under the hatchways and iron gratings. In ammunitions stands in the saloon there were pistols and rifles with fixed bayonets, ready for use against any Chinese who became violent.

CHAPTER XV

Adventurers of the Cross

MISSIONARIES OF CHRIST, from the time of John of Montecorvino and Francis Xavier, went with the first white men to China. While the pioneer shipmasters and traders fought for entrance along the coast, the missionaries with their gentleness and learning won the friendship of the emperors, the mandarins, and the people. They found that the tolerant Chinese, devoted to learning, would give them their ears if not their hearts; indeed the edicts banishing all Christian missionaries came not from enmity to their religion, but from the quarrels of the several Catholic orders among themselves. These quarrels were healed by the time the Americans came, and the homesick priests were glad to greet foreign travelers or traders of any faith.

Catholic and Protestant joined in revering John of Montecorvino, Rome's first apostle to the Chinese, whose record of conversions seemed miraculous to the later missionaries.

Arriving in India in 1291, and from there traveling to the court of Kublai Khan, John was permitted to erect a church at Peking, and the three bells he hung in its tower eventually called to prayer 6,000 converts.

"It is now twelve years," he wrote at last "since I have heard news from the west. I am become old and grayheaded, but is rather through labor and tribulations than through age, for I am only fifty-eight years old. I have learned the Tartar language and literature, into which I have translated the New Testament, and the Psalms of David, and have caused them to be transcribed with the utmost care. I write and read, and preach openly and freely the testimony of the law of Christ."

The second Catholic entrance was undertaken by Francis Xavier, who about 1552 started from Goa in company with a Portuguese ambassador to China. He arrived at the island of St. John, an island thirty miles southwest of Macao, but this St. Paul of Roman missionaries died before he could feel the thrilling satisfaction of entering the forbidden land.

His successor, Valignani, gazing across the sea at the stern hills of China despaired of achieving the same goal. "Oh mighty fortress!" he cried. "When shall these impenetrable brazen gates of thine be broken through?"

The Italian Jesuit Matteo Ricci, who followed him, did not spend time in lamentations. He came humbly and sociably and, having literary gifts, associated the Christian and Chinese faiths in a way acceptable to the leaders of China. Finding that the Chinese believed their country was the Middle Kingdom, the heart of the universe, he prepared a map to show its ruler that this was true.

Against a colorful background of Catholic history in Macao and Canton, the Protestant missionaries from England and America moved. Among them were influential men who praised the work of the early Catholic teachers. Especially liberal in their tributes were Drs. Milne and Medford, of England, and S. Wells Williams and Chaplain Taylor of the United States.

The European Catholic bodies were quick to take advantage of the opening of the treaty ports. When the Seward party visited Peking in 1870, they found the Roman Catholic missionaries active throughout China. The Church had divided the empire into eight bishoprics or more, which were in charge of sixty priests from abroad, and twenty native priests. Adjoining the stone Catholic cathedral was a nunnery whose sisters were French and Irish. They were lamenting the death of Sister Louise, slain in a native uprising, whom they affirmed to be a noble martyr.

The Protestants could never bring themselves to use dramatic spectacles and processions to impress the Chinese, but Chaplain Taylor, the scholar from Yale, reported with respect the solemn procession of Corpus Christus at Macao:

"The military," he wrote, "were drawn up at rest, in a line extending from the church on their left far down the wide street. The church was filled to the jam, by Portuguese women kneeling in a mass, and most of them with the light shawl thrown over their head, while the dark lace veil formed the head-dress of the better class of worshippers. The governor was kneeling near the altar, and other military officers occasionally entered, with a genuflection, and left again, watching the progress of the service, and being in readiness to move, at the signal for the elevation of the Host.

"The mass was over; and the sacred emblems were borne by four or six priests followed by the vicar general, the governor, and the separate orders of Dominicians, Franciscans, and others.

"As they passed on from the gate of the church, the military, already formed, wheeled in platoons to the left, uniting with the procession, and the band of musicians struck up their solemn and fine music, as the procession moved on in measured and martial step towards the senate house—passing through several streets and back again to the church. All were uncovered, the soldiers carrying their caps in their hands, as their muskets were pressed at their breasts. The intense tropical sun beat alike upon the venerable head of the governor and tonsure-priest, and darker and thicker locks of the soldiery. Minute guns from the fort bore their testimony that the devotees were on their solemn march; which, with the circumstance and pomp and respectful demeanor of the joiners in with the procession, and the mass of spectators that crowded each side of the street, or thronged the windows of the houses, presented at once an imposing and impressive scene."

In sketching the story of American preachers who pioneered at Macao and Canton, it is worth noting that they were conveyed to the Orient by American ship owners, whom Preacher Abeel referred to as "the servants of Christ engaged in foreign commerce." Representative of these was David W. C. Olyphant, a merchant of Scotch descent who was born in Rhode Island and as a youth went down to Manhattan to work for the shipping house of King & Talbot.

David Olyphant's religious zeal had been further quickened by what he had seen of the pitiable state of the masses of China, and when he met in a Manhattan prayer-meeting the Reverend Robert Morrison, he became an active supporter of the English missionary.

Born at Newcastle-upon-Tyne, England, and possessed by a fervor to carry gospel to the heathen, Morrison declared that he "would station himself in that part of the missionary field where the difficulties were the greatest, and, to all appearance, the most insurmountable." Timbuctoo was the field he first had in mind, but when China was proposed by the London Missionary Society, he gladly accepted the commission, and sought passages to Canton in an East Indiaman. He met his first serious obstacle—the East India Company refused to give him passage.

At that time the Company, pressing the Chinese government to open other ports to it and to increase its trade privileges, had aroused bitter opposition among the Celestials. Its directorate feared that the bringing of an English missionary would awaken suspicions and renew the conflict over religion, and that the Company's interests would suffer.

Morrison decided to take the American way to China. Crossing the Atlantic in a packet, he stepped ashore into the hospitable company of the churchgoers of Manhattan. An influential group of merchants led by Olyphant prepared the way for his going to the Far East. Secretary of State Madison gave him a letter addressed to Consul Carrington in China, requesting the latter to aid the missionary in finding protection and lodging in China. Sailing in an Olyphant ship, Morrison was cordially received and housed by Carrington.

As he watched the troubled dealings of the East India Company with the Chinese Viceroy at Canton, the missionary acknowledged that if he had come on an Indiaman to preach under British sponsorship, he might not even have gained a foothold.

David Olyphant became the prime mover in sending American Protestant missionaries to keep Morrison company in China. He began by offering to pay the expenses of a missionary for one year, besides providing the passage. The Reverend E. C. Bridgman was chosen, and sailed for Canton in the Talbot and Olyphant ship *Roman,* commanded by Captain Lavendar.

With Bridgman sailed the Reverend David Abeel, of the Dutch Reformed Church, whose letters and later book kept the missionary fires burning back home. Abeel started a movement to establish mission stations at wild coasts of the Indian Ocean, even though the natives were cannibals and pirates.

He pointed out that missionaries might dare to attempt it if they knew that ships from the United States would come to them several times a year. Ships bound for Canton, and "out-of-season" ships, might visit these dangerous coasts on their voyages back and forth, and thus sustain the health and morale of the devoted missionaries.

After Abeel's vessel was approached, off the Pelew Islands, by a native proa in which were six men and women, "perfectly naked," he became more urgent that they be taught manners and decencies.

As Olyphant's firm expanded, it opened a branch in Canton under partner C. W. King, who was as zealous in missionary work as was Olyphant himself. The partners helped Morrison establish himself at Macao and attended his services.

Mr. and Mrs. King entertained sociable Chaplain Taylor when his ship touched at Macao. Mrs. King, he wrote, "was an attractive young woman who wore a dark silk dress of American fabrics and mode." She had delicate features and glorious blue eyes and the brightness of her smile, he said, was emphasized by her gleaming, perfect teeth. She pleased him because "her feelings and action had been elicited for the moral welfare of the native females of China."

The East India Company, after having rejected Morrison as a passenger, employed him as an interpreter. Since much of its business was opium, this was a hampering connection for the missionary, but circumstances forced it. It became Morrison's custom to travel along the coast or to islands near by on board the ships of the Company, but since their sailings were often a long time apart, the Olyphant firm provided their friend a swift ship called the *Morrison*. Apart from this service, the *Morrison* pioneered the way for Perry's fleet in opening the closed door of Japan.

The incident we are about to relate throws an odd light on the character of King, a zealot in soul-saving, yet willing to resort to guns when aroused.

When the *Morrison* arrived at Whampoa in the late spring of 1837, the season was too far along to obtain a return cargo. Rather than have the ship remain idle in port, King decided to use her to explore the coast of Japan. There was at Macao several ship-wrecked Japanese, and the return of them to Japan provided a good excuse for the voyage. To avoid the appearance of force, King decided that the *Morrison* should go unarmed. The hospitality of the firm to the work of missions is reflected from these names of passengers: S. Wells Williams, editor and printer of the American Board of Foreign Missions; Rev. Peter Parker, M. D., of the Ophthalmic Hospital at Canton, and missionary, Charles Gutzlaff.

The Christian-minded voyage was a failure. Anchoring in the Bay of Yedo, King received in reply to his advances gunfire from the forts. He tried the port of Kagoshima, but here also the cannon answered.

Roused to fury, King wrote home urging our Government to resent the insult to the American flag and demand a treaty with Japan. Passenger S. Wells Williams, a well-balanced man, warned him that such a warlike attempt would be attended with "fatal influences."

Our Government did nothing then, but King had made a path for Commodore Perry.

The most distinguished person in promoting good will between the Chinese people and Americans in the earlier days of Chinese-American relations was probably Peter Parker of Massachusetts, the first American medical missionary to China. You met his bride in a previous chapter.

Peter Parker was born in 1804 at Framingham. His father Nathan was a farmer, and his mother Catherine was a farmer's daughter. They were Congregationalists, and sent their son to Amherst, but he later decided to complete his college education at Yale.

At twenty-seven he applied to the American Board of Foreign Missions for an assignment as medical missionary. Three years later he was ordained as a Presbyterian minister and sent to China; but when he found that the Chinese government restricted missionaries to Macao, he studied the language among the many Chinese at Singapore. Returning to China he lived at Canton, in the quarters of Olyphant, King, and Company. The Cantonese grew friendly towards him when they discovered that he could work miracles in healing eye diseases and in removing tumors.

Dr. Parker gave Chaplain Taylor a gracious welcome when the latter went ashore at Canton, and the account the chaplain gives of a journey with Parker through the streets of Canton shows vividly what a Godsend the physician was.

"Towards evening I took a stroll with Dr. Parker, passing up old China Street, one of the widest streets in the city, and composed of respectable shops on either side; and in a short time we had wandered through a number of streets, presenting at once the variety of this extensive mart of the East. The streets are narrow, serving only for foot-passengers, flagged with quarried granite. . . .

"I had ample opportunity to witness the doctor's popularity, and the impression he has made, as I walked with him through the streets. He was often recognized, and an undertone of respect would now and then be heard among the crowd, saying, 'The good heart' . . . 'The doctor who cures blind eyes' . . . 'The doctor with the pitiful heart' . . . 'The *no cash* doctor'—alluding to the circumstance that Dr. Parker would take no pay for his cures and practice.

"And the doctor's large hands, too, seem here to attract general attention, which seem not only to ennoble our benevolent physician but tend to add profoundness to the almost superstitious veneration with which they regard his person. 'What hands!' the less instructed in decorum, as the crowd gathers round, sometimes exclaim, in surprise and astonishment, as if he were indeed of the race of the gods they worship, which are in all their temples represented in their huge proportions. And the amiable physician hesitates not to let them compare their own tiny fingers and palms with his, when their curiosity has surprised from them the ejaculation. . . .

"Indeed, his reputation as 'the foreign physician who cures all things, and particularly restores sight to the blind,' has spread throughout the empire, more or less, and has drawn from various parts, and from the capital itself, patients seeking relief."

The pity of Dr. Parker and his associates was quickened by the sight of the blind beggars of Canton. With an unafflicted youth to guide them, or depending on the instinct of a blind leader, a number of blind beggars strung themselves in a row, and went through the narrow streets invoking celestial charity with infernal noises, crying shrilly to the accompaniment of the beat of iron pans, and the sound of unmusical Chinese musical instruments. Sometimes groups of these beggars united in voice and music, and a hideous concert resulted.

The beggars had their czar, chosen from their own ranks, and he was expected by the authorities to keep some sort of order among them. The beggars were forced to pay an admission fee into the union which they called "The Heavenly Flower Society." Whatever rules the king of beggars imposed, cleanliness was not one of them, and visitors shrank from their filth. Their hair was matted; their exposed bodies covered with dirt and vermin; and the loathsome creatures went about eating decayed cast-off fish and vegetables. The peak of misery among them mounted in the person of the lepers, who were obliged by law to wear a peculiar hat, and a mat around the shoulders, much after the custom of the Israelites in ordering that the leper's clothes be rent, his head shaven, and his upper lip covered.

Medicine in China was in a lamentable state when Dr. Parker began his work. There were no schools of medicine, and a beginner must engage himself to a practitioner. The doctor's fee was a copper coin, but if he treated a mandarin he received four coppers. The physicians of the Emperor's household were chiefly eunuchs.

As to smallpox, the Chinese had noted that it attacked a person only once, and had gotten into the habit of exposing the young to it, in the hope that it would be a mild infection. The success of this method led them to devise a crude inoculation against smallpox.

Blindness or sore eyes were more prevalent in China than elsewhere, so that western physicians who could treat eye diseases were especially welcomed.

Many Chinese doctors created their own quack medicines and advertised them by handbills, giving testimonials as to resulting cures. One sect of physicians advertised that they had exclusive possession of the medical secret—"not to die."

Speaking of the eagerness with which suffering people sought the hospital, Dr. Parker told the chaplain:

"I observed some of them, with lanterns, with which they left their homes at two or three in the morning, in order that they might be at the hospital rooms in season. When the days of admission were limited, they sometimes came the preceding evening, and remained all night, that they might secure a ticket in the morning. . . ."

The doctor had indeed need of the companionship and care a good wife gives in times of trouble and overwork. "I have more work," Parker wrote, "than one mortal can perform. Never were my professional services sought with more avidity than now. Officers of high distinction seek them; and crowds of all classes; but oh how I long to be laboring directly for the soul's salvation."

In explaining his method of teaching, Dr. Parker said, "One of my most respected medical teachers told his students: 'When the materia medica of earth fails, point your patients to that of heaven.' When hopeless cases have come to me, I have pointed these patients to the world above where none are blind, none deaf, none sick."

As our story proceeds Dr. Parker changes from a medical missionary to an officer in the diplomatic service. One reason for the change was lack of appreciation or lack of funds in America for his ministry of medicine. A blundering official at home suggested that since Parker's work lay almost entirely in the field of medicine, he should look for support to the British Medical Missionary Society which had a station in Canton. The vigorous reply he made revealed the hurt of his feelings.

Discovering his need of an income, the worldly merchants of Canton called on him to be their physician. Caleb Cushing, the new United States Commissioner to China, appointed him secretary of the expedition and gave him his first experience in what was for him the unfortunate field of diplomacy.

CHAPTER XVI

How Opium Came to China

THE CHINESE THEMSELVES were great sea-traders, but their quest when visiting India was not the fruit of the poppy-opium.

Centuries before the coming of the white men, the seaports of China—Hangchow, Fuchow, Chinchow and Canton—were trading with ports of the East Indies. They carried to Indian harbors cargoes of sugar, tea, ginger, rhubarb, silk, porcelain, jade, and lacquerware. They brought back to China brocades and cotton fabrics, cloves and pepper, the sandalwood so much desired by woodcarvers, precious metals, ivory, and mother-of-pearl; but they carried little opjum.

It remained for the enterprising English, in association with the native growers of the poppy in India, to discover the Chinese as an immensely profitable market for opium. The British East India Company, driven to produce dividends, became the principal carrier of the drug from India to the coasts of China.

British public opinion was in the main opposed to participation in drugging the people of China. The historian Green declared that it was an offense to the public conscience, and in 1843 Lord Ashley told the British parliament that it was "utterly inconsistent with the honors and duty of a Christian kingdom.'

But on the other hand, there was the fact that the East India Company, with many influential and common investors, was earning dividends because of its part in sending the drug into China.

In 1833, opium formed about one-half of the total value of British imports to China, and the amount of opium brought in by British ships was greater than the amount of tea exported by the Chinese.

The wrath of the Chinese court against Britons for their activity in the opium trade became furious when the Company's monopoly expired in 1833 and was not renewed; for the Company's moderation in the opium traffic—induced by British public opinion—was replaced by greedy and indiscrimate opium running by independent British shippers.

In the spring of 1834, when the fleet of free-trading British merchant-ships began to arrive via India to load tea at Canton, opium sales leaped.

The center of the narcotic trade was originally at Macao, but the greed of the Portuguese promoters had caused the Chinese to drive it to the nearby island of Lintin. Here opium was kept stored in armed ships and delivered to the Chinese smugglers by written orders from agents at Canton, who operated swift river-boats called "fast crabs" or "scrambling dragons," very much like the recent slick rum-runners off our Atlantic shores. By 1837, the trade had been driven farther to the east, to the coast of Fokien, where a fleet of twenty ships were engaged in it, including several American vessels.

Yankee skippers, tempted by opium profits, had succumbed also.

Ships from Philadelphia and Baltimore having started the custom of carrying opium directly from Turkey to China, the shippers of New York and New England took over the trade and by 1824 were responsible for most of America's wholesale opium trade.

When in 1798 Captain Joseph Ropes, in the ship *Recovery* of Salem, reached Mocha, Arabia, on the Red Sea and opened the coffee trade, he discovered the source and market for opium. Soon American ships were sailing between Mocha and Smyrna, and from Smyrna to China, the medium of exchange being Turkish opium.

The early engagement of American ships in carrying opium to China is revealed by the manifest of the ship *Lion* which sailed from New York in 1816 with 60 cases of opium in her cargo, which had been brought to New York through the system of ships abroad using goods instead of specie in exchanges. There was no intention on the part of the shipowner to engage in the opium traffic. The cases, valued at $30,015, were used to solve the problem of exchange. The Boston merchant Thomas H. Perkins stated that "Our funds arise from the export of opium from Turkey, British goods from Great Britain, lead and quicksilver from Gibraltar, and the same articles on a large scale from Trieste."

Opium obtained at Smyrna by Yankee ships was paid for with funds derived from the sale of American cotton goods and other commodities to the merchants of that port.

After the first few years, opium shipments direct to China from Turkey were discontinued, and the drug was shipped to American ports and then transhipped to China, or transferred to China-bound English vessels.

The Chinese did not like the Smyrna opium as well as that of India, but there was a market for it among the addicts who must buy cheaply, and among cheating traders who used it to adulterate the fine stuff.

The early American skippers, through their cargoes of Turkish opium, became so identified in Chinese minds with Turkey that, in 1839, a high mandarin at Canton asked if Turkey did not belong to the United States, and was amazed to learn that it was distant by a month's sail.

As American participation grew, the hong merchants at Canton who were security agents for American shipmasters were ordered by the harassed Viceroy to examine every arriving American vessel to see that no opium was aboard. He issued an edict that singled out the ship *Emily* of Baltimore, saying that "the said vessel came for no other purpose than to sell opium—INFINITELY DETESTABLE." He pointed out that while China exported tea, rhubarb, etc., for the health of the people of other nations, foreigners, with no gratitude, smuggled in prohibited opium, "which flows and poisons the land."

Another Baltimore ship, *Wabash,* which was boarded by Chinese pirates who killed the chief mate and some of the crew, was found guilty of opium smuggling. In making a report to the Secretary of State, Consul Wilcocks said that in counting the loss, he did not mention to the Chinese authorities that the cargo contained opium. However, when the pirates were arrested, the opium was found on them.

The Chinese leaders, in ordering foreigners to stop bringing the pernicious drug to China, repeatedly included the Americans with the British and the Portuguese.

Hu Kiu, Canton Viceroy, demanded the departure of nine persons, among whom were several Americans. When he ordered that a subject found guilty of opium smuggling be executed, "having taken into consideration that his penalty of death was the result of the pernicious introduction of opium into Canton by depraved foreigners," the spot selected for the strangling was at the flagstaff flying the American colors, but was shifted when the Americans resisted.

Active as certain American merchants were in the opium traffic the part of the United States in the trade was always a minor one. The carrying of opium to China in American ships was never more than one percent of the British trade in narcotics; and never more than ten percent of the total value of America's export business with the Chinese empire.

CHAPTER XVII

White Sails and Dark Cargoes

THE OPIUM RACES were beginning!

In 1831, American shipmasters in China were watching with grudging appreciation the busy plying between India and China ports of three small English opium schooners, the *Jamesina,* the *Lord Amherst* and the *Sylph,* which tended towards the clipper model and were very fast. There followed excited correspondence between the Americans in China and their houses in the United States. Discovering that fast little ships could pile up fortuntes for their owners, they reported that the *Jamesina* had sold Indian opium valued at more than a million and a half dollars to Chinese agents in the ports of Foo Chow, Amoy, Ningpo, and other harbors.

The American commission house of Russell & Co., were among the first to accept the challenge of the British opium schooners. From Brown & Bell, New York shipbuilders, they ordered the

Angola, which sailed for Hong Kong as the pioneer opium clipper.

The fever spread to New England ports, and soon Puritanland was in the trade with the *Zephyr,* 150 tons, the brig *Antelope,* 370 tons, built by Samuel Hall at East Boston, and the *Ariel,* 100 tons, built by Sprague and James, Medford.

Against this competition the British firm of Jardine, Mathewson & Co., added the *Torrington,* a clipper schooner, to their fleet, and other swift little ships soon came from British yards

The Americans then entered the *Minna* and *Brenda,* 300 tons each, both owned by John M. Forbes, and the British sent out the *Wild Dayrell,* 253 tons.

Built for speed and easy handling so that they could overcome the adverse tides along the China coast, make haste despite the monsoons, and elude the pirate junks propelled by sweeps which lay in wait for unwary ships along the Chinese coast, these clippers composed a distinct class. With their rakish masts carrying clouds of canvas, they were envied by crews of sluggish vessels.

Opium was shipped from India to China in its raw state, rolled up in balls the size of billiard balls, and wrapped in poppy leaves. The receivers boiled it down, refined it several times, and prepared it for smoking.

At the close of the Government opium sales in India, the new crop was shipped in such clippers, which had to race in all seasons and in all kinds of weather. The northeast monsoon resisted their going and tried to drive them back with a heavy head sea and a strong adverse current, but they thrashed their way to the China coast. The value and comfort of their cargoes made them especially the objects of pirate fleets lurking along the way.

The sailing of the tricky ships required officers of bravery and skill, and the passage from India to Macao or Lintin was a great training ground for sailors and fighters. The officers of the English ships were usually ex-naval men, and many of the young officers were sons of highly-respected parents—the younger sons of the nobility, or the offspring of clergymen. Induced by fabulous pay and exciting adventure, these young men served their period in the trade, and went back with fat wallets and bank accounts to become attorneys defending the law, or clergymen preaching against evil habits.

Captain Basil Lubbock discovered in an old American book of voyages this stirring account of the first opium run of the *Antelope*, under Captain Watkins:—

"With her low, black hull, tall rakish masts and square yards, she was a regular beauty," the narrator wrote:. . . ."We went aboard to take a look at the beauty and before we left her had shipped for the voyage. The Captain was a lank West Indian, a nervous creature, who looks as though he never was quiet for a moment, even in his sleep, and we afterwards found out he didn't belie his looks. After taking a cruise around Calcutta for a couple of days we went on board, bag and hammock (for no chests were allowed in the forecastle). Our pay was to be 80 rupees per month with a half month's advance.

"The vessel was well armed, having two guns on a side besides a Long Tom amidships. Boarding pikes were arranged in great plenty on a rack around the mainmast, and the large arms chest on the quarter-deck was well supplied with pistols and cutlasses. We were fully prepared for a brush with the rascally Chinese, and determined not to be put off our course by one or two mandarin boats.

"We sailed up the river some miles to take in our chests of opium and, having them safely under hatches, proceeded to sea. With a steady wind we were soon outside the Sandheads. The pilot left us, and we crowded on all sail, with favoring breezes for the Strait of Malacca. If ever a vessel had canvas piled on her it was the *Antelope*. Our topsails were large enough for a vessel of double her tonnage. We carried about all the flying kites that a vessel of her rig has room for. Skysails, royal studdingsails, job-o'-job, staysails alow and aloft, and even watersails, and save-alls to fit beneath the foot of the topsails.

"She steered like a top, but our nervous skipper, who was not for a moment day or night at rest, but ever driving the vessel, had one of those compasses in the binnacle, the bottom of which, being out, shows in the cabin just how the ship's head is at any moment. Under this compass, on the transom, the old man used to lay himself down, when he pretended to sleep (for we never believed that he really slept a wink); and the vessel could not deviate a quarter of a point off her course, or while we were on the wind royals could not left in the least, before he was upon the helmsman, cursing and swearing like a trooper, and making as much fuss as though she had yawed a point each way. It was the season of the southwest monsoon, and of course we had nearly a headwind through the Malacca Strait. But our little craft could go to windward, making a long tack and a short one, nearly as fast as many an old cotton tub can go before the wind.

"Our crew consisted of seventeen men, all stout, able fellows. There were no boys to handle the light sails, and it was sometimes neck-breaking work to shin up the tall royalmast when skysails were to be furled or royal studdingsail gear rove. We had but little to do on board; to mend a few sails and steer the vessel was the sum total of our duty. On board these ships the men are wanted mainly to work ship expeditiously and to defend her against the attacks of the Chinese officers, whose duty, but ill fulfilled, it is to prevent the smuggling of opium into the country.

"Once past Singapore we had a fair wind, and with studdingsails set, made a straight wake for the mouth of the Canton River. As we neared the Chinese coast, preparations were made for repelling any possible attacks. Cutlasses were placed on the quarterdeck ready for use, pistols loaded, and boarding nettings rigged to trice up between the rigging some ten feet above the rail, thus materially obstrucing any attempts to board the vessel when they were triced up.

"It did not take our little clipper many days to cross the China Sea. We had passed the Ass's Ears, the first landfall for China-bound vessels, and were just among the Ladrone Islands, which are the great stronghold of Chinese pirates, when we beheld starting out from under the land two of the long mandarin boats. They appeared to know our craft or to suspect her business, for they steered straight toward us. With the immense force they had at the oars it did not take them long to get within gun-shot range, which was no sooner the case than our skipper, taking good aim, let fly a shot from Long Tom in their midst. This evidence of our readiness to receive them took them all aback, and after consulting together for a little, they showed themselves to be possessed of the better part of valor—prudence—by retreating to their lurking place behind the land. We knew that so long as we were in clear water and had a good breeze, there was but little to be feared from them. The only danger was in case we should be becalmed when we got under the lee of the land, as they would be keeping a constant watch upon us and perhaps capture us by mere superiority of numbers. As may be imagined, we were all determined to defend ourselves to the last, even the black cook, whom we called "Doctor," kept his largest boiler constantly on the galley stove, filled with boiling water, wherewith to give the rascals a warm salute should they endeavor to board.

"What we feared shortly came to pass. In less than two hours after we had seen the boats, we lay becalmed under the land. The little vessel was perfectly unmanageable, drifting at the mercy of the current. Had we been far enough in shore we should have anchored. As it was, we could neither anchor, nor could we manage the vessel to turn her broadside towards the enemy.

"It was not long before they made their appearance. They had in the meantime obtained reinforcements, and four large boats containing from sixty to a hundred men each, now shot out from under the land, and came toward us with rapid sweeps. We did not wait for them to come to close quarters, but sent some shots at them from Long Tom. These, however, did not deter them. The calm had given them courage, and after discharging their swivel-guns at us, with the hope of crippling the vessel by hitting some of our top-hamper, they rushed to the onslaught.

"We now rapidly triced up our boarding nettings, and lying down under the shelter of the lower rail awaited the attack. The boarding nettings they were evidently unprepared for, as at the sight of them they made a short halt. This the old man took advantage of, and taking good aim, let drive Long Tom at them and luckily this time with good effect, knocking a hole in one of their boats, and evidently wounding some of her crew. Taking this as a signal to advance, and leaving the disabled boat to shift for itself, the remaining three now rapidly advanced to board. Taking advantage of the unmanagableness of our vessel, they came down immediately ahead, to board us over the bow, a posi tion where, they all knew, they were secure from the shot of our two light guns, which could only be fired from the broadside.

"Cocking our pistols, and laying the boarding pikes down at our sides ready for instant use, we waited for them. Directly twenty or thirty leaped upon the low bowsprit, some rushing to the nettings with knives to cut an entrance. We took deliberate aim and fired, about a dozen falling back into the boats as the result of our first and only shots. Dropping the firearms we now took to the pikes and rushed to the bow. Here the battle was for minutes pretty fierce, and a rent having been made in the boarding net the Chinamen rushed to it like tigers, but as fast as they came in they were piked and driven back.

"Meantime one of the boats had silently dropped alongside, and ere we were aware of it, her crew was boarding us in the rear. But here 'the Doctor' was prepared for them, and the first that showed their heads above the rail received half a bucketful of scalding water in their faces, which sent them back to their boat howling with pain.

" 'That's it, Doctor, give it to them,' shouted the old man, who seemed to be quite in his element, and he rushed down off the poop, whither he had gone for a moment to survey the contest, and taking a bucketful of boiling water forward he threw it among the Chinamen, who were still obstinately contesting the possession of the bow. With a howl of mixed pain and surprise they retreated, and we succeeded in fairly driving them back into the boats.

"A portion of us had before this gone to the assistance of the cook and had succeeded in keeping them at bay aft. To tell the truth, the hot water frightened them more than did anything else, and the boat's crew alongside required all the urging of their mandarin officer to make them charge at all. Luckily, at this moment a squall which had been some time rising broke upon us, and the brig began to forge ahead through the water. With a shout of victory we made a final rush at our assailants and, driving them back into their boats, cut them adrift, giving the one alongside a parting salute of half a dozen shots in her bottom, thrown in by hand. Making the best of our way from the scene of action, we steered towards Lintin Bay, where we were so fortunate as to meet a little fleet of opium boats, who quickly relieved us of our cargo, and we were no further molested."

So much for an opium clipper on the run; as for the activity of one in a Chinese harbor, Osmond Tiffany, Jr., the Baltimore observer who was in China at this time, gives this account:

"As we anchored in Macao Road, we saw a heavy armed brig going about two knots to our one. She overhauled us, and went past us like a flash, dropped her anchor, rounded to, and fired her guns.

"She had no name on her stern, and we concluded that she was an American government brig. In an instant her yards were swarming with men, and the sails were furled in man-of-war time and precision. We soon learned that she was an opium clipper, carrying twenty heavy guns, and a crew to match.

"Besides the men and officers, the smuggler employs a 'schroff' or assayer, a native whose music has been the jingle of dollars, and whose sight is so keen that he can look further into a lump of sycee silver than any ordinary gazer.

"The vessel makes sail with a freight of the 'pernicious drug,' and wherever an opportunity presents along the line of the coast, she anchors, and a trade is at once begun with the Chinese, who are always ready for the bait.

"The chests are brought on deck, the opium examined, and paid for in the unalloyed metal; the schroff turns over every piece, and hammers into it with an iron spike, and having thoroughly tested and valued it, the bargain is made, the opium sent over the ship's side, and the vessel proceeds on her errand.

"Vessels will thus sometimes make very successful voyages, remaining some months on the coast, and returning with a valuable ballast of the best silver."

CHAPTER XVIII

American Business Men in the Opium Trade

WE INTEND TO show now the part played by American individuals and commission houses in the opium crisis at Canton. There has been so much speculation as to the part opium played in the building of substantial American family fortunes, that it has seemed worth while to us to search out the facts. Our chief dependence is the Personal Reminiscences of Robert Bennet Forbes.

A man frank and unashamed, the world is indebted to his memoirs for facts historians and family chroniclers have avoided.

There is something considerable in his contention that his Yankee compatriots who were engaged in rum and slave running were hypocritical to frown on the engagement of commission houses like his Russell and Company in opium commerce.

In 1818, an important date in Chinese-American commerce, Samuel Russell of Middletown, Connecticut, and Philip Ammidon of Providence formed the significant firm of Russell and Company, and took in as partners Edward Carrington, Cyrus Butler, and T. V. Hoppin.

In 1828, D. W. C. Olyphant, who had been supercargo and agent for the frenzied tea operator Thomas H. Smith, organized the firm of Olyphant and Company, salvaging what he could of the bankrupt Smith's business in China. The firms of Russell, Olyphant, Heard, and Wetmore became the Big Four of the China trade.

Working together against the European competitors; becoming agents for shippers in India and Batavia as well as in the United States; employing swift ships and manning them with minimum crews of high efficiency as sailors, American firms in the first three decades of the nineteenth century almost ruined the China business of the East India Company.

Russell and Company accepted opium shipments, but Olyphant didn't. Both were successful. By material standards, no judgment can be made.

Perhaps it was under the influence of the Chinese, who put

poetic meanings into their trade names, that the firm of Olyphant named one of their swift clippers *The Wild Pigeon.* There are many lovely names in the lists of tea and opium clippers. The selection of them indicates that the literary mandarins were impressing the practical Yankee.

We start our Russell and Company story with the youth of Robert Bennet Forbes. Less pious, he is a more dramatic figure than Olyphant, but we choose him solely because he gives us the clearest, swiftest penetration into the trade we are curious about.

The white-painted store beside Foster's Wharf, Boston was a ship-chandlery shop bearing the name of Perkins Bros. and Cabot. The Perkins brothers, James and Thomas, have recently gone into the shipping business with James Cabot.

The War of 1812 had ended, and the merchants of Boston were reviving their trade with the West and East Indies, and were hoping that the confounded Marylanders who had brought on the war would not provoke the British navy to resume the blockade.

To schoolboy Ben Forbes, England and France were just names his elders mentioned with bitterness, but the name China was both magical and familiar. His cousin, Tom Cushing, had gone there and, while the American coast was blockaded, had opened a profitable commission business.

His uncles employed Ben to sweep out the store, make the fire, copy letters, and collect bills. One day while he was at Central Wharf watching the loading of the firm's fascinating square-rigger, the *Canton Packet,* his uncle James came along and said, "Well, Ben, which of these ships do you intend to go in?"

The boy answered promptly, "I am ready to go in the *Canton Packet.*"

That was enough. James Perkins sent him to Gedney King, the ship chandler, to buy a quadrant, a Bowditch's Navigator and a log book, and to a "slop-shop" for an outfit of sailor's clothes: checked shirts, duck trousers, a pea-jacket, socks, and shoes. His concerned mother had quite a task altering the duck trousers to fit the thirteen-year-old sailor.

Ben's uncle bought him a mattress filled with pig's hair, a

couple of blankets, an iron spoon and several knives. His mother, meanwhile, was filling his ditty bag with well-darned socks; well-patched clothes, and a supply of thread, needles and buttons. His aunt sent him a Testament, and neighbors gave him gifts—a bottle of red lavendar, one of essence of peppermint, and a small box of broken sugar; if he got seasick, he was to put drops of lavendar or peppermint on a lump of sugar, to settle his stomach.

A family friend, William Sturgis, gave him an admonition which, as to the first part, Ben faithfully followed:

"Always go straight forward, and if you meet the devil cut him in two, and go between the pieces; if anyone imposes on you, tell him to whistle against a northwester, and to bottle up the moonshine."

The *Canton Packet* was commanded by kindly Captain John King, of Medford, who, the roguish Ben said, had a nose "of the shape and about the size of our storm staysail." The voyage began October 19, 1817, and the boy in his checked shirt and duck pants waved goodbye to his mother and sister keeping back their tears. And so began the career of a man who became one of the most dynamic partners of Russell and Company, the commercial colossus of the Far East.

When the *Canton Packet* anchored at Whampoa on March 13, 1818, Ben for the first time grasped the fact that his relatives the Perkinses were almost as important on the Canton river-front as they were on the wharves of Boston. His cousin, John Perkins Cushing, met him. Cushing had become head of the branch of Perkins and Company, Canton.

Ben Forbes stayed with Cushing during the three months the ship was at Canton and proved himself so handy at weighing teas and packing silks that Cushing was eager to keep him; but his uncles in Boston had selected him as a sailor to train him to be a commander, as was the custom, and he stuck to the ship. When the *Canton Packet* arrived at New York, after a run of 172 days, he sought out his uncle, Colonel James Grant Forbes, and was welcomed.

On Ben's second voyage to China, a nest-egg of a box of dollars was put aboard the ship as a present to Ben and his brother Tom, from James and T. H. Perkins.

They advised Ben to consult Cushing at Canton as to the best way to invest the dollars, and suggested that it would be profitable to purchase crepes for the New York market.

Ben and Tom invested the money in silks and shipped them to New York in the *Nautilius,* where they were sold by the Hones, selling agents for the Perkinses. The profits were substantial, but when the Hones came to settle up years later, they paid simple interest instead of compound, which disappointed the youths in their expectations of having $16,000 each when they came of age.

Ben was told by his uncles that, since he was not very "stout," he need not stand watch to Gibraltar, but that thence to China and back he must keep watch as the others did. He was to prepare himself for promotion by studying practical navigation, and was to take the sun regularly and keep a regular journal throughout the voyage.

On arrival at Canton, he again lodged with Cushing and worked as junior clerk alongside John Hart, chief clerk. There he met merchant Philip Ammidon of Providence, whose nose, he noted, was even longer and sharper than that of Captain King. The Ammidon nose, however, was keen enough to smell a good worker in Ben, and when Cushing renewed his offer to the youth of a clerkship, Ammidon asked Ben why he did not accept.

"Because I promised my uncle Perkins to stick to my ship until fit to command her."

Ben also had it in his mind that his brother Thomas, in the Perkins office at home, was the logical candidate for the good job at Canton.

Cushing wrote comfortingly to Ben's mother that he would answer for the lad's being at the head of his profession in a few years. He also wrote to Thomas H. Perkins that Ben already had the stability of a man of thirty and was more competent to transact business than half of the supercargoes sent out. Since Ben chose to be a sailor, Cushing urged that he should be promoted to an officer.

It is evidence of the spirit of the women of those times that when Ben spent a short time at home between voyages, his eldest sister Emma said that maybe his leaving them so soon was for the best, since the long enjoyment of the pleasures of home might make him reluctant in resuming his profession.

Ben at eighteen had been promoted to second mate of the *Canton Packet,* and on a later voyage was offered that of chief mate, but told his uncle that he was too young, and went as second mate.

When twenty, he was given the work of fitting out his uncles' favorite ship, the 264-ton *Levant,* and while he was attending to details, Colonel Perkins came aboard of her and told his nephew that it was time for him to be looking for a mate.

Bennet stammered that he was too young, but his uncle brusquely told him that if he were not then fit to command he never would be, and the young man accepted command of the *Levant.*

His crippled father—an old man at fifty—died at the time fixed for sailing and told his son that he died content, knowing that Tom and he could support the family.

Ben's mascot was a poodle dog he had bought at Rotterdam, whose hair was trimmed round his face and legs to show ruffs. The poodle's accomplishments were that he could sit up and howl or sing at command, tend a weather-brace in setting a royal, drag the goat aft to be milked, and drive the pigs to the quarter-deck.

To plain-living New England brothers like Tom and Ben Forbes, life in China offered temptations to luxury it took strong moral fibre to resist. To be waited on by a Chinese boy in the Russell factory, for instance, could lead a poor youth to imagine himself a millionaire, and the enjoyments of the young clerks and supercargoes—races, gambling, and sometimes courtesans—could tempt a youth to grasp for money so that he might indulge himself.

Ben felt like a mogul at breakfast when the Chinese servant brought coffee or tea, crisp white perch, and snowy bread, or for lunch served plantains and a bottle of Calcutta beer that had the same popping power as Burton's ale. At dinner the same servant boy—handsomely gowned—joined with his fellows in serving a grand sociable feast, but was always careful to serve only the man whose chair he had pulled out.

How good it was, at afternoon dinner, when there were usually fifteen or twenty diners, from the chief partner to the humblest Portuguese clerk, to have one's own servant bring in delicious mutton from the mountains, which epicures declared was like the Southdown of England in flavor and tenderness, and then a course of teal or reed birds, with excellent potatoes grown near Macao and other enjoyable vegetables. Afterwards came small thin-skinned oranges with blood-red juice and a large oval fruit tasting like a gooseberry and so called by foreigners; litchi, pomegranates, walnuts, chestnuts, wine, and cheroots—they indeed dined like lords in the hong dining-rooms.

After dinner a young Yankee sailor could grow envious watching the smart young junior partners and better-paid clerks go off to the boats they had had built by some famous Chinese builder and sail in their yachts modeled after those in New England havens, or challenge each other to races in their sleek eight-oared cutters. These races had become an institution, with starter, umpire, and European and Chinese spectators lining the banks.

There was a piano in the hong, and someone always owned a guitar or a flute; at the risk of homesickness they sang favorite songs of their native land.

Evening came, and a visiting young man should reject the thought of the Chinese girls on the pleasure boats anchored at Whampoa, or a companion's suggestion about a river girl who was kind to foreign young men. And if a young man had money, and wished company virtuous or loose according to his tastes and morals, there was such company and pleasures at Macao; and it was said that oddly-entertaining company could be found at the new "Astor House" in Hong Kong.

If a white man did not have a wife or lady love waiting for him, fair enough "China coasters" could be found at the bars— girls attracted there by their loose male kind—scoundrels and loafers who had drifted there when the atmosphere of London or other places en route grew dangerous for them.

There was a romantic side to the river girls. Through some mysterious backing, or through her own industry, many a river girl had acquired her own sampan, which was her home, her boudoir and her means of livelihood. A group of these single young women anchored at the shorelines of the ground occupied by the foreign factories, and there they stood waiting to go to where a prospective passenger signaled. In the stream their voices could be heard calling, "Come in my boaty!"

They were pretty and flirtatious, and they wore glossy black tresses braided into a queue and ornamented with glass. The fact that the hair was not gathered in a knot showed that they were single, and open to casual courtship. On their foreheads the hair was brought down almost to the level of their eyebrows, and cut square, and under this black fringe the eyes that regarded the "foreign devils" were serene if roguish.

Little pictures and ornaments meagerly brightened a girl's floating home. They had been given to her by some foreign admirer.

Like Major Shaw, Ben Forbes' heart was at home.

At thirty, he married Rose Green Smith of Boston, and bought a house in Temple Place. A financial panic came, however, several of his ventures went bad, and he felt it necessary to go to China to recoup his fortunes.

Arriving at Hong Kong in 1838, he was welcomed by the principal partner of Russell and Company, John C. Green, and the junior members of the firm, Messrs. Abiel Abbot Low, Edward King, and William C. Hunter. His cousin and early backer, John Perkins Cushing, organizer of Russell and Company at Canton, had strongly recommended him to that firm.

Having made his fortune, senior partner Green wished to return to the United States, and he felt that Forbes was the man to take his place. The arrangement went through despite the opposition of one member, Joseph Coolidge.

Becoming general manager of Russell and Company, Forbes faced a crisis in the attempt of the Chinese government to drive out foreign-owned firms located in China.

The Russell commission business had increased so rapidly in Canton that there was always a scarcity of partners capable of carrying their share of the burdens. Samuel Russell, whom Cushing had inspired to begin the partnership in 1824, retired in wealth from the firm twelve years afterwards, and thereafter it was carried on by numerous partners—Augustine Heard, William G. Low, John C. Green, John Murray Forbes, Joseph Coolidge, Abiel Abbott Low, Wm. C. Hunter, Robert Bennet Forbes, Warren Delano, Jr., Russell Sturgis, Daniel Nicholson Spooner, Joseph Taylor Gilman, Paul Sieman Forbes, George Perkins, Edward Delano, William Henry King, John N. Alsop Griswold, and as many again.

Augustine Heard deserves more than mere mention. In Baker Library, Harvard University, there are 450 bound and unbound volumes of manuscripts relating to three generations of the Heard family.

Augustine, in his twentieth year, went to China as a supercargo. The shrewd John Perkins Cushing marked him as a likely fellow and, after the youth had proved himself, took him into the firm of Russell and Company. In 1833, Augustine was the sole partner of the firm in China. Breaking under the strain, he returned to Boston. Afterwards, with Joseph Coolidge, former Russell partner, Augustine formed the firm of Augustine Heard and Company, which became, with the firms of Russell, Olyphant, and Wetmore, the Big Four. Augustine brought four nephews into the firm. As traders in tea and opium, the Heard firm pursued the same activities as Russell and Company. Ben Forbes tells that when Augustine was in China, his recreation was to ride a pony about the compound; the antics of the animal, new to the Chinese, fascinated them.

When Chinese business men in Canton wished to buy opium for their own retailing, they went to the offices of the foreign merchants and bought certain amounts of opium at the market price, and the merchants' clerks issued an order to the commander of the firm's receiving-ship, to deliver the amount purchased. Then the purchaser went to the storage-ship at Lintin and, after examining the contents of the chests, employed native wherries to deliver the drug on shore. These paid regular fees to the custom-house and the military posts, but resisted the demands of any other government or pirate boats, desperately fighting the attackers.

For the Russell partners and some of their competitors, there was a fascinating element of speculation in the opium traffic. When the price of the narcotic became depressed the rich members of foreign firms bought it up cheap and stored it in their warehouses, with the result that a chest bought for $150 could be sold for $500 or $700; and when there was a great scarcity, the demand forced the price up to $1000 or more. But it was as easy to lose several hundred dollars on a chest as it was to gain that amount.

A sidelight on the Yankee part in the opium trade at that time comes from the visitor from Baltimore, Osmond Tiffany:

"The English are not the only people who deal in opium; the Parsees and Arab merchants are very fond of dabbling in it, and the model republicans, the universal Yankees, are by no means to be held blameless. Many of the fastest vessels that scour the coast, and prove so instrumental in filtering the poison through the reservoirs of the empire, sail under the American flag, and their owners would be very indignant if they were supposed to belong to any other nation."

Yankee Robert Bennet Forbes of Russell and Company was so free of shame as to opium cargoes, that he named his first steamship of the opium run after his daughter Edith.

The ship was a challenge to the wood-and-sail tradition as well as to the critics of the narcotic trade. While most of the Yankee firms refused to recognize the threat of the steam-driven vessel, Forbes was open-minded, and when the British builders began to experiment with iron vessels and steam power, he invested heavily in the same type.

As to the *Edith,* a bark of steam and sail built in 1843 by Samuel Hall, with engines by Hogg and Delamater, she arrived sensationally at Bombay and found in port the naughty brig *Antelope,* Captain Dumaresq.

Both sailed for China loaded with opium, though the underwriters at Bombay feared that an opium cargo would be ruined by the heat from the engines. The *Edith* made better time only because she was able to steam six or seven knots through the Straits of Malacca, while the *Antelope* was becalmed.

Partners Warren Delano and Paul S. Forbes watched the

arrival of the *Edith* at Hong Kong, but remained skeptical as to the efficiency of the iron ship with auxiliary engines.

Commissioner Lin, with special authority from the Emperor, was on his way to Canton to put an end to the opium traffic. Heads might fall; grafting officials might be tortured; war might be provoked with the stubborn English traffickers—any of these measures he was prepared to put in force. The Opium War of 1840-42 was beginning.

A splendid-looking man was Commissioner Lin. He was brilliant of eye, tall, and well-proportioned, and was blessed with the paunch Chinese ladies admired. A man of the people, who had risen to eminence by passing literary examinations for public office, Lin had won the trust of the weak Emperor who in sending him to Canton had wept and said: "How may I die and go to the shades of my imperial father and ancestors until these dire (opium) evils are removed?"

On the Commissioner went with his troop, the imperial "tigers," accompanied by standard-bearers, mandarins, attendants, musicians, executioners, and palanquins carrying women of pleasure.

It was a procession Gilbert and Sullivan would have been delighted to send onto their stage. The foot-soldiers wore red garbs faced with white, and carried on the chest and on the back an oval of white calico on which was written in large black letters the name of their regiment. Their heads were covered with tall conical hats decorated with stripes of various colors. Those who could afford it carried heavy, awkward swords; and if they were sufficiently rich, they bore two or three of these unwieldy weapons. The cavalry was mounted on miserable hacks and wore long blue cotton robes; their only weapons were bows and arrows.

Lin's journey was a continual triumphal procession. Passing through the Chinese section of Macao, the people erected honorary portals for him and put up laudatory scrolls "in order to manifest their profound gratitude for his coming to save them from a deadly vice. . . ."

The English official whom Commissioner Lin was to deal with

was Captain Charles Elliot who had become superintendent of British interests in China. Elliot found himself in a delicate position. He was the representative of the British conscience as well as its treasury; but because of the Chinese edicts, he found himself protecting opium traders who wanted Great Britain to go to war to protect their investments and profits.

Writing to the home office, he said that "the Chinese government have a just ground for harsh measures," and thus stated his personal conviction: "No man entertains a deeper detestation of the disgrace and sin of this forced traffic"; and: "I see little to choose between it and piracy."

On arriving at Canton on March 10, 1839, Commissioner Lin found that there were several British merchants in the river with opium aboard, and that there was, on ships and in factories, 20,000 chests of the drug, valued at millions. He demanded that the chests be given up to be destroyed, and then began a battle of wits between the mandarins and the foreigners as to how much of the opium could be salvaged. The British and American commission houses decided to ignore the order, but they found this time that they were dealing with an official who could not be cajoled or bribed.

Without stopping to arrest brokers or to parley with foreign officials and merchants, Lin issued a proclamation demanding of the foreign community the instant delivery of every chest of opium in Chinese waters. The hong merchants, agents for the foreign commission houses, were threatened with death if the mandate were not at once obeyed. To show his earnestness, Lin commanded a walkout of all native employees of the hongs, and when these had left he surrounded the foreign compound with troops.

Then the luxurious merchants and clerks, who had each had a coolie to wait on him, were forced to do the cooking and housework themselves. Surrounded by savage soldiers, threatened by swarms of Cantonese beyond the troops who at a word could be aroused to massacre the foreign devils, the Americans and Europeans went on living, and even made fun out of the situation.

Fortunately the food supply was not shut off—provisions came in the shape of pens of chickens, and pigs and sheep on the hoof.

Clerks were assigned to herd and butcher the livestock and other duties were distributed.

These notes from leader Forbes' journal give an intimate account of the confinement:

"J. C. Green sweeps the dining room and makes tea.

"R. B. Forbes attends to the glass and silver.

"A. A. Low set the table.

"Warren Delano—head cook.

"W. C. Hunter—lamps.

"Gilman attends to the wine, beer and cheese.

"Miranda and Silva wash the dishes, clear the table, and clean knives.

"Every man is required to take care of his own rooms."

Mr. Snow, the United States Consul, was then an old man, but he carried water to the upstairs rooms.

The imprisonment lasted for five or six weeks, and to relieve the irksomeness, sports were arranged that amazed the watching Chinese soldiers.

There being many terrier dogs in the factory, rat hunts were organized which the troops outside watched enviously, thinking that the Americans would have fine repasts of rats and beer. There were foot-races, cricket and ball matches, and the climbing of flagstaffs.

Grave rumors and happenings made such diversions a welcome relief. There was the sorry day when Houqua and Mouqua appeared with chains around their necks to show that the Commissioner meant what he said when he declared that he would execute the hong merchants if their clients did not surrender the opium chests, and there was a more ominous occasion when the mandarins of Canton tried to force Mr. Dent, head of an English house which was one of the principal holders of opium, to surrender himself to the Commissioner as a hostage for the delivery of the opium.

Then the Chamber of Commerce met, and British, American, and Parsee merchants in its membership gave up, as individuals, 1037 chests. Later, upon Lin's insistence, they gave up the balance.

"Be careful," Lin had warned, "and do not view this document as a matter of form, and so tread within the net of the law, for you will find your escape as impracticable as it is for a man to bite his own navel."

The surrendered opium was conveyed to Chunhow, near the mouth of the river. There the chests were emptied into prepared trenches and the opium mixed with lime, salt and water, after which a channel for the mixture was dug to the sea. Thus supposedly flowed away narcotics valued at twelve million dollars, Spanish money.

In reporting on the opium war at Canton, Dr. Peter Parker wrote to his friends that—"The officers who have sailed the Viceroy's boats have been arraigned and convicted, and they have implicated the Viceroy himself, who, they say, has received one-half of the profits, so banishment may be his lightest punishment . . . according to a custom well understood, the Emperor will not pass sentence of decapitation, but will send a golden cord concealed in a box, which the Viceroy will open, and seeing that his services are no longer acceptable to the Emperor, forthwith he must be his own executioner, and must strangle himself with the Golden Imperial Cord."

Forbes testified that it soon became apparent to the Chinese and foreign merchants that to destroy part of the crop was to enhance the value of the remainder, and those firms who had cargoes of opium waiting outside were not slow to use the usual means of disposing at an enormous profit of the opium they retained. Small owners of the drug lost greatly, but the big commission houses profited greatly in the end.

When Captain Elliot and Commissioner Lin came to an agreement, and the imprisoned merchants were released, the head of each foreign house was made to sign a bond pledging never to have anything to do with opium within the waters of China. This pledge was generally kept until the British by force caused the emperor to admit the drug on payment of duty; then the American houses that had handled opium before resumed the trade.

The opium chests surrendered, the English merchants retaliated against Canton by shutting up their factories and moving to Macao. Elliot tried to persuade Forbes to shut up the factory of Russell and Company and leave Canton with the English.

"If your house goes," Elliot said, "all will go, and we shall soon bring these rascally Chinese to terms."

Forbes made a memorable reply: "I have not come to China for health or pleasure. I shall remain at my post as long as I can sell a yard of goods or buy a pound of tea. We Yankees have no Queen to guarantee our losses."

"Are you willing to do business with a chain about your neck?"

"The chain is imaginary," Forbes said, "but my duty to the customers of Russell and Company is real. I will buy and sell at Canton and Whampoa as long as I find people to deal with!"

The new trading season had come. The few months of its duration were rich in chances for wealth. The American firms kept on in Canton and obtained the general business the English firms had temporarily abandoned.

Loading ships with tea and silks, they sent them to a Dutch East Indian port, where the cargoes were transferred to British bottoms. The great British firms of Jardine and Dent then began to send their accumulated goods into Canton under the American flag, and the Yankee ships they hired navigated the river with their holds packed and hills of cotton goods on their decks.

Forbes set the American pace in these dealings. When the Salem ship *Navigator*, Captain Bridges, anchored at Hong Kong with a cargo of betel nuts and rattan, Forbes persuaded Bridges that rattan did not count at that time, and that, with cotton bringing seven dollars a bale, he should pile the rattan on deck and cram the between-decks with cotton bales. The captain did so, obtaining thousands of dollars of added profits.

The opium crusade having made idle the Russell receiving-ship *Lintin,* its owners sent her on several profitable trips up the river, with her upper spars down. Her decks were piled with cotton and tea and silks. Chinese boats were employed to assist her in towing her up and down the river. The freight charged for silk or cotton was from five dollars to seven dollars a bale for a trip of ninety miles up the river, which was more than the freight cost per bale to carry the same bundle to America.

Forbes and all the Russell partners found themselves called on more and more to defend their part in the opium trade. Peter

Parker preached against it before the Congress. The rival firm of Olyphant & King was praised as a supporter of missionaries and an abstainer from the opium traffic.

Forbes' defense for the part his firm of Russell and Company took in the opium traffic was that it was a commission house and that the opium sent to them from India belonged to Parsees—planters of small means who had chosen Russell and Company as their consignees, sending it in a season opium of a total value of $800,000.

As to the open part of the partners of Russell and Company played in the opium business, their defense was generally accepted as being in accord with the commercial standards of the times.

The point of view of the Russell partners was that dealing in opium was not a smuggling business so long as the drug was sold in waters outside the jurisdiction of China; that it was a legitimate trade at Singapore, Manila, and Macao.

Forbes said boldly: "... I considered it right to follow the example of England, the East India Company, the countries that cleared it for China, and the merchants to whom I had always been accustomed to look up as exponents of all that was honorable in trade—the Perkinses, the Peabodys, the Russells, and the Lows."

Perhaps the reason Robert Bennet Forbes' book, "Personal Reminiscences," went into several editions was the honesty and frankness of the author.

Fortune, throwing together the preacher opposed to opium and the commission merchant engaged in the business, created amusing situations. We tell of one, the occasion being a passage to America in which Dr. Parker and Robert Bennet Forbes were shipmates.

The season was bad for a voyage across the China sea; the ship was a cranky one and was undermanned as to crew but overcrowded with passengers.

A gale sprang up and the barometer fell, and Forbes, the shipowner and master, decided to "haul on a wind" and await a better chance to run into the Straits. He had to carry sail to keep the vessel's offing, and in a squall the ship heeled over, and China and glassware showered the cabins.

Dr. Parker poked his nose out of the cabin while the sails were splitting and inquired if he could be of any service.

"Go back," the irate master said irreverently, "and pick up all the crockery playing Isaac and Josh in the cabin!"

In the procession of American diplomats who influenced relations between China and the United States was New Yorker Townsend Harris of the cocked hat, gold braid, and gilt shoe buckles, who concluded the first treaty of commerce with Japan after Commodore Perry's treaty of peace and friendship. Harris quarreled with the American commission houses in China and wrote home complaining about them. All American commission houses in China, he said, except D. W. C. Olyphant and Wetmore and Company, were engaged in opium smuggling.

Investigating these charges, Secretary of State Marcy wrote to Paul Sieman Forbes, a partner of Russell and Company, but Forbes replied evasively that so far as he knew "Russell and Company had never smuggled a chest of opium."

When the expected British blockading force under Sir Gordon Bremer arrived in Chinese waters, the partners of Russell and Company had time to reorganize the firm. The interests of members of the firm was renewable at certain periods, and when one withdrew, another was chosen to become partner in his place.

There was a separate firm named Russell, Sturgis and Company operating at Canton and Manila, and Forbes proposed that either of the two active members, Russell Sturgis or Warren Delano, brother of the grandfather of Franklin Delano Roosevelt, come into the firm in the place of a retiring member. Warren Delano became a member on January 1st, 1840. His partnership continued until 1866. In 1844 his younger brother Edward Delano became a member of the firm.

Opportunities to obtain lucrative places as members of the house increased as new ports were opened. The firm established itself as the exchange bankers of the harbors they entered, successfully competing with branches of London banks. It became an international network with banking and shipping branches in Europe,

India, Boston, Salem, New Bedford, New York, Philadelphia, and Baltimore.

We have not felt that the work of American consuls in China comes within the scope of our book, especially since the reader has available such a splendid work as Eldon Griffin's *Clippers and Consuls*. We permit ourselves, however, to give this glimpse of the duties and difficulties of these unhonored officials:

As to the difficulties our consuls met in performing their duties, these words by Wood, a resident, are revealing:

"The consul is the judge, a sheriff. He daily makes arrests (of obstreperous sailors), holds court, and is sustained with great physical ability by a stout marshal. The theatre of all these dignified doings is a little out-building just ten feet square, and alongside the door the eagle, with outstretched wings, is painted on a sign in the most ferocious attitude . . ."

The writer went on to say that after the consul had tried his erring countrymen, he had no prison to put them in.

Commission merchants, allied with shipmasters, often became antagonistic to consuls who stood up for State Department rules. For instance, in 1857, when the American inspector, Dr. Fish, made an adverse ruling against Russell and Company's claims as to cargoes of the bark *Quickstep* and the brig *Spec,* the firm used its private police force against the inspector, and indirectly intimidated the Chinese port authorities.

In 1853 Russell and Company was the first firm to use the port of Foochow as a shipping point for superior teas to England, though the port had been opened to the English by treaty ten years before. All the trade they had done there in the ten years was in opium, piece goods, and common Bohea tea; but a shrewd Chinese employee of the Russell house showed the firm that they could obtain in the country and send to Foochow the same fine teas the English merchants bought and shipped at Shanghai, and that the cost from the plantation to Foochow would be two to four taels less than shipping it to Shanghai. Following his advice, the Americans obtained "an edge" in profits when shipping to the London market.

Along toward 1860 the American firms began to 'lose profits.

The British banks began to take the exchange business away from them, and the British merchants competed successfully with them in the American market. Chinese competition grew strong again. While a vast amount of business was being lost, costs were increasing. Like the American clipper ships, the American commission houses they had helped to found were passing away.

Major Shaw, dreaming at the opening of the century of organizing a commercial colossus doing business in all harbors, had a sound ambition, even if he died before the vision became a reality. After the Chinese Government had been forced to open treaty ports, the American Commission houses, often in connivance with influential port officials, had founded depots in these places:

Russell and Company: depots at Shanghai, Hong Kong, Canton, Foo-Choo, Kiu-Kiang, Hang-kow, and Tien-tsin;

Augustine Heard and Company: Shanghai, Hong Kong, Canton, and Foo-Choo;

Olyphant and Company: Shanghai, Hong Kong, Canton, and Foo-Choo;

Bull, Pardon and Company: Shanghai, Hong Kong, Canton, and Foo-Choo;

Smith, Archer and Company: Shanghai, Hong Kong, and Canton;

Silas E. Burrows and Company, and E. J. Sage and Company: Hong Kong;

H. Fogg and Company, and A. C. Farnham and Company: Shanghai.

Time and again in stories of travel in China, the researcher discovers praise of the hospitality extended at treaty ports by the various managers of Russell and Company. The travelers entertained would have felt a little less easy if they had known that General Manager Robert Bennet Forbes was drawing adverse conclusions about such sociability:

"Individual expenses," he noted, "greatly increased, houses and social arrangements became more luxurious, and with the great increase of society attendant upon the advent of ladies at all the ports, social entertainments became more general and costly."

There is a comment in Seward's journal which penetrates to the eason why Russell and Company and other great commission houses went out of business at last.

Seward observed as to conditions at Hangkow on the Yangtze: ". . . There are six foreign houses, one of which is American (Russell and Company). The high expectations of increase have been disappointed, not because the trade was misestimated, nor yet because it failed, but, strange to say, only for the reason that the native merchants have learned the respective wants of foreign markets, and the ways of supplying them."

It will probably be asked what part the American Navy took in suppressing the opium trade. At the period of which we now write, there was little grounds for blaming it. The chief offenders, in its eyes, were partners of Russell and Company.

The commission merchants, resenting naval interference, were barely polite to officers of the fleet who craved shore lodgings. Spalding, a naval officer, made this sarcastic complaint:

". . . should you be a merchant-man, and indebted to their brokerage for the purchase of tea and silk, or the sale of opium, their spacious chambers are soon placed at your disposal; but if unfortunately an officer for some national vessel, your way to the single Chinese hotel, with its pent-up rooms, infuriate mosquitoes, and pleasant fried-rat odors, will not be impeded by them."

Reporting from China to the Secretary of the Navy, on May 29, 1843, Commodore Kearney said:

"The American flag is now the only cover for this illicit trade, Sir Henry Pottinger having issued a proclamation against it; and the English craft having been turned away from the rivers has placed the Americans in a peculiarly advantageous position, as freighters, under the flag of the United States. . . .

"With regard to the *Ariel*" (a Russell ship), "I have taken her papers and colors from her; and I have obliged her master to discharge the whole of her cargo (at Amoy), and then he is to return to Macao. Her papers are endorsed by me in a manner which will render them unavailable, and are returned sealed to the consulate. Were it not for the risk, I would send her to the United States; but she capsized once or twice in Boston harbor before she sailed, and is now a dangerous vessel. Should I fall in

165

with any seaworthy vessels of her character I shall send them home, that their case may be properly decided by the laws, of which the owners, as well as the consular establishment of the United States, seem to have been clearly regardless in making transfers that are illegal. These sham sales are well known, by which our national character is daily losing ground, and will so continue to do while the public consular duties are confined to merchants whose interests are so deeply involved in the transactions before cited."

The ground on which Commodore Kearny seized the *Ariel* was not that she was smuggling opium but that, owing to a juggling of ownership papers, her owner professed to be an American citizen, though he had not lived in the United States for six years.

Commodore Foxhall A. Parker, commanding the East India squadron, had afterwards received from the Navy Department orders similar to those given Kearny: he was to impress upon the Chinese authorities that "one great object of your visit is to prevent and punish the smuggling of opium in China either by Americans, or by other nations under the American flag, should it be attempted."

Parker was not as forceful as Kearny. While Parker was at Bombay awaiting the arrival of Commissioner Cushing, whom he was to convey from that port to China, the Russell brig *Antelope* arrived with Fletcher Webster, Secretary of the Mission, aboard. And after Webster disembarked, the skipper of the *Antelope,* with Parker watching, began to load opium chests for China.

"I cannot find any law," the Commodore reported to the Secretary of the Navy, "which will authorize my interfering to prevent or punish smuggling by Americans or others in foreign countries. The only course that appears proper for me to pursue is not to interfere in their favor, should they be taken by the Chinese authorities."

According to a note we have come across, State Department and naval policy must have relaxed afterwards with regards to discouraging the carrying of opium by American vessels, or else the opium thus carried was just part of a cargo and was intended for medicinal purposes. One is astonished to come upon this note in the diary of Executive Officer John Philip of the U. S. Warship *Massachusetts*, which was on pirate patrol off Hong Kong in the sixties:

"Our store ship *Supply* left the harbor for Yokohoma, and the *Parsee* with her from San Francisco. As the route of the two vessels is the same for a long distance, we did not convoy the *Parsee* out. The pirates will be disappointed, (at the convoying by the *Supply*) as they had been waiting for the ship for a long time. She has a valuable cargo of opium."

A shipment of opium to America as late as the sixties is incomprehensible unless the drug was to be used for pharmaceutics.

In 1856 the Navy made the first display of American force against the Chinese. Commodore Armstrong, while in Chinese waters, assigned Captain Andrew Hull Foote of the *Portsmouth* the duty of protecting American residents against the rebellious mobs in Canton, who at one time even set fire to the American factories.

The Cantonese were bitter against both English and Americans, and did not care to distinguish one from the other. Indeed, one of the massive Chinese forts along the river fired at Captain Foote himself as his small-boat was being rowed past it. Though his boatmen waved the American flag and the Commodore fired his revolver in protest, the fort continued firing and the next fort, when Foote's sampan was 200 yards away, let loose with grapeshot.

The *Portsmouth* bombarded the fort the next day, and several days later the *Portsmouth*, the *San Jacinto* and the *Levant* repeated the assault. With 287 men armed with five howitzers, Captain Foote attacked the first fort in the rear and killed forty of the fleeing Chinese soldiers: then he turned the guns of the fort on the second one and silenced it.

As early as 1871, the Koreans demonstrated to the American Navy a truth it was to re-discover in the war with Japan—that the people of those islands will die rather than give in.

The American schooner *General Sherman* having been destroyed in a river of Korea by a band of pirates, the State Department felt that it was high time to do something about protecting American shipping in those waters; Mr. Low, minister to China, was instructed to obtain a treaty from the Korean Government assuring safety for American sailors.

The Minister went in Perry-fashion, attended by a squadron of naval vessels under Admiral Rodgers, and anchored in the Salés River without opposition, but when surveyors from the ships were at work charting the harbor, they were fired upon from the shore. Rodgers demanded an apology from the ruler, and when ten days had passed without an answer, he bombarded the harbor forts. Under cover of the cannon, Lieutenant-Commander Casey led a landing party of 575 sailors and Captain Tilton joined with 105 marines.

They went ashore at low tide, plowing through mud that came up to their knees, just as American boys of later times were to plow in through the shallows to take Japanese-held islands. Captain Collum of the Marine Corps wrote: "The hillside was very steep, and the walls of the fort joined the acclivity with scarcely a break in the line."

The Koreans made a brave stand, throwing rocks when ammunition gave out. They would neither give nor ask for quarter. The indomitable Americans captured the fort, but the Koreans fought them until the last man went down. Out of the garrison of 263 Koreans, only twenty prisoners were taken, some of them wounded.

CHAPTER XIX

Those Racing Clouds—the Tea Clippers

A SENSATIONAL NEW triumph for Baltimore was heralded in 1832 when financier Isaac McKim of Maryland brought about the making of a ship that was to challenge and give new ideas to both Yankee and British builders concerned with the China trade. This ship, the beautiful *Ann McKim,* was herself a development of recent Maryland progress in swift-running China ships. The

Maryland brig *Argyle*, for instance, had sailed from Canton to Baltimore in the astonishing time of ninety days.

Sent to Europe by his father—of a Londonderry family—young Isaac McKim had shown from the first distinct qualities of leadership, and when the captain of his ship declared her to be unseaworthy, the youth dismissed him and brought the vessel home under his own command.

Isaac became a flour-producer and a copper exporter. He helped organize the Baltimore and Ohio Railroad. He also built ships to send goods produced inland to the West and East Indies. The sea being his chief love, in 1832 he gave shipbuilders Kennard and Williamson of Fell's Point his own plan for a speedy vessel. In naming the lovely ship they launched after his wife, he paid the wife a worthy compliment.

Entrancing to the eye, the *Ann McKim* also satisfied her owner as to speed. Describing an early run the *Baltimore Sun* of November 7, 1838, exclaimed editorially: "Baltimore shipbuilders against the world for building fleet craft!"

In 1840, the *Ann McKim* brought to New York from Canton the first news of the outbreak of the "opium war," and the arrival off Macao of the British fleet from India.

In 1842, on East Indian runs, the ship went like the wind, and her swift voyages without doubt influenced her later owners, Howland and Aspinwall, to compete more strongly in Oriental trade.

Northern shipbuilders said that the *Ann McKim* was a luxurious and expensive ship, and that her cargo space had been skimped to achieve her slender lines. The same speed could be obtained, they said, without so great a sacrifice of precious cargo space; and years later, these shippers hurrahed when the substantial China packet *Helena* made as rapid a run with almost twice as much cargo per ton.

The young marine architect John Willis Griffith of New York, who created the model of the forthcoming clipper, *Rainbow,* with its sharp lines and hollow bows, had undoubtedly been inspired by the graceful *Ann McKim.*

It fell to the lot of Captain Land to take the 750-ton *Rainbow* on her first run. She broke the record for the round trip to Canton, and Captain Land declared: "She is the fastest ship in the world!" On her second voyage to the China coast, against the stubborn resistance of a northeast monsoon, she made port in ninety-two days and came home in eighty-eight days, apparently warranting Master Land's further affirmation: "No ship can be built to outsail the *Rainbow!*"

Few ships broke the *Rainbow's* records on the run to Canton and return.

"Old Man Land," they called her master. It was the day of young men, and he was flying the white banner of age; but the owners of the *Rainbow* gave him command of the lofty, radical ship and were well rewarded by his astoundingly swift voyages. Making a championship run to Hong Kong in the *Challenge,* he died as he drove her to anchorage at the chosen port.

The *Rainbow* responded to a second master just as splendidly. In 1847, Captain William H. Hayes brought her in from Canton in eighty-five days, beating by three days her astonishing time on her second voyage. She came, however, to a mysterious end, fading from marine history as untraceably as the rainbow itself. On Hayes' fifth voyage in the adored ship, New York to Valparaiso, the *Rainbow* vanished, and the fate of officers, crew and ship became one of the unsolved mysteries of the ocean.

Captain Bob Waterman, employed by Howland and Aspinwall, was determined also to make a name for himself as a speedy and successful master in the China trade. He got his training on Atlantic packets. At twenty-five Howland and Aspinwall gave him command of the *Natchez,* a New Orleans packet whose run to that port had been discontinued, for the purpose of taking goods from northern ports to Valparaiso. He shook up the old ship so that she made unexpectedly swift voyages and in 1842 took her from Valparaiso to Canton. Rounding the Horn, he made the run in time that would have been creditable for one of the new clipper ships.

Men explained the new swiftness of the old *Natchez* by saying that Waterman crowded on extra canvas and kept it drawing to and beyond the last moment of storm danger, and that he worked his men for all they were worth in energy. In 1845, in the same ship, he actually beat all records by coming home from Macao to New York harbor in seventy-eight days. Howell and Aspinwall rewarded him with the best of sea-laurels—they built for his command the biggest and swiftest ship in the tea trade.

Reminiscent of the *Ann McKim* was this new ship, the glorious *Sea Witch,* which on the eighth of December, 1846, was launched by Smith and Dimock, who had built the *Rainbow.*

The *New York Herald* said of this new ship: "The *Sea Witch* is, for a vessel of her size, the prettiest vessel we have ever seen."

The decorations on her hull were fascinating to the crowds who watched her rising in the yard at the foot of Fourth Street; she was painted black with the old-fashioned American bright stripe, and had for a figurehead an immense gilded Chinese dragon to denote her engagement in the China tea trade.

Having personally supervised all details of spars, sails, and rigging, Waterman, on December 23, 1846, left the thronged, cheering wharves of Manhattan and sailed the *Sea Witch* out to sea in spite of a strong northwest gale, voyaging to Canton via Rio de Janeiro. Carrying clouds of canvas—three standing skysail yards, royal studding sails, large square lower studding sails with swinging booms, ringtail and water sails—she matched in speed the new ocean steamships and was for three years at least the fastest ship that sailed the seas.

Perhaps it was for debt, perhaps it was for his habit of driving his men, that Waterman got into trouble on a certain occasion. While he was in New York between voyages, a "sea lawyer," learning that he was getting ready to sail, came down to the office of his firm to serve him with a legal notice. From this awkward situation, his amused employers rescued him. Gardner G. Howland and William A. Aspinwall, warned by a clerk that the process server was in the outer offices, schemed with Waterman to escape.

The *Sea Witch* lay at anchor at their wharf across the street. Keeping the man of law waiting, the partners got out of their ships' stores a boatswain's chair, a rope, and a tackle block, and fastened the rope to the flagstaff on the roof of their building at 55 South Street. Then they rigged the chair and threw the other end of the rope to a sailor in the street below, who ran with it to the deck of the *Sea Witch,* where an officer wound it around the lower part of the foremast.

Receiving a signal, Waterman sat in the chair and slid down the rope and over the side of the ship. At the same moment the tug that had been held in readiness to tow the vessel pulled her into the East River and down the Narrows. When the hounder discovered the trick, his quarry was gone.

It was the auspicious year of 1849, linking the Atlantic seaboard with the west coast. The California run around Cape Horn was to cap the immense demands made on Atlantic shipyards by the markets of the world. While the China commerce continued, the California clipper trade was gripping the interest of shippers and shipbuilders.

Along South Street, New York, the talk was mainly about western expansion. Railroading, ranching, lumbering, city-building were new topics crowding out the talk of Oriental manifests. Tea, porcelains, rugs, and mattings were dwindling in importance beside the demands the developing West was making for flour, clothes, furnishings, guns, and powder.

It was an omen of the swift decline of the China clippers that the merchants of New York in this year of 1849 had forgotten that dramatic Captain Waterman had sailed to China in the beautiful *Sea Witch* and was hoping to lead the flock of tea clippers into harbor. Even with an amazingly fast flight, he could not be expected before the second week in April, and here on March 25th there was little reason to let talk of the China run interrupt the talk of the coming race to the Pacific.

The lookout at Sandy Hook sent word to the tea houses along the water front that a big clipper had been sighted, a square-rigger with her great rakish masts carrying bellying clouds of canvas. The owners, suddenly became intent on the immediate ship making port.

As she drew near and took in sail, her private signals became distinguishable and were recognized by a single group—the owners of the *Sea Witch.* Other shipowners threw up their hands in mock despair. Captain Bob Waterman had again done the impossible; he had brought in his China cargo a fortnight before the rest, making the passage in seventy-four days, and fourteen hours, breaking all records for the China run.

Captain Nathaniel Brown Palmer, who had gone to sea at fourteen and at eighteen had sailed on a sealer around Cape Horn, found time while resting up on his Connecticut farm to read the shipping news. Fascinated by the career of the *Ann McKim,* he wished for a chance to command a new swift vessel in the China trade and was happy when John M. Forbes, partner of Russell and Company, built the *Paul Jones* and offered him command of her.

Sailing out of Boston harbor for Hong Kong, he made the voyage in 111 days, but was eager for an opportunity to better that time.

On the homeward voyage of the *Paul Jones,* Captain Nat had as passenger William H. Low, one of the partners of A. A. Low and Brother, a New York firm which was already important in the tea trade. Low noted that Palmer, besides being a dependable skipper admired by his crew, was a keen judge of ship design. He watched the captain whittle a model which, Nat said, would outsail any other ship in the China trades. Catching Palmer's enthusiasm, Low took a three-quarter interest in the projected ship and persuaded his brothers to back the enterprise. She was the swift *Samuel Russell.*

Becoming a shipowner in his own right, Captain Palmer gave his newly-acquired ship the name *Houqua,* after the venerated dean of Chinese merchants, and employed a skillful woodcarver to make as a figurehead an image of the Chinese financier and trader.

Proud and amused was Palmer at the sensation created among the junks and sampans crowding Pearl River, Canton, when he poked his ship's sharp bow, overhung by a noble bust of the familiar Houqua, among them.

These courtesies to China, shown in the dragon figurehead of the *Sea Witch* and the bust of Houqua on the vessel of that name, were returned in a way when the 300-ton teakwood junk *Keying,*

173

flying the dragon flag of the Emperor of China, visited New York.

Lowering her matting sails and dropping her ironwood anchors close to Castle Garden, she rode there, an object of curiosity and speculation.

High of bow and stern, with a yellow hull and a huge painted eye on her bow, the *Keying* was odd also because of the nine big black, white, and red mats that hung along the gunwales like the shields of Viking serpent-ships.

Those who were permitted to go aboard her marveled at her colossal rudder which, with rudder-post, weighed seven tons. It was a perforated contraption and could be let down twenty-two feet when required to steady the vessel's sailing.

The word went around that this could be no other than one of the delightful Mr. Barnum's humbugs; but New Yorkers were somewhat let down when they heard that the junk, with its crew of thirty-six Chinese and twenty Europeans, was owned by Charles Kellett and associates of England. It was, however, true that she had sailed from Canton on a voyage that lasted seven months, and that she would return there. Her European sailors, growing confidential with American visitors aboard, whispered that they were fed up with their primitive quarters and hoped for a chance to desert.

Rebuking "Skipper" of the *New York Herald* for failing to mention in a published list the *Samuel Russell,* "one of the sweetest craft that ever danced through Old Neptune's dominions," a correspondent of the *New York Herald,* issued September 23, 1851, wrote:

"When I made a voyage to China in that 'ere ship, under the command of old Captain Nat Palmer (a captain, let me tell you, as is a captain) we had an experience of so wonderful a character that it had often been a wonderment to me that the ship's owners, or some of her relations, did not blow on it through the newspapers. Scores of vessels, on the same tack with ourselves, were overhauled and ran away from with just the same ease as the *America* beat the royal yachts of England. Occasionally, to be sure, some brother Yankee would put the good ship to her mettle before we could shake her off; but as to anything foreign—whether English, or French, or Dutch, or what not, and we had chances with all sorts of them—why, Lord bless you, sir, it was the merest baby play in the world.

"But, lest you consider this only a sailor's yarn, also to give you a more definite idea of her performances on the voyage, allow me to state one fact that may be proved from her log-book. One day, we took a pretty smart breeze upon our starboard quarter, and it continued to blow tolerably steady for the space of ten days. At the end of that time we had skimmed upwards of 45 degrees, making, you will perceive, hard on to 3200 miles in ten days."

Most of the group of skippers we have been telling about were attracted by the sea from boyhood, but Captain Philip Dumaresq was different. Son of a sturdy Maine family, his sickliness worried and shamed his parents.

"Send him to sea," the doctor said. "Send him a long way—to China!"

And so young Phil Dumaresq went aboard a tea clipper, faced seasickness and endured sea fare, and came home so robust that the physician's reputation was enhanced. This intimacy with the sea worked a further wonder on Phil Dumaresq. Announcing that he was going to follow it, he took hold so briskly and capably that at twenty-two he was given command of a vessel, and toward the end of his dramatic career in the tea and opium trades, earned this tribute from his employer Captain Robert Bennet Forbes: "He was the prince of sea captains."

Alarmed at the growth of American world trade, Great Britain in 1849 repealed its historic but handicapping navigation laws. The Government decided to give a push to England's backward shipbuilders. It reasoned that if British shippers bought vessels from American yards, they would get the advantage of the improvements the Yankee had made. The new Act made it possible for British merchants to build or buy ships in any country for the promotion of British world trade, and also invited foreign vessels to compete with the British in their own home markets.

The alert partners of Russell and Company were quick to take advantage of the repeal and seized the opportunity to ship tea direct from Canton to the London market.

When A. A. Low and Brother's magnificent new clipper *Oriental,* 1003 tons, under Captain Theodore Palmer, which left New York in May, 1850, arrived at Hong Kong, Russell and Company chartered her and loaded her with tea for the English market.

Slower English ships with lower freight charges were available for the voyage, but Russell and Company reckoned that a swift voyage would bring prices for the tea cargo in London which would more than make up for the higher freight cost Captain Land charged.

Bringing the first tea of the season, she anchored after a record-breaking run of eighty-one days from Hong Kong at West India dock, London, on December 3, 1850, the first of a flock of swift Yankee clippers—whose long hulls and raking masts were closely studied by British shipbuilders.

Since American clipper ships had demonstrated that they could speed past the almost becalmed Indiamen in the Chinese seas and Indian Ocean, there was nothing to do but copy their lines or to order ships of similar fashion from the Yankee shipbuilders. When the gold rush to Australia began in 1851, the two big clippers *Marco Polo* and *Lightning,* which carried crowds from England to the goldfields, were built in American shipyards for British owners. Within five years, Cutler states, there were twenty-four American ships carrying cargoes of tea to England.

For a time after the Repeal, British shipping tonnage was cut in half and the empire's foreign trade figures dropped alarmingly.

The determination of the British to restore supremacy in the Far Eastern trade was shown at a dinner of shipowners given in London in 1850. Among the speakers was builder Richard Green, who had dared to support the movement for Repeal.

Called upon to speak after the Secretary of the American Legation had made a florid speech, Green said:

"We have heard a great deal about the British Lion and the American Eagle, and the way they are going to lie down together. Now, I don't know about all that, but this I do know, that we, the British shipowners, have at last sat down to play a fair and open game with the Americans, and by Jove we will trump them!"

Richard Green resolved to invest personally in defeating the audacious Yankee traders, and he built the *Challenger,* to beat the record of the American ship *Challenge,* which Captain Waterman had driven from Canton to London in amazingly fast time. Historian Lindsay wrote that the *Challenger* "thoroughly eclipsed the *Challenge."* We fear he used an obscuring term. The two ships were never directly matched, though both were among the ships racing home in 1852. Then the Yankee *Challenge,* sailing from Whampoa, beat the English *Challenger,* sailing from Shanghai, by eight days.

The Scotch shipyards gradually restored the confidence of the British shipping interests by matching American ships for speed, and excelling them in strength and durability.

The battle of British iron and steam versus American wood and sail had its first skirmish in the Far East when the iron steamship *Lord of the Isles,* built by Scott of Greenock, made the run from Shanghai to London in the remarkable time of eighty-seven days during the northeast monsoon.

It became a battle of historians as well as of skippers:

In 1856 Captain Maxton sailed this ship home from Canton against A. A. Low and Brother's saucy clipper *Maury,* Captain Fletcher. The object was to encourage fast loading and sailing, and a premium of one pound sterling per ton was offered for the season's first ship home from Foo Chow, regardless of time of passage. British writer Lindsay states that the *Lord of the Isles* beat two of the fastest American clippers, whose tonnage was double that of the British vessel, and that she delivered her cargo "without a spot of damage." American writer Arthur H. Clark says that the *Lord of the Isles* loaded and sailed four days ahead of the *Maury.* Both arrived in the Downs the same morning. When they passed Gravesend the *Maury* was leading, but Captain Maxton of the *Lord* obtained the smartest tug and, getting his ship first into dock, won the prize. It was a fair victory, but Lindsay's claim of a spotless cargo is met by Clark's statement that the *Lord of the Isles* was the only tea clipper built of iron at that time, and that she sweated the tea in her hold, though otherwise the cargo arrived in excellent condition.

Another race in amusing dispute was that of the British ship *Ganges,* Captain Deas, a vessel that, after the Repeal, went out of Leith to challenge the Americans. Lindsay quotes T. C. Cowper, who had sailed from China in the *Ganges.*

"We loaded," the narrative runs, "new teas at Whampoa, and sailed on the first of September, 1851. Two of the fastest American clippers, the *Flying Cloud* and the *Bald Eagle,* sailed two or three days after us. A great deal of excitement existed in China about the race, the American ships being the favorites. The southwest monsoon being strong, the *Ganges* made a rather long passage to Anjer, but when we arrived there we found that neither of our rivals had been reported as having passed. We arrived in the English channel on the evening of the 16th of December. On the following morning at daylight we were off Portland, well inshore and under short sail, light winds from the northeast, and weather rather thick. About 8 A.M. the wind freshened, and the haze cleared away, which showed two large and lofty ships two or three miles to windward of us. They proved to be our American friends, having the Stars and Stripes flying for a pilot.

"Captain Deas at once gave orders to hoist his signals for a pilot also, and as, by this time, several cutters were standing out from Weymouth, the *Ganges,* being farthest inshore got her pilot first on board. I said I would land in the pilot-boat and go to London by rail; and would report the ship that night or next morning at Austin Friars. (She was consigned to my firm.) The breeze had considerably freshened before I got on board the pilot cutter, when the *Ganges* filled away on the port tack, and Captain Deas, contrary to his wont, for he was a very cautious man, crowded on all small sails. The Americans lost no time and were after him, and I had three hours' view of as fine an ocean race as I can wish to see; the wind being dead ahead, the ships were making short tacks.

"The *Ganges* showed herself to be the more weatherly of the three; and the gain on every tack inshore was obvious, neither did she seem to carry behind in forereaching. She arrived off Dungeness six hours before the other two, and was in the London

SOUTH STREET, NEW YORK, 1878

HE VISIT OF THE JUNK KEYING TO NEW YORK, 1847
noramic painting by Samuel B. Waugh

Peabody Museum, Sale.

WHAMPOA ANCHORAGE IN THE 1840's
Painting by Youqua

MODEL OF THE BALTIMORE CLIPPER ANN McKIM (183?

Phillips Academy, Andover, Mass.

docks twenty-four hours before the first, and thirty-six hours before the last of her opponents."

Clark points out that while story-teller Cowper stated that the race began at Whampoa on September 1, 1851, records show that the *Flying Cloud* arrived at San Francisco on the day before August 31, 1851, and that the other ship mentioned, the *Bald Eagle,* was not launched until 1852. Cowper may have watched such a race, but the Yankee ships concerned were certainly not the *Flying Cloud* and the *Bald Eagle.*

It was difficult to determine which of competing British and American ships were the swiftest. They never left at the same time; and the fitful monsoons and occasional typhoons made tests of speeds unsatisfactory. But the rivalry had taken a sporting turn, and in September, 1852, the American Navigation Club of Boston challenged British builders to a ship-race from a port in England to a port in China and back, the ships to be modeled, commanded, and officered entirely by citizens of the United States and Great Britain. Later the amount offered, £10,000 a side, was doubled, but the challenge was not accepted. It was urged in vain by the London *Daily News* that Great Britain should make good her claim to maritime supremacy by accepting the challenge and winning the race.

Proud of their *Nightingale,* under Samuel Mather, the firm Sampson and Tappan of Boston, which was not a member of the Navigation Club, made its own wager of £10,000 that their clipper could lick any ship, American or British, in a race to China and back, but there were no takers. Her passage in 1855 from Shanghai to London in ninety-one days, averaging 197 miles per day, indicates that she would have been a formidable contender. A sharp lofty ship, she was also a wet one. Sailors said her captain drove her into one side of the sea and out of the other. Her crew, holding on for dear life when she plunged into a wave, called her the "Diving Bell."

Yankee clippers continued through the fifties to show their sterns to the British ships. The arrival of the new American clipper *White Squall* at Hong Kong caused further alarm among the British merchants. She was the longest and sharpest of the new clippers, and her log registered the marvelous speed of fifteen knots. Captain Lockwood had brought her from San Francisco to Hong Kong in the fast time of thirty-eight days, twenty-two hours. The Hong Kong *Register* warned British shipbuilders that if they meant to successfully challenge Brother Jonathan, "they had better be about it, and that speedily."

Captain Lockwood died before he could take the *White Squall* to London, but under Captain Goodwin she showed that the Hong Kong editor had good grounds for warning British builders. Although caught in a terrible typhoon, he beat the *Chrysolite,* fastest British ship of the season. Back of the Yankee tea clippers were fifty years of designing and sailing with the object of speed, and it would take a decade and more for the British shipbuilders to learn the tricks.

In 1853, twenty American ships in various China ports started for England. The beautiful, celebrated *Oriental,* in charge of a Chinese pilot in the treacherous waters of the River Min, China, was irrecoverably wrecked. The large American clipper *Celestial* saved the honors that year for the Yankees. The next year, the American ship *Golden Gate,* Captain Samuel F. Dewing, collided with the barque *Homer* in the China sea and was laid up five days by a fog off Beachy Head; still she made the voyage from Shanghai to England in a time that has never been equalled, defeating the crack English clippers *Spirit of the Age, Lady Hotchkiss,* and *Northfleet.* In the same season the Yankee *Comet,* with a handicapping cargo of coal, made the voyage from Liverpool to Hong Kong in eighty-three and a half days, a record run between England and China.

When Hall and Company of Aberdeen had launched the successful *Torrington* for Jardine, Mathewson and Company, it received from the latter an order to produce "a ship as sharp as those of any American, but of superior strength." The "strength" was to come from the historic English oak, instead of the cheap and uncertain American white oak. The ship was the *Stornoway,* Captain Robinson, which broke all British records for a passage between Hong Kong and London. Following it came the 471-ton *Chrysolite,* Captain Enright. They were fast ships, but the Americans were making ships double their size, and it was not until Hall and Company built the larger *Cairngorm* for the Jardine firm that an equality in speed was attained.

It is amusing, since the opium trade was mainly in British hands, to find the English historian Lindsay writing that the *Torrington* was sent out "to compete with the Americans then engaged in the coasting trade of China, and in the still more lucrative opium trade."

The British shipbuilders made headway. The American ship *Maury,* and the British ship *Lord of the Isles* raced from Foo Choo Foo to Gravesend, and were within sight of each other after a voyage of 127 days, with the *Lord of the Isles* slightly astern.

Veteran master Philip Dumaresq was still in the running, but this skipper of many triumphs was to be in command of the *Florence* in the year 1859 when, for the first tea season since the repeal of the Navigation Laws, an American ship failed to be first to arrive at an English port. Despite Dumaresq's frenzy for carrying sail, the *Lord of the Isles* beat his ship by ten days. This year marked the close of active American participation in the tea run from China to England. The tea merchants of Boston, New York and Philadelphia required their ships for their own services to and from California and China.

The third generations of the families that had founded the great American commission houses in the Far East had in the fifties lost interest in Asia as a field for careers and had turned to the American West for employment and investment. This fact, along with such factors as the American Civil War, the successful revival of British competition in banking and shipping, and the activity of Chinese and Japanese industrialists in taking over the trade of their coasts, led to the decline, withdrawal or failure of the American firms. Olyphant and Company failed in 1878, and Russell and Company in 1891. British and German firms took over their business. The Chinese Government, which had been both a rival and associate of Russell and Company in coastwise and ocean trade, lost heavily in the Russell failure.

A veteran of the matting trade, H. S. Wheeler of Caldwell, New Jersey, who began his business career as a youth in the floor-covering department of W. and J. Sloane, recalls that even after the triumph of the steamship the square-yarders and brigatines were still in active use in the China trade. He remembers when the big sailing ships came into New York harbor, lowering their topmasts to get under Brooklyn Bridge and dock on the East Side, at the foot of Market Street.

Wheeler is an example of the uncelebrated travelers to China who had much to do with expanding the Chinese-American trade. He was sent by his firm to open a branch at Canton, for procuring the mattings then in vogue for floor covering in the United States.

The Chinese themselves were only slightly interested in mattings for bedding and floors, and used it mainly for the sails of seagoing junks and river boats. It was so cheap that a sail of 400 square feet could be obtained for ten dollars. Wheeler finally extended his purchases to Kobe, and in one year shipped home 119,000 rolls of matting, 40 square yards to the roll.

As to steamers in the Far Eastern trade, he recalls the early voyages of the Standard Oil steamers *Kobe* and *Baring Brothers,* which carried to China and Japan as many as 120,000 cases of the famous five-gallon tins containing highgrade "Westminster" illuminating oil—for the first time giving to millions of Orientals light for night reading.

A wider variety of Chinese goods came to the United States through the Standard Oil custom of permitting its shipmasters to bring back whatever kind of goods they thought saleable in the United States. Using Chinese manganese ore for ballast, they packed on it the lighter, bulky stuff, such as chests of porcelains, rolls of matting, and bamboo poles.

For a long time we have been treasuring a letter from "Bill Adams" (Bertram Martin Adams). The original of this letter was written by Bill at our suggestion to Commodore Chapman, Editor of *Motor Boating,* and the copy he sent seemed to bring ocean combers dashing against our uptown Manhattan window. With a salute to Bill, wherever he is, we use his rhapsody of square-riggers to close our chapter on the racing tea skippers and tea ships.

"Those old windjammer days were great days, I went to sea under a Blue Nose skipper. On my first night at sea we were caught under topgallant sails by a very heavy squall. A pitch-dark night. Black as the old Pope's hat. My memory of that night is somewhat confused. She lost everything. Topgallant sails, foresail, mainsail, cross jack, three upper and three lower topsails, flying jib, jib, foretopmast staysail, main, mizzen, and jigger top-mast staysails, were all whipped to ribbons. When dawn came the ship was a picture! I can see that dawn well. Somehow or other we had managed to get a new main lower topsail aloft and set in the night. She was running for shelter under that one sail. Her main deck was a grand picture, as she rolled first one rail and then the other down under the sea. Two weeks in port, making repairs.

"There were ships in those days. I've seen a hundred square riggers at anchor in one harbor. I've seen fifty-two ghosting along under full sail with the sun on their canvas, all coming together from ports all over the world. And I've seen dismasted ships off the Horn, and ships with the smoke curling up from their ventilators; cargo afire. And I've held a ship's wheel many a time in the trades, with the stars up above her and the sea all phosphorus lighted below and around her.

"If there's more joy to be found on earth than that that comes to a young man when he's steering a 1500-ton square rigger through a starry trade-wind night with a stiff squally wind a point or so abaft the beam, I don't know it. All the sermons that a man might hear in a long lifetime won't sink as deep into his soul, nor anywhere nigh as deep, as the voice of this swinging universe will sink into him on a night such as that.

"I can shut my eyes, and feel the wheel spokes under my fingers yet; feel the lift, the dance, the eager beauty of a ship. All alone under the stars, with the dusky squall clouds flying up from south-east one after another. Put your helm up a little, just a little, as you see the squall coming up. Let her just be beginning to pay off as the squall strikes in her shadowy canvas; and the strike of the wind will luff her again, counterbalancing the bit of weather helm that you've just let her have. She'll fly along, straight on her course then. And as she jumps to the squall's music you'll put your helm down the little touch you have just put it up, so that, as the squall passes, she still lays her course.

"A man don't know what living is till he's stood at a fine square rigger's wheel in a brisk windy dawn with another fine ship a mile or so to windward, laying the same course. Everything set. Both ships with every sail sweated up to the finest touch, every sheet and halliard just as a sheet and halliard ought to be. Sprays smashing up over both fo'c's'le heads. Two skippers on deck, each with hard sharp ferrety eyes on the rival vessel. All hands handy. Hour after hour of it. Mid ocean. Six thousand miles of sea astern, six thousand miles of sea ahead. I've sailed like that for days together, day on day, night on night, for a full week. Neither ship able to gain a foot on her rival. And at the end of the week maybe a black night with downpouring rain. Another dawn and the rival not to be seen. Thick weather.

"And I've sailed from the line in the Pacific to the line in the Atlantic, to St. Paul's rocks, without so much as catching a glimpse of the royals of any other ship over the sea rim. . . .

"Windjammer days. Windjammer sailors.

"*Ships.* There aren't any ships today.

"It's an old man's privilege to say that sort of thing. We say it to ease a hurt.

"Any man who follows the sea, who lives at her edge and loves the old grey lady with her eyes now green, now blue, now darkling, can't help but get a something of her message, of her beauty. She'll whisper to him, and she'll win him, bind him. He'll answer when she calls."

CHAPTER XX

Coolie Cargoes

In July, 1836, an English shipmaster brought to his home port as part of his general cargo a mysterious substance.

"Here's some gu-an-ner," he said to the owners, Messrs. Myers and Company. "They say in Peru it's a wonderful help to growing things."

184

Dubiously the ship owners fingered and smelled it. They wished their captain had had the good sense to fill the space it occupied with some material more certain as to profits, but rather than dump it overboard, they gave it away to farmers and gardeners.

Lo and behold, the plants sprang up like Jack's beanstalk from the ground where the stuff had been spread. News of guano's wonderful fertilizing powers spread through Britain, and four years afterwards Myers and Company sent a brig to the coast of Peru to bring back an entire cargo of it—the first of many full cargoes of the fertilizer.

We tell the story of the bringing of guano to England because the Chinchas—a group of islands on the Peruvian Coast, a hundred miles south of Calloa—was one of the chief destinations of the Chinese coolies who were tricked into bondage.

The exporting of cargoes of coolies by trickery and force to the New World began about 1850 when the Spaniards began to entice them to Cuba. The cruelly enslaving coolie trade to Peru and the Chincha Islands began about the same time.

The coolie traffic centered at Macao, adding to the wickedness that gave the lovely city the reputation of a modern Gomorrah. Coolie commerce is a mild term for a business almost as cruel and shameful as the slave traffic. When Edmund Roberts, American envoy to Cochin-China and Siam wrote, "Macao is one of the most immoral places in the world," he was speaking of a condition that included coolie running among its cardinal sins.

The activity in shipping coolies had several causes: the need of labor arising from the discovery of gold in California and Australia, the lack of cheap labor in the West Indies and parts of Latin America, and the suppression of slave labor in the United States.

Of the half-million coolies transported during a quarter century, many of them were Taiping rebels.

An example of mutiny and murder aboard a coolie runner is that of the *Waverly*, in September, 1855, which took out 353 coolies from Amoy and 97 from Swatow.

In their misery below decks the men from the two ports began fighting with each other; then some of them, finding that they had been deceived as to their destination, rose in mutiny and were killed.

Others committed suicide. When the commander of the ship, changing his course in desperation, landed the survivors at Manila, 138 went ashore alive out of the 450 that had been snared aboard her.

In another case, Acting Consul Albert L. Freeman went aboard the ship *Wandering Jew* and found 236 coolies in the hell below decks. Freeman and the accompanying United States marshal found out that 117 of them had been kidnapped, lured by promises of employment on the ship, or of jobs at Shanghai. Instead they were bound for the sugar plantations of Havana.

When the coolie trade shifted from Macao to the port of Swatow between 1852 and 1858, American ships took away 40,000 coolies.

As to the profits that induced ships to transport coolies, the New York shipping list gave the vessel *J. Wakefield,* chartered at a cost of $14,000, as bringing to Havana a cargo of coolies valued at $45,000.

The work of converting free hard-working Chinese peasants into peons was carried on by coolie brokers, a slimy breed of Portuguese and Chinese who beguiled and trapped Chinese rustics. Coming to Macao to trade and see the sights, the simple peasants were lured into gambling houses and other gaudy dens. These houses of seeming pleasure had once been handsome residences, but now behind their trappings they were actually coolie barracoons.

When the hour came for the ships to sail with human cargoes, the barracoons gave up their victims, who had been beguiled aboard by stories of the coasts of fortune and luxury to which they would sail. They were fiddled on board and given presents of cheap toys, and they comforted themselves during the voyage by picturing themselves on the way to become princes of fertile, houri-crowded islands, where they could indulge by day in the pleasures of the hunt and in the evenings in the delights of the seraglio.

Some of the victims were young Chinese who had been sold to

the brokers by poor relatives. A father and son might be together aboard, because the sire in his passion for gambling had staked himself and his son on the outcome of the game. Losing, the pair had been traded by the gambling-house owner to the coolie broker, but had been buoyed by the prospect of new prizes in the romantic islands of the West.

Crowded into stifling holds, suffering under tropic heat or the pounding of typhoons, for any comfort at all they had to cling tenaciously to their dreams.

The Chinchas were dots of land called by men who knew, "Islands of Hell." There were deposits, unbelievably immense, of the bird-droppings called guana, which the demands of agriculturists had made a profitable item of trade. When in 1856 the British ship *Martello Tower* had touched at the Chinchas, the Government of Peru had farmed out the guana rights to a Don who had been named by sailors "The Guano Governor." Dwelling on the island of suffocating fumes and dust, he fully earned what revenue he received. Under the guns of his guards, the population of 5000, mostly Chinese coolies and Peruvian convicts, excavated 2000 tons daily, which were "shot" into the ships that waited under clouds of dust.

Yellow men doomed to work in yellow dust . . . coolies always breathing the ammonia fumes, and often bleeding from the nose or ears because of the strength of the inhalations . . . coolies who wore handkerchiefs tied around their mouths to keep from choking. The negro slave condemned to work in the rice fields of the deep South was far better off.

Where were the luxuriant green islands that had been promised John Chinaman? Where were the voluptuous young women eager to flock into his harem? He could only obtain them in the dreams that broke in on his sleep of exhaustion, and even then, his wives and concubines must come in cloaks of yellow dust, perfumed with ammonia.

In a conversation between Secretary Seward and American Consul Drew at Ku-Kiang, the coolie traffic was mentioned. Drew having suggested that the United States should increase American prestige by force, Seward replied:

187

"If the United States, during the last twenty years, had pursued a policy of intimidation toward China, do you think we would have been able, at the same time, to draw from the empire an emigration of seventy-five thousand laborers to build the Pacific Railroad, and open the mines of the Rocky Mountains?"

It was an effective argument against Drew's ideas, but this policy of importing coolies to work in the United States had already boomeranged against Seward. They remained in California as cheap labor to compete with the oncoming American workmen, and their low standards of living permitted them to work for wages no ambitious and self-respecting American workman could accept.

In the American south there were politicians and business men who were watching the coolie problems of California, speculating as to whether Negro labor, upheaving as a result of the War between the States, could be replaced by Chinamen. The interest of these promoters, however, never got beyond the speculative stage.

When Seward went to San Francisco for the purpose of boarding a steamer to take him to the Far East, he was invited by the anti-Chinese party to explore the Chinese quarter, so that he might see, they said, how unfit its inhabitants were to become citizens of the United States. At the same time he received an invitation from a group of Chinese settlers requesting him to make the same tour, so that he might see how harmless to the United States, and how profitable to American industry, Chinese colonization was.

Because of the opposition to Chinese immigration in California, Seward made a close study of the methods of emigration while in China, and approved the established way of clearing them through the port of Canton, under the laws of the United States that required a certificate and consular examination. He was horrified, however, at the coolie trade as practiced at Macoa, and the part Americans played in it. The editor of his journal, his daughter, Olive Risley Seward, made this statement:

"The emigrant to the United States (from Canton) is contented and cheerful. It is not so, however, with the emigrant who embarks at Macao. The system of abduction prevailing there is an abomination scarcely less execrable than the African slave-trade.

The emigrants are promiscuously taken by fraud and force; ignorant of their destination, and without security for their labor or their freedom, they are hurried aboard sailing-craft. These vessels are built in the United States, and they appear at Macao under the United States flag, promising to convey the emigrants to our country. So soon as they have cleared the port, they hoist the colors of Peru, San Salvador, or some other Spanish-American state. It is when this fraud is discovered that scenes of mutiny and murder occur, of which we have frequent and frightful accounts. It shall not be our fault if, in the cause of humanity, the United States Government is not informed of this great outrage against our national honor."

Seward might scoff at the opposition to Chinese cheap labor gathering strength in California, but three years after he sailed from that port to the Orient riots broke out that influenced the Congress of the United States to pass laws against Chinese immigration. The Workingman's Party had become violently active, and led by the "Pick-handle Brigade," they fought for two hours on the docks and steamers of the Pacific Mail Steamship Company to prevent Chinese passengers from being landed. They won their battle, and met later attempts by threats to blow up the company's steamers and docks.

Denis Kearny, himself foreign born—a drayman from County Cork, Ireland—led the Workingman's Party. He was a sober and industrious fellow, and his leadership carried weight in political circles.

The Chinese who came to San Francisco in the "coolie ships" came without coercion and were self respecting. The contemptuous class term "coolies" was not deserved by most of them, for they came from families in China whose sons rose to good position in commerce and teaching. Those that spent their savings to go to California were lured by highly-colored posters put up in Canton by immigrant agents—alluring pictures of the "Golden Hills." Having had unusual liberty in their own land, the Chinese adventurers were unprepared for the hostile and restricting reception that afterwards developed in free America.

The women who came with them were of a different character. Forbidden to take wives—as the Europeans and Americans were forbidden to take wives to Canton—the Chinese shipped women without virtue, and their presence in California hurt the race in general. William Speer, D.D., Missionary to China and to the Chinese in California, was an ardent defender of the Chinese immigrants, but admitted that the 8000 Chinese women then in California were the scourings of "boat-people," "an ignorant, vicious race inhabiting the boats upon the rivers and in the harbors of Canton province."

The Chinese, who loved and desired sons, were forced to marry or consort with this class—the secondary mates, "the Hagars and Zilpahs of their Oriental domestic life."

CHAPTER XXI

Yankee Side-Wheelers Churning the Yangtze

THE SIDE-WHEEL steamships puffing and churning in the obliterated track of the sailing ships brought their own peculiar kind of adventures.

Transpacific passenger and freight service as we know it in our day had its beginnings in these side-wheelers which followed the triumphant transatlantic *Great Eastern*.

We will give quick glimpses of the side-wheelers that started in the Argonaut days of San Francisco and stemmed the Pacific, and paddled in rivalry with the British up the speculator Yangtze River.

The first threat of steam against sail in Chinese waters was made forty-three years after the *Empress of China* dropped her sail at Whampoa. A Chinese newspaper recorded: "Early in April 1828 there came suddenly from Bengal a 'fire-wheel' boat (steamer)."

In 1836 the British steamship *Jardine* excited the mandarins and the people along the river by making a passage from Macao to Canton. Her skipper invited the amazed Chinese admiral to come aboard and he came with one hundred fearful attendants. Exhilarated by the experience, he requested the captain of the

Jardine to tow his junk, and was given a ride at a fast pace in the "Demon Ship."

The marine engine, first employed to propel vessels across the Atlantic, was installed in wooden vessels with paddle-wheels. American builders retained this model long after the invention of the screw propeller, and the steamers that plied between San Francisco and China in the seventies were paddle-wheelers.

In the matter of steam navigation the Chinese were not as backward and adverse to foreign inventions as the general impression is. In 1847 they imitated the British builders and constructed a steamer at Canton. The only trouble with it was that it would not go—nothing could move the paddle-wheels.

There was coming along, however, a Chinese official, Tseng Kuo-Fan, who was to build steamships in China and make them go. This leader presents an interesting case of an official torn between resentment at foreign powers and the desire to have his country adopt their inventions.

During the Anglo-Chinese Opium War, Tseng remained in obscurity at the Hantin Academy of Peking, but in 1852, while visiting his home in Hunan, he was aroused against the Taiping rebels who were using the rivers to ravish the country, and became a captain of war, earning the title "Scholar-General." He interested himself in the improvement of ships and weapons, and, having failed in his attempt to build rafts steady enough in the water to permit the accurate firing of cannon, he became ambitious that China should construct its own steamships. In a small way, he was the Peter the Great of China. Encouraged by Li Hung Chang, he built a Chinese navy, and used foreign devices and workmen to complete the fleet.

Interviewed at Shanghai by a reporter for the *North China Herald,* he thus set forth his idea about dealing with foreigners: "There are three friendships that are advantageous and three which are injurious. Friendship with the upright, with the sincere, and with the man of much observation—these are advantageous.

"Friendship with the man of specious airs, with the insinuatingly soft, and with the glib-tongued—these are injurious.

"I think foreigners belong to the latter class and shall be cautious in my intercourse with them."

For all his suspicion of foreigners, Tseng had the sense to consult Englishman Sir Robert Hart and American Anson Burlingame. He sojourned in Shanghai, studying the western science of navigation, and he encouraged the sending abroad of young Chinese to acquire technical knowledge.

Fortunately for the progressive but hesitating scholar-general, he had a young friend Yung Wing. Yung Wing, with other pig-tailed Chinese boys, had been educated at Yale. He was its first Chinese graduate—class of 1853. They played baseball with local teams and refreshed themselves at home-plate from a large tea-pot. When Prince Lung authorized Tseng to build steamers for the defense of the Yangtze, he enlisted the aid of the capable and progressive Yung Wing.

Tseng insisted that the war steamers be built in China, and planned to build shipyards operated by foreign machinery. He sent Tung Wing to England, France, and America to choose the equipment. The contract went to two American firms—the Putnam Machine Company and Warner and Whitney of Fitchburg, Massachusetts.

With the aid of foreign engineers, Tseng used the machinery to successfully build five steamers. The first three he named *Dignity and Tranquillity; Controlling the River;* and *Fathoming the Sea.* This scholar, who went among his English, French, and German assistants wearing on his cap the red coral button and on his robe the open-jawed dragon, brought in a new epoch in Chinese military and industrial history.

Living in the times of the repressive Empress Dowager, it is remarkable that Tseng was so progressive. He was, in a way, the morning star of the world-minded Chinese Republic.

In 1855, Robert Bennet Forbes sent to China the first iron paddle-wheel steamer. She towed an American sloop-of-war into action against the forts below Canton. In 1861 he sent to China, in the bark "Palmetto," a steam paddle-wheel boat in sections. She was named the *Hyson* and was a profitable venture. He repeated this method of sending steamboats in sections for sale in the Chinese market.

Robert Bennet Forbes in May, 1870 was a passenger on the first Pullman train to San Francisco. In an address he spoke of the contrast between his first visit in 1825 and his present trip.

"Instead of now and then seeing a rusty-looking whaleship, or a Boston hide-drager, with a Dana before the mast . . . I find clippers of wood and clippers of iron, pilot boats, tugs, yachts, steamers of all sizes, dredging machines, spite drivers, centerboard barges, and boats of every kind."

Speaking of the future of California, he said:

"She must have steam lines to Australia, China, the Pacific Islands, Japan, Alaska, and the West Coast, second to none in the Atlantic.

"The paddle-wheel must give way to the propeller."

In 1867, the Pacific Mail Steamship line was established by an act of Congress, which granted the line a subsidy over ten years of about $4,500,000. The intended route was to Shanghai and Yokohama by way of Honolulu, but later the Company shortened the distance by omitting the stop at the Hawaiian Islands. Its most profitable cargo was cheap Chinese laborers.

Typical of the transpacific side-wheelers of the seventies was the *City of Peking,* built at Chester, Pennsylvania and launched in the Delaware River for the San Francisco-Yokohama route. She covered the 4750 miles in fifteen days and nine hours.

Japan lost no time in starting upon a program of shipbuilding, and, entering the California and China trade, became through low costs and rates a crushing competitor of expensive British and American lines.

Retiring as Secretary of State, William H. Seward, leading American expansionist in the Pacific, had decided to take the track he had advocated. In 1870, at San Francisco there was waiting for him handsome and comfortable accommodations for the voyage. The Pacific Mail line had developed a fleet of ocean-going side-wheel steamers surpassed only by the passenger steamers on the Hudson River and Long Island Sound.

The ship on which he passed through the Golden Gate was the *China,* 4300 tons burden, the upper deck of which had a promenade space of 700 feet. Her passenger list summed up the human traffic of the seventies between the United States and the Far East:—General Vlangally, the Russian Minister returning from St. Petersburg to Peking; several English civil officers returning to their posts in Japan and China; a company of American missionaries with their wives and children, voyaging trustfully to perhaps violent places in Japan, China, Siam, and India; United States naval officers on their way to join the Asiatic squadron; college students on a tour of the Far East; and sundry adventurers.

The men went in for sports; the women devoted themselves to music and books; the youths explored the families aboard to find young ladies free enough for promenading. In the evening, Japanese jugglers entertained the company in the cabin.

In the steerage, 500 coolies, returning home, slept on the floor. In the middle of their floor space they had erected a room of canvas for opium smoking, and this and their incessant gambling had become subjects for whispering among the shocked younger missionaries going to the Far East for the first time.

In contrast with the simple commodities carried by the first square-riggers, the freight of the side-wheeler *China* was Mexican silver dollars, manufactured goods, agricultural machines, furniture, flour, butter, fruit, drugs, and patent medicines. She would bring back the traditional cargoes of teas, silks, and rice—plus Chinese emigrants.

Six days out, just as the captain had predicted when boasting of the regularity of steam over sail, the *China* hailed the side-wheeler *America* of the same line, eighteen days from Yokohama. She was coming in a direct line with her square sails set, and it seemed to the delighted, then alarmed passengers that there was bound to be a collision. An exchange of signals, however, caused the *America* to divert her course, and they stopped close to each other while a gig from the *America* brought the mail aboard.

Twenty-three days out, in preparation for the end of the voyage, the ship was thoroughly scoured, tarred, and painted, and for the cleaning of the steerage the Chinese passengers are brought on deck. The craning white women discovered a dozen Chinese women among the Celestials jammed in a rope enclosure on the forward deck, and chattered about the evidences of Chinese religions exhibited by the women in their scattering of rice and small pieces of colored paper on the waters, to propitiate the gods of the sea so that they might arrive safely.

At Yokohama, the United States steamship-of-war *Monocacy* under Captain McCrea met the *China,* and Seward went aboard her.

American steamboats, competing with British steamers, were busy then in the coasting-trade. One of these, the *Kin-San,* carried the Seward party from Hong Kong to Canton. The lower deck was given over to Chinese traders who paid the fare of a Mexican dollar for the voyage of ninety miles. The purser rejected many a dollar offered because the edge had been clipped. The Chinese passengers brought along with them the art of opium smuggling. Looking down at them from the upper deck, the Americans saw a native trader step up to the bulwark and throw overboard small bundles of hay and straw; then they watched natives in small boats pick up this refuse. Passengers who knew the ways of John Chinaman informed the Americans that the bundles contained packages of opium. Another trader sealed in a bottle a paper containing the prices of opium current in London, and threw it overboard. His partner, a smuggler in that region, recovered it and used the prices in his business.

A peculiarly American ambition had been to open the Yangtze to steamboats as far as Nanking, "the Southern Capital." Humphrey Marshall was the first to propose it; Commissioners McLane and Parker had kept the idea alive; but Commissioner Reed stopped pressing the matter, feeling that the Chinese had the right to absolute sovereignty over their rivers, and having in mind what the wise S. Wells Williams had written—that the privilege of running steamers should belong to the Chinese, and that if they yielded to greedy foreigners the people would lose their control over their own territory. Lord Elgin, pressing his demands on China at the time of the opening of new ports, insisted that the deep and wide Yangtze be opened as far as Hankow and later to other ports. His zeal for England and disregard for China is revealed in a letter to his family quoted by Dennett:

"I sent for the Admiral (British); gave him a hint that there was a great opportunity for England; that all of the Powers were deserting me—on a point which they had *all,* in their original applications to Peking, demanded, and which they all intended to claim if I got it; that therefore we had it in our power to claim our place of priority in the East, by obtaining this when others would not insist on it. Would he back me? . . . The treaty was signed that evening!"

The Yangtze has its sources in the mountains of Thibet and flows sinuously to the Pacific through the central region of China. Nanking, situated in an amphitheater of hills on the south side of the river, was the capital of the empire before the conquest by Kublai Khan, and it was the center from which the Taiping rebels waged war against Peking.

The United States Navy was busy protecting American residents in the years of the Chinese rebellion.

When the robber bands who claimed to belong to the Taiping army of rebels began raiding along the Yangtze, Captain Shufeldt of the *Wachusetts* was assigned the duty of patrol. A special object of his trip was to awe the chief mandarin of Hangkow, a city 618 miles in the interior of China, who held the general idea that the United States was a small place, a subject nation to China. The old fellow was entertained on board and was duly impressed by the evidence of power the commander exhibited.

Five missionaries and their families visited the ship, and the officers in turn went to their homes and were pleasantly entertained. Executive Officer Jack Philip commented, "The missionaries here and at Foo-Chow are the nicest families we have visited in the East. They seem more homelike."

The *Wachusetts* made a trip up the Yangtze to punish a band of "swordracks" or robbers who, roving the country, had murdered American citizens and assaulted Consul Knight and his coolie. Alarmed at the ravages of the bandits, the foreign residents at the town of Yangtze were drilling under the British consul, Mr. Meadows.

The elusive mandarins, when rounded up by an American force, promised to punish the local members of the robber bands, but the bandits daunted them by posting placards—an old Chinese custom—which contained threats that if their brother-bandits were executed on the demands of the American commander, they would descend and kill all the foreigners in the town.

Forced by the American captain, who threatened to appeal to Peking, the mandarins at last arrested eight of the bandits, leaving at large the robber chief Hon and his sons, who stayed boldly in the town when the American expedition arrived. When Executive Officer Philip with a group of his sailors went to his house, Hon met them defiantly.

"We will drive all foreign devils into the sea," he said. "If you lay hands on us, bands of patriots will come and kill all the foreigners in this place."

Philip decided that it was high time to show American authority and might, and in a midnight raid seized Hon and his sons and rushed them into the brig. The mandarins heard the news of his arrest in great agitation.

With thirty armed men, Jack Philip attended the trial of the first group of bandits. By the Chinese law, a person could not be punished until he made a full confession and in this case the officiating mandarins, thinking that the accused men were lying, spent the first day in subjecting them to various tortures.

With one of them, Chung, the leading mandarin wrote down what he thought the prisoner should say, and when he would not acknowledge it, tortured him again until he fainted. At last the judges announced that the prisoners had voluntarily confessed to being leaders in the deadly assault on the American consul.

Fearing revenge by the gangs of outlaws after the American ship had left, the local mandarins asked the American commander to let the Chinese law take its course with Hon and his boys. Captain Shufeldt, called away by other duties, was forced to depend upon their promises, and gave up the captives. He got up steam and sailed down the river, suspecting that the robbers would be released as soon as they were out of sight. However, Consul Knight boarded the *Wachusetts* and then took passage on an English vessel bound for the port of Peking, where he meant to complain to the Emperor.

At Teng-Chan-Fut on the Yangtze, a mission of a similar kind awaited the *Wachusetts*. Hostile natives had attacked American missionaries and desecrated American graves. The ship went there and awed the townpeople by gun pointing, but could not stay, and missionary Hartwell and his associates were left to the protection of other foreign ships in the harbor.

In 1861-62, when the Taiping Rebellion was put down, and the forceful British opened the Yangtze to foreign shipping and trade, British-American rivalry became keen again. This time the competition was between steamboats instead of windjammers.

Sir James Hope, admiral of the fleet, was also superintendent of British trade. He was prejudiced against the Americans, and asserted that they never took part in movements that benefited all foreign nations operating in China, but always took great advantage of any openings the others made. He was especially bitter against Russell and Company, and when he sent an inspection party up the river on a British steamer to decide what ports to open and what locations to choose for factories and grounds, he excluded members of the Russell firm. The competitors of the firm exulted at this barrier to the spread of the Russell network, but they rejoiced without reckoning the resourcefulness and enterprise of the Russell partners who, depending on their connections with influential Chinese mandarins and merchants, succeeded in turning the tables on the British. Chinese favor was more useful to the Americans than the good opinion of the English. When the cards went down, Russell and Company held trumps in the shape of the best wharfage sites.

When the river trade began, the large commission houses gave orders for the building of large steamers in America and England. Russell and Company organized the Shanghai Steam Navigation Company with European, American, and Chinese investors, capitalized at $5,000,000, which operated a first-class line of eighteen steamers. Working with the navigation company, the Russell firm established nine depots and flourished until the Government subsidized Chinese interests to compete with foreign ownership.

BOOK TWO

The Ship of State in the Far East

CHAPTER XXII

Caleb Cushing—Pioneer of the Open Door

IN THE FIRST half-century of Chinese-American relations, the Ship of State hesitated in entering the seas of the Orient. Perhaps it was best for the United States that such was the case.

The important change in State Department policy which spread the flag behind American merchants and missionaries came about after the British with their ready might had obtained the treaty of Nanking, August 25, 1842. The opening of several new ports under the treaty was taken as a summons by American shipping firms and missionary societies, and together the Cross and the counting-house moved in. Settling among swarms of Chinese easily moved to violence against "foreign devils," it became, as we have seen, necessary for the United States to put protection behind them. Then also, matters of international politics had become a motive for changing the shadowy Ship of State into a threatening or persuasive substance.

Great Britain had made Hong Kong the China outpost of her Indian Empire, and American administrations began to interest themselves in blocking British efforts to convert Shanghai into a British port, and make it instead an international one. The pull of trade, religion, and diplomacy had at last brought the Ship of State into the waters of the Far East; and where American commission houses bargained with local mandarins for trade privileges in ports besides Canton and daring missionaries opened their chapels among the hazards of superstitious masses, American naval ships began to go frequently.

Our story now concerns itself with the adventures of some of the more important homespun politicians American administrations sent to cope with subtle mandarins and with smooth European diplomats who knew what they wanted in China. Plunged into situations of European aggressions, native uprisings against both the "foreign devils" and the Manchu dynasty, and actions by Yangtze merchants contrary to United States policy, these politicians turned diplomats had careers as curious and dramatic in their way as were those of the skippers and traders who opened the road. Following their stories, we trace the history of the Open Door policy.

It was Daniel Webster who sent the first resident commissioner to the China post. He chose Congressman Caleb Cushing, son of a Newburyport ship-owner. Cushing's mission was a pickaback one—he was to obtain for the United States, in the wake of the triumphant British, equal treaty rights in the ports of Amoy, Ningpo, Foochow, and Shanghai.

The policy of President Pierce and Secretary of State Daniel Webster had outlined from him was really to get a free ride on the English bus into China. It was the policy which was to cause Admiral Sir James Hope, at the opening of the Yangtze River to foreign trade twenty years afterwards, to complain that the Americans did nothing for the common good of foreign nations in China, yet always reaped the greatest advantage. His irritation can be understood, for American shrewdness had from the first merchant in China stressed to the viceroys that the British were aggressors, while Americans had only the axe of trade to grind.

A graduate of Harvard, a newspaper editor, lawyer, and Congressman, Caleb Cushing was better equipped for his mission than several of the home-made diplomats who followed him, but he consented to a whim of President Tyler which put him in a ridiculous light when he appeared before the level-headed American merchants in China. Believing that his ambassador should sail with the pomp and grandeur of an English plenipotentiary, Tyler had provided Cushing with the escort of a frigate, a sloop of war, and one of the newly-invented steamboats. The embarrassed minister wore the uniform of a major general, with extra gold braid to impress the mandarins. Tyler gave him a letter that vied with those of the Emperor's proclaimers of the Middle Kingdom in boasting about the magnificence and might of the United States.

Niles Register published this mocking picture of Caleb Cushing at Macao, as seen by a merchant correspondent:

"When at Macao I had the honor of seeing much of his excellency, who had spurs on his heels, and mustachios and imperial, very flourishing!"

Cushing was to assure the Chinese government that he was "a messenger of peace, sent by the greatest power in America to the greatest Empire in Asia." He was told to point out that the Americans sought only opportunities for friendly commerce and had no desire to acquire territory. He was also given leave to inform the Emperor that the Americans had also fought against China's late foe, the British Empire.

For all of this, he was to threaten China if necessary.

"Finally," his orders ran, "you will signify, in decided terms and positive manner, that the Government of the United States would find it impossible to remain on terms of friendship and regard for the Emperor, if greater privileges or commercial facilities should be allowed to the subjects of any other Government than should be granted to the citizens of the United States."

Cushing as a diplomat skillfully blended polite persuasion and force. Availing himself of the service of the highly-esteemed Dr. Peter Parker, he used the doctor to convince the Chinese that the American Government had no desire to aid in the partition of China. When subjected to the usual Chinese evasions and delays, he notified the Viceroy of Canton that the United States warships *St. Louis* and *Perry* would soon arrive, and that the American Government had decided to enlarge its fleet in Chinese waters. Responding to this insinuation, the Viceroy informed him that the Emperor had appointed Ki-ying, who had negotiated the treaties with the victorious British, to make an agreement with the Americans, and that the Commissioner was speeding to Canton. When the haughty Ki-ying sent him a letter with the name of the United States lower than that of the Chinese Empire, Cushing sent an indignant protest and extracted an apology. Then Ki-ying sent this message:

"In a few days we shall take each other by the hand, and converse, and rejoice together with indescribable delight."

Cushing got his treaty—one that he told Ki-ying was just and honorable to both China and the United States. With no strong fleet to enforce his demands, he obtained a most-favored-nation agreement as to newly-opened ports. Despite the fury of the Chinese Government at the opium trade, he phrased the document so that his Government was not called on to police American opium runners. American firms at Canton were delighted that beside other savings, the agreement reduced tonnage duties per vessel from $4000 to $400. The general effect of Cushing's mission was to introduce the policy of the good, ungrasping neighbor into Chinese-American relations.

While in Canton, the minister perceived what a wall of superstition must be broken down before the East and West could understand each other. He had given the American consul at Canton an arrowed weathervane to adorn the flagstaff. The arrow, shifting with the winds, seemed bad magic to the Cantonese. The country around was suffering from a drought, and alarmists among them said the arrow had been raised to bring unfavorable winds. When a mob gathered to chop down the flagstaff, Cushing agreed that the arrow be removed.

When years afterwards the American Commissioner Anson Burlingame returned to the United States from China in the rôle of leader of the first Chinese mission to foreign powers, Cushing, an old man, creator of the first guidepost to a fair American policy toward China, sat in the audience approving Burlingame's generous sentiments.

CHAPTER XXIII

Humphrey Marshall and the Chinese Pretender

GENERAL PATRICK HURLEY, going recently to China to try to reconcile two mighty parties of Chinese, had an early counterpart in the martial Humphrey Marshall, who stepped ashore into the greatest civil war in history.

The Taiping Rebellion at its climax reached from the south to within one hundred miles of Peking. It laid waste some of China's best provinces, and in its fury fully 20,000,000 Chinese perished. It raged for fifteen years and was finally stopped by the Imperial forces aided by the English "Chinese Gordon" and his Ever Victorious Army, which had been created by the American, General Ward.

We are seeking to determine today whether or not China can ever be depended upon to be a nation united under one ruler. A study of the Taiping Rebellion may give us the answer.

Commodore Perry on his mission to Japan, and Humphrey Marshall on his mission to China, chanced to arrive at Shanghai when that port was under the black shadow of an invasion by the rebel army, which had taken over a rich stretch of the Yangtze, and was occupying Nanking, nearby.

It was long ago thought by thinkers in China that the empire had grown too big to be held together by one central government, and that it would be better for it to become what it was three hundred years after the death of Confucius—a federation of various kingdoms.

Chinese members of the secret societies of Canton who had traveled through China told their friends that the several countries composing the Emperor's dominions were enormously distant from each other, differing in manners, laws, and speech, and that one ruler's code could not satisfy all the people. The way to be free was by federation, not by abject submission to one throne.

Let no one think that the secret societies were composed of men of wicked designs. Their members were patriots like those of the underground of Europe during World War II, and their chief design was to rid their China of the effete Manchu dynasty. From their beliefs and plotting sprung the Taiping Rebellion which, though at last apparently extinguished, was the prophesying star of the later revolution led by Sun Yat-sen.

In 1850, sixteen horsemen, called "Fuma" or "Flying Horses," set out from the imperial palace at Peking to carry the tidings to the various provinces that his Celestial Majesty had departed for the abode of the gods, and had transmitted the throne to his son Se-go-ko. This twenty-year-old son assumed the name of Hièn-foung, which means *Complete Abundance,* and ignoring the troubled state of the empire, plunged into the pleasures of the harem.

When at last he exerted his authority, he dismissed the ministers his father had honored and thus incurred the displeasure of the people. A revolt broke out in a great province, and a movement toward Peking began, led by the mysterious Pretender, King Tien-wang.

The Pretender's own story of his career stated that:

"I am a native of Hang Chang, and am thirty years of age . . . from my youth I addicted myself to letters; I have undergone several examinations, but as the examiners would not recognize in me a talent for composition, I became a bonze. Again I presented myself for examination and was rejected as before. This made my heart swell with resentment. I took to studying all our books on the military art, in order that I might become skillful in war . . ."

He tells how with other members of the secret Triad Society, which had heard of a celestial father called God, and a celestial brother called Jesus, he organized a Protestant Society, and was given the title King Tien-wang, *Celestial Virtue*. He wore an embroidered robe and a high yellow hat, and the four lesser kings who marched with him wore like hats, embroidered in red. The rest of the officers wore embroidered yellow aprons and carried yellow flags into battle. In the official palace, Tien-wang wore a yellow robe.

The missionaries who later discovered Christ-like qualities in the Pretender were perhaps ignorant of the fact that he traveled in an imperial palanquin followed by thirty women in chairs richly painted and gilded.

The rebellion, in spite of reverses, spread through the empire, and its fleet appeared before Nanking. The Chinese government beseeched the British and American ministers to call their warships to Nanking and destroy the rebel fleet, but it then seemed to the British that the rebels were the winning party, and for their own fortunes in China they did not want to offend Tien-wang. Besides, the Christian preachers were saying that the new leader was an envoy of the Almighty, sent to clear the way for the march of Christianity through China.

The Taiping Rebellion began when the people began to accept new religious beliefs, largely inculcated by the Protestant-Missionary Gutzlaff, a German-Mongol employed as interpreter by the British Government at Hong Kong, who had devoted his entire life to converting Chinese and Siamese to Christianity. He spoke the language like a native and, knowing all the dialects, could converse with all sorts of natives as he traveled on their junks. The ministers of the Emperor called him a foreign propagandist, and there was some grounds for the accusation, but he worked with missionary zeal rather than to advance the interests of foreign powers.

Other missionaries joined him in supporting the rebel movement, and in their enthusiasm they wrote home to England and America that the advantages of victory for the revolutions were these:

The country would be opened to the preaching of the Gospel; idolatry would be put down by a strong hand; the opium traffic would be stopped, because the rebel leaders would make no treaty with a foreign power without abolishing the trade; and China would be fully opened to foreign commerce, science, and all the influences of western civilization.

Studying these things, we can understand why in the first years of the revolt, the Taiping leaders nearly won the European powers to their side. When the powers took a larger look, they decided that a China made up of federations instead of one ruler would be hard to deal with; then, putting religious objectives aside, they supported the Manchu throne.

The missionary supporters of the Taipings were bitterly disappointed when their governments turned against the Taipings, but they probably would have been just as disappointed with the brand of Christianity the rebel princes would have promoted.

These were the conditions when Caleb Cushing's successor as American commissioner to China, Humphrey Marshall, arrived in the Orient. He was a vain, narrow, belligerent fellow who with all his faults of temperament was to serve his country well. The first American diplomat to inform his countrymen that the partitioning of China would be a matter of grave concern to the United States, he suggested that a wise course for the United

States would be to strengthen and support China against aggression.

Landing in China at the time of the outbreak, Marshall found it to his advantage that his training had been a military one. Born in Frankfort, Kentucky, he was appointed at sixteen to West Point. Graduating from it in 1832, he became a lieutenant of Mounted Rangers, and four years after graduation raised a company of Kentuckians to help in the Texan battle for freedom. In 1846 he raised the First Kentucky Cavalry for the War with Mexico, and as its colonel, led several brilliant charges at Buena Vista. Practicing law in intervals of peace, he became a Congressman and, while being urged for the Supreme Bench, accepted the appointment as resident commissioner to China. There both his legal experience and his military gifts had full play.

Egotist met egotist when Commodore Perry and Commissioner Humphrey Marshall opposed each other in Chinese waters.

Arriving at Hong Kong in the steam frigate *Mississippi,* Perry expected to find there the *Susquehanna,* which was to be the flagship of the Japanese mission. But Marshall, seeking to impress the rebel army, had borrowed the sensational steam frigate for the defense of Shanghai.

Impatient to proceed to Peking, Perry lost his temper when the American merchants told him that it was more important to keep the newly-arrived fleet in China than to go seeking an entrance in unimportant Japan.

Returning, Commissioner Marshall defied the raging Perry and supported the traders. Both sides appealed to the Congress, and the chances were that Marshall and the commission houses, having the strongest influence in Washington, would have won. Perry, however, sailed away before orders could reach him.

One of the chief opponents of Marshall in the Taiping affair was the zealous missionary from Tennessee, Issachar Jacob Roberts, who was as fiery in his way as Marshall was in his.

Devoted to practicing his Lord's commission to "go ye forth into the world and preach the Gospel to all creatures," Issachar Jacob Roberts, born in Sumner County, Tennessee, was ordained as a Baptist preacher at twenty-five. Circuit rider, camp-meeting preacher, river baptizer, the call came to him in the isolated hill country to be a missionary to the Chinese.

Owning property in Mississippi valued at $30,000, Roberts took literally the Biblical warning as to the difficulty of a rich man entering the Kingdom of Heaven.

Answering the call, he used his fortune to organize the Roberts Fund and China Mission Society, and took passage in a clipper to Macao. There he worked as a saddler while learning the language, and if no mention of him is found in the journals of American travelers to China during his period there, it is because he chose as his first field to preach to a colony of lepers and was therefore shunned by fastidious visitors.

Opening a Baptist mission at Hong Kong, he ministered to the British troops as to the natives. Afterwards, he moved to Canton and with his own funds bought a lot and built a chapel. When the Cantonese rose against the foreigners, his house was mobbed, and at a later time an attempt was made by hostile natives to murder him.

The Reverend Roberts was always taking his life in his hands. If he ventured into the interior, deprived of all protection, he became the "foreign devil" who had helped to plunder and sicken China. Facing the superstitious Chinese masses, he stood on the edge of a volcano. That he would be cursed and stoned were certainties, and he must depend for shield on his gentle tones, and the light of the Gospel shining in his face.

Following his custom of chapel preaching by renting a shop on a city street open to passers-by, he provided rude benches and waited for the people to come in. Curious at the sight and sound of a "foreign devil" singing, a crowd began to gather. It would not do to open the meeting with a prayer—they would think that he was asking his god to cast a spell on them. The way to start was to preach the Gospel to them simply and directly. Fortunately, Jesus himself was an Oriental and taught in parables. If a Western preacher were wise enough, he could use the divine Oriental's method of talking to Orientals. They approved the Commandment, "Honor thy father and thy mother."

People came and went. Tea was served between talks, tracts were distributed, and the Bible offered for sale.

So the Reverend Roberts went from town to town, finding out where a fair was to be held, and going there on foot, by wheelbarrow, cart, sedan-chair, or boat. Finding a place among the bawling venders, he shouted his holy wares, continuing his talk-sermons as long as he had voice. Sometimes he preached beside a village well, where women listened too, and so it was that he was heard by the village youth who became the leader of the mighty Taiping Rebellion.

It was at this period of danger that there appeared in his Canton congregation Hung, future leader of the Taipings. This young man sat under Roberts and then disappeared. Five years after Roberts had given instructions to the lowly Hung, that self-glorified young man, as Commander Tien-wang, asked the missionary to come to Nanking, the center of the rebellion, and instruct his people.

The native Chinese had thrilled at the ruthlessness of the rebels toward the Tartars in the garrisons of the Manchus. When the rebels in 1853 besieged and conquered Nanking, the rich capital of the last native dynasty, they put the entire Manchu garrison and their families to the sword.

At the same time they pleased the missionaries by their observation of the Jewish Sabbath, and by the singing of hymns by their soldiers. In this worship by hymn-singing, the Pretender was something of an Oriental Cromwell. The preachers who supported him and then fell away from him comforted themselves by the thought that his campaigns had introduced the Christian Bible into many a wild tribe which would not have otherwise learned of it for decades.

Highly delighted was the pretender and the five subordinate kings to have captured Nanking, for what Paris was to the world before the great wars, Nanking was to the Chinese. Peking was the seat of government, but Nanking was the residence of men of learning, painters, poets, dancers, jugglers, and famous courtesans. A witty traveler said of it: "In that charming city are held schools of science, art, and pleasure; for pleasure is, in that country, both an art and a science."

Now, however, Roberts came in conflict with Commissioner

VIEW OF THE FOREIGN FACTORIES IN CANTON
Chinese export porcelain about 1800

TODDY JUG
WITH
PORTRAIT OF
WASHINGTON
AFTER AN
ENGRAVING
BY
DAVID EDWIN
Chinese export
porcelain
about 1805

Metropolitan Museum of Art

FAN SHOWING THE EMPRESS OF CHINA, FIRST AMERICAN SHIP
TO SAIL TO CHINA, AT THE WHAMPOA ANCHORAGE. About 1785

PLATE WITH THE EMBLEM OF THE ORDER OF THE
CINCINNATI

Part of the dinner service owned by George Washington, Chinese export porcelain about 1785.
Metropolitan Museum of Art

Humphrey Marshall, who decided that the European powers would walk in if China was divided into groups, and that it was best for the United States that the Manchu dynasty be upheld.

Disobeying the orders of Marshall, Roberts made his way to Shanghai in company with two Chinese whom the rebels called princes, and finally reached Nanking. Appointed assistant to Kang wan, the Chief Minister of State, the Tennessee missionary was soon advanced to Minister of Foreign Affairs, and sat in dignity wearing a yellow robe and a crown.

The rebellion dragged on, and Roberts' office continued, but an anticlimax came when Roberts accused Kang wan of murdering his servant. Kang wan doused the magnificent Roberts with a cup of tea, and, fearing a lethal attack, Roberts put aside his crown and robe and fled to Shanghai, where he declared that Tien-wang, the "Heavenly King," was mad, and his cause hopeless.

One cannot, however, end the story of Issachar Jacob Roberts on a note of raillery. Remembering his missionary apprenticeship among the lepers of Macao, we record that he died of leprosy at Upper Alton, Illinois.

Roberts was just a minor annoyance to Commissioner Marshall. A far more serious reason for worry was his discovery that some of the foreign powers were disposed to favor the Taiping rebels and take advantage of their inroads. He confided to Secretary of State Marcy his suspicions that Great Britain was plotting to set up a protector of the Taiping pretender, and that if Hung gained the throne the British might obtain an inland port in western China and secure the right to navigate the Yangtze with the new steamboats British yards were turning out; this gain would bring British trade close by portage to the important British-controlled Irrawaddy River in Burma.

Marshall was somewhat of an imperialist himself, and he appreciated the strategy of Great Britain. His opposition to the plan did not spring from mere jealousy; he himself had proposed that the Yangtze be opened to steamboats, but he wanted the concession to go to the United States, and the boats to be American built and operated.

Fascinated by the game of diplomacy, the Commissioner from Kentucky began to trace the Russian designs. He saw that with Great Britain tending to support the rebels, Russia appeared to be on the way to back the established Manchu government. Then her arms would be used to drive the rebel army from the seaports and the roads leading to them. If this happened, he reported, China might come under the official protection of Russia, or the Lion and the Bear might declare a truce and agree to divide China between them.

A keen observer was Humphrey Marshall, and he seemed to realize that he was watching a long, long game of competing foxes and luscious grapes—the foxes being Great Britain and Russia, and the grapes the mellow Chinese empire.

At the period of Humphrey Marshall's mission in China, the Russian strategist Muriaviov, Governor-General of Siberia, had seized the Amur River route through Chinese territory to gain a passageway from Siberia to unfrozen ports of the Pacific, and it was apparent then that Russia coveted China to offset Great Britain's control of India.

Interesting for the future was this warning Marshall sent to the State Department:

"I think that almost any sacrifice should be made by the United States to keep Russia from spreading her Pacific boundary, and to avoid her coming directly to interference in Chinese domestic affairs; for China is like a lamb before the shearers, as easy a conquest as were the provinces of India. Whenever the. avarice or ambition of Russia or Great Britain shall tempt them to take the prizes, the fate of Asia will be sealed, and the future Chinese relations with the United States may be considered as closed for the ages, unless *now* the United States shall foil the untoward result by adopting a sound policy."

For better or for worse, the United States supported the corrupt Manchu dynasty.

CHAPTER XXIV

Dr. Peter Parker—A Good Physician in a Diplomatic Pickle

THE NOBLE WORK as a healer of Dr. Peter Parker, the first American medical missionary to China, did much to create good will for the United States among the violent Cantonese. But his out-of-character career in the American diplomatic service is a curious case which those who like to probe psychological mysteries will study with sympathy.

When Secretary of State Daniel Webster in 1843 queried importers as to what to do to assure the success of the mission of Caleb Cushing, seven Boston merchants suggested that Dr. Peter Parker, medical missionary at Canton, be selected as Cushing's interpreter and guide. Parker was the physician of their partners in Canton, and if he healed their bodies, they were willing to listen to his condemnation of opium trading. Accordingly, Parker was made a member of the Cushing mission; and the Reverend E. C. Bridgman was appointed chaplain. The team coached Cushing effectively in the ways of the Chinese court.

When discreet Commissioner Cushing returned to the United States, he deputized Commodore Foxhall A. Parker, U. S. N., who commanded American naval ships engaged in suppressing piracy and opium-smuggling, to succeed him. Dr. Parker volunteered to act as secretary to Commodore Parker—without pay.

Later he was given a salary of $2500 and for about ten years, under successive ministers including the vigorous Humphrey Marshall, managed the embassy.

Parker's association as Secretary with Robert M. McLane, U. S. Commissioner to China in 1854, contributed strangely to making the man of peace a disciple of force. With an important naval force at his service, McLane worked to obtain a fuller recognition of the rights of the United States and cooperated in using pressure with the British and Portuguese to open Peking to foreign diplomats.

The American warships engaged in the move toward Peking

were the *Powhatan,* the *John Hancock,* and the *Fenimore Cooper.* Along with them went the British warship *Rattler,* and a lorcha. "May this important mission," Parker wrote, "be successful and redound to the best good of the nations concerned. All my trust is in God."

His health suffering, Parker went back for a time to the United States, and despite his illness, spent his time to good political effect. In 1855, he returned to China as U. S. Commissioner, at a salary that was to become fixed at $12,000. He was imbued with the idea that the United States should protect its dignity in China, and that contemptuous and insolent viceroys must be made to stop their insults.

When he was acting envoy, Parker urged President Polk to send an ambassador of the first rank to compete with the British ministers, but when he was appointed minister, his views changed, and he was so eager to go along with Great Britain and France in their plans to force upon China the so-called benefits of Western civilization that he journeyed to his Oriental post by way of London and Paris, to discuss joint British-French-American action in China.

The foreign offices of England and France, however, were wary of Dr. Parker. They appear to have suspected that his temperament did not fit him for the smooth cooperation required.

Working to obtain a modified renewal of the treaty Caleb Cushing had negotiated at Wanghai, Parker insisted on the privilege of residing in Peking.

Viceroy Yeh, with Canton threatened by the powerful Taiping rebels, was refusing personal interviews with similarly insistent foreign ministers. He received Parker's messages in contemptuous silence. The physician's wrath grew hot when the official letter to the Emperor he had borne from the President of the United States, which he had delivered to a high mandarin, was returned to him without an answer, but with the seals broken and bearing marks of disrespect.

"This is an insult to the American nation!" Parker declared. Calling on Commodore James Armstrong, of the U. S. frigate

San Jacinto, Parker asked to be taken to the mouth of the Pei-ho for a personal journey to Peking.

"I will demand an apology from the Emperor for the insults of his officials," he vowed. "I will open the treaty negotiations in Peking!"

Armstrong, in a dilemma, told him that the *San Jacinto* had been disabled by an accident, and Parker was left fuming at Canton.

In seeking for an explanation of Parker's change from a man of peace to one of violence, we turn to Tyler Dennett. The missionaries had sympathized with the insurrectionists. The Manchus feared that the missionaries were working to ruin their dynasty under the cloak of religion. They saw missionaries Bridgman, Parker, and Williams acting as advisers and interpreters to the commissioners of the United States and watched with astonishment the peaceful Parker become bellicose. He who goes out to win peoples for the Prince of Peace cannot wield a bludgeon.

Further inflamed by fresh hostilities, Dr. Parker wrote out a violent prescription for this trouble and sent it to Secretary of State March, who read it with dismay. The physician-diplomat proposed that the three representatives of England, France, and the United States use their respective naval forces to insist that the French flag be hoisted in Korea, that the British banner go up again at Chusa, that the Stars and Stripes be raised in Formosa, and that these territories be held until satisfaction for the past and a right understanding for the future be granted. Instead of the exact terms of medicine, the doctor had learned the vague language of diplomacy: "satisfaction for the past," and "a right understanding for the future"—meaning, of course, reparations and concessions.

President Pierce and Secretary Marcy were greatly disturbed at Parker's violent recommendations and were further troubled when the news came that James Keenan, American consul at Hong Kong, had aided the British forces attacking Canton and had carried the American flag over the walls of the city. Marcy wrote to Parker: "The President sincerely hopes that you, as well as our naval commander, will be able to do all that is required for the defense of American citizens and the protection of their property, without being included in the British quarrel, or disturbing America's amicable relations with China."

Fearing that he would soon be superseded, Parker put into action a long-nursed design to establish an American protectorate over Formosa. His actions thereafter gave a shocking aspect to his earlier proposal to the State Department that the Stars and Stripes be sent up over Formosa. He appears to have been unduly influenced by an old friend, one Gideon Nye, Jr., an American at Canton. Formosa had been found to contain deposits of coal which seemed to be better than those brought out from Liverpool for the steamers, and it had already become a source of supply of raw camphor for the markets of Europe. Aware of these resources, Nye and a partner Robinet, had obtained a monopoly of the camphor trade and had built an establishment at a convenient harbor, where they exacted $100 tonnage duty from each vessel that came to load camphor. Being Americans, they had hoisted their country's flag and ruled independently of the Formosa government. The honest if foolish Parker came into the position of protecting the type of reckless Americans who looked to the flag to protect their dangerous operations.

Gideon Nye, Jr., merchant, orator, social leader, pamphleter, and expansionist for personal profit, was, as is often the case with a man of many interests, a failure in business.

Nye was friendly with the British, admired their aggressiveness, and was given to writing to the State Department and the New York *Herald* urging action against the Chinese to advance American privileges in China.

As conductor of "Canton Social Evenings," he himself filled many of their programs, and being in money at the time, had his lectures privately printed in Canton. Read today, they are enjoyable reflections of his exuberance and egotism. We catch him on the human side in one of them, "The Morning of My Life in China."

"So early as the year 1817, my Kinsmen (my father being also part-owner) sent a ship hither, and in her came my cousin Ezra Hathaway as supercargo; but my immediate exemplar was his youngest brother Mr. Francis S. Hathaway, who came here first

216

in 1827; and who, when about to return here to reside, in 1833, invited me to accompany him.

For business reasons, Nye's cousin wished to enter Canton before his ship came in from Macao, and the only way to do this was to be smuggled in bodily by night. If they could reach the house by the river of the friendly Chinaman "Boston Jack," agent for incoming foreign vessels, they would be successful in escaping arrest and imprisonment.

At 4 P.M. the cousins went aboard a small boat and hid under a low deck. When passing a mandarin guard-boat they heard the little hatchway closed over them and almost died of suffocation. Further on, passing close to the sentry houses of the Bogue forts, the hatch was shut again, and in addition they were covered with cloth so that they were almost stifled.

"Then," Nye related, "we ran alongside a large East India Company's ship . . . I carry in the retina of my eye until this day, the bright welcome light that shone from the open port of that ship's gun-deck upon the gloom of that night of anxiety, assuring us that our greatest perils were over and that we had but to resume our course for a few hours longer to reach the neighborhood of the Whampoa shipping.

"At length, when really asleep with excessive fatigue, we were aroused by the announcement that we were at Boston Jack's landing steps, but must still be silent until within his premises . . ."

Smuggling of opium . . . merchants . . . wives . . . these were dangerously tempting sports for Englishmen and Americans on the stretch of river between Macao and Canton.

Eldon Griffin, authority on American consuls in China, gives a favorable verdict on the business operations of Gideon Nye, Jr. When Nye's firm failed, a local newspaper said that he commanded well-merited respect, and that the Chinese merchants had the warmest sympathy for him. Robinet, Nye's partner in the later camphor monopoly, appears to have been an imperialist greedy for trade and fortune. The group of traders of which Robinet was the center loaded seventy-eight vessels with camphor valued at $400,000. Robinet bought out the rest of the group, but local camphor gatherers rebelled against his methods. It was to this dubious combination that Dr. Peter Parker, in an excess of patriotic enthusiasm, gave his support, seeking to persuade the United States to secure a degree of control over Formosa. When the State Department declined, the camphor monopoly passed into British hands.

Having their own military forces, Nye and Robinet proposed to Parker that they set up an independent government in Formosa under the protection of the American Government. Parker approved, and wrote to the State Department endorsing the proposal from Nye, which he forwarded.

The Secretary of State must have indeed thought Parker out of his mind when he read such urgings as this: "It is much to be hoped that the Government of the United States may not *shrink* from the *action* which the interests of humanity, civilization, navigation and commerce impose upon it. . . .

". . . Great Britain has her St. Helena in the Atlantic, her Gibraltar and Malta in the Mediterranean, her Aden in the Red Sea, Mauritius, Ceylon, Penang and Singapore in the Indian Ocean, and Hong Kong in the China Sea. If the United States is disposed and can arrange for the possession of Formosa, England certainly cannot object."

The State Department made no reply to Parker's proposal that the United States take over Formosa. As to his proposition that England, France, and the United States raise their flags in separate Chinese territories, Marcy told him plainly that the military and naval forces of the United States could only be used by authority of the Congress, and that "while it might be expedient to increase our naval forces in Chinese waters, the President would not do it for aggressive purposes."

Emerging exhausted from the maelstrom of Far Eastern politics, Parker came under healing influences when he returned to the United States. The friends who gathered about him were those who remembered vividly his sacrifices as a medical missionary. They revived his interest in medicine and religion. He lived for many honorable years and died remembered chiefly for his earlier career in China, when he served as the good physician, without recompense, to the suffering poor of Canton.

Parker's successor, Wm. B. Reed, formerly professor of American history in the University of Pennsylvania, had as his main duty the business of persuading the Chinese authorities to permit Americans to reside in open ports without opposition. Commissioner Yeh, the Emperor's delegate at Canton, refused to receive him, and let him know that the proposed revision of the treaty was unnecessary. This treatment inclined Reed to go along with the Allies, and he watched with some satisfaction the arrival of the allied squadron from Hong Kong, with the British Lord Elgin and the French Baron Gros in command. From a safe place he saw the fleet bombard the city of Canton, and after its capitulation observed the arrest of Commissioner Yeh, who was sent as a prisoner to Calcutta.

Reed was eager to be cordial to the allied commanders, but Lord Elgin was distant and the French Baron Gros followed suit. Their idea was that those who would share in the spoils should put their warships into the campaign. Thus rebuffed, the lonely Reed was glad to find a friend in Count Putiatin, the Russian commissioner who had come warily on the scene with no intention of officially supporting the British-French attack. It interested Reed to learn that Putiatin had advised the allied commanders to menace Peking by occupying the seaport nearest to it—Tientsin; and it interested him still more afterwards when he heard the Muscovite envoy accused of offering arms and ammunition to the Chinese army to help turn the invaders back from the capital.

Putiatin's main purpose was to obtain a treaty confirming Russia's recent seizure of the left bank of the strategic Amur River, and the control of the Amur down to the Ussuri and then to the Pacific Ocean. He told the Chinese that, in seizing the Amur, he was protecting China and Siberia from a British advance from the Pacific.

At this time, though, Putiatin's paw was one of sheer friendship for the American Reed, and the Yankee's grip was a sincere one. When the aloof British lord and French baron moved toward Pekin to enforce their demands that ports and rivers be opened and that diplomats be allowed to visit if not reside at the capital, the yielding Chinese Commission asked the Russian and American, who had watched the attack on the forts, not to withdraw;

therefore behind the steamer bearing the allied leaders to the peace negotiations puffed the small Russian steamer *Amerika*, flying the Russian and American flags, and probably well stocked with vodka and caviar. (The correspondents who were mystified or amused by the appearance of a Russian steamship in the harbor of San Francisco during the security conference of 1945 may now know that such a ship is a traditional part of a Russian peace conference.)

With this not very glorious entrance, Commissioner Reed came to the allied feast and obtained for the United States the same travel and trade privileges granted the allies and the independent Russians, though the right to reside at Peking was still denied.

Three-quarters of a century ago, when Secretary Seward arrived in Peking, he found that the Russians had already developed the art of getting along with the Chinese authorities. The Russian minister, distinguished by service in the Crimea, was discreet and intelligent, and since his nation for the time had abandoned the use of threats, he exercised a strong influence over the Chinese cabinet. He lived in an elegant residence with a personnel which impressed the Oriental mind. Beside it the residence of the able Mr. Low, American minister, was to the Chinese officials, unimposing. It reflected stinginess upon the part of the announcedly great United States.

CHAPTER XXV

Commodore Perry—Prophetic Imperialist

AN ECCENTRIC COMMODORE commands a place among diplomats of the China Seas. Recalled to the minds of Americans by the war with Japan, the comment now is that it would have been better for civilization if Matthew Calbraith Perry had not pushed open the door of Japan. Nevertheless, he assumes a large place among our voyagers to the Far East, for he is, in a naval way, the Fremont of our military expansion in the Pacific.

Matthew, the brother of Oliver, hero of Lake Erie, was the first naval officer to foresee that American traders and whalers were shaping the destiny of the United States in the Far East, and that his country would need stations close to China and Japan. His plans and arguments for American expansion became obscured by the war at home, but Secretary of State Seward and the Navy Department remembered them. Today several islands he wished to take over are included among those over which the United States requires control.

Before we show Commodore Perry's bold and aggressive policy, let us glance at his contradictory personality.

He was a Quaker, and yet a militant fellow given to pompousness; while a man of big ideas, he was at the same time narrow and cantankerous; though devoted to justice, the evidence is strong that he obtained the command of the historic mission to Japan through political scheming that worked an injustice on a brother officer. Edward M. Barrow's book, "The Great Commodore," gives an excellent portrait of the erratic Perry.

The move of Congress in 1845 to open diplomatic and trade relations with Japan having been agitated years before, Perry, a student of the Far East, had become ambitious to head the diplomatic expedition to Nippon. He knew of the exploit of his former associate Commander Biddle in rescuing in the U. S. S. *Preble* fifteen castaway sailors of the whaleship *Lagoda* of New Bedford, who were in jail at Nagaski. He knew also of the later frustrated attempt of Commodore Biddle to communicate with the Japanese authorities when in command of the East Indian squadron.

As an American naval officer whose duty it was to protect American shipping wherever the seas rolled, he felt that our whalers, eighty-six of which had visited Japanese waters in one year, should be protected from ill treatment if shipwrecked on any of the islands of Japan.

Though he had little use for business men, the Commodore was willing to be the spearhead for the movement on Japan which they were urging the Congress to launch. The whaling interests of New Bedford and Nantucket were pressing their Senators and Representatives. The traders at Canton having watched the British open up China and gain extraordinary trade privileges, were eager to take advantage of Great Britain's surprising backwardness as to Japan.

Commodore J. H. Aulick, a veteran of 1812, was next in line for the mission to Japan and, to Perry's chagrin, was appointed. Aulick's cruise, however, was a timid and colorless one.

Steam having begun its challenge of the clippers, Aulick went in the new steam frigate *Susquehanna* and spent some time on the China coast organizing his squadron. While at Macao, he received orders relieving him of his command. It appeared that an efficient little group of politicians in the Navy Department, who supported Perry's ambitions, had brought charges against Aulick, who had a clean record. On his indignant demand for a court martial, Secretary of the Navy Dobbin—a name that suggests docility to politicians who had the reins—wrote him a letter exonerating him from any misconduct. The charges were of the flimsiest nature: he had paid the personal expenses of the Brazilian minister whom the *Susquehanna* had transported from Macedo to Rio de Janeiro, and he had taken his own son on board as a free passenger without first obtaining authority from the Naval Department.

Free of the charges, he had no other solace. Wishing to be restored to his command, he found that Perry had already sailed to take his place.

Since one of the charges made against Commodore Aulick was that he had taken his son as a free passenger, it is interesting to note that Perry could have been charged with the same offense, though he managed it in a way to avoid being brought to book. Wishing to take his son Oliver Hazard Perry on the voyage to Japan, he sent Oliver to Macao by a passenger ship and then took him aboard the *Mississippi* with the rating of clerk.

Having contrived to have the mission given more power and grandeur, Perry glorified himself to awe the Mikado. The ceremony of going ashore in Japan to present the President's letter to the grand ruler was worked up into a diplomatically threatening spectacle of one hundred marines and two hundred sailors, carefully picked for size. Behind the receiving Japanese official and his interpreter who led the procession marched this American brigade; then came the two tallest seamen, carrying the Stars and Stripes and the flagship's pennant; then the Great Commodore;

then two ship's boys carrying gold-inscribed rosewood boxes containing the letter from the President and the Commodore's credentials, and then, as Perry's bodyguard, two giant negroes he had picked up on the African coast. They were dressed with the utmost flair, and bristled with arms.

Commodore Perry, having decided to make the Great Liu-Chiu Island (Okinawa) a stage for rehearsing his drama with the Mikado, refused to receive the two little men who came out in caps of bright yellow and garments of gay grass cloth to welcome him. Ignoring the red card of Japanese paper which contained a polite salutation, he ordered "non-fraternization," and the next day refused to receive the same two ceremonious visitors who offered another red card and wished to present a boatload of pigs and vegetables. What he wanted was to meet the Regent himself, and he behaved rudely to force the Regent to receive him.

There is a historic contrast to Perry's bullying approach to the mandarins of the Liu-Chiu Islands. It is supplied by the British Commander Maxwell, who could be a bully too, but who could be cordial when occasion required.

In this case, the charming Captain Basil Hall, R.N., F.R.S., was aboard Captain Maxwell's ship, and we take his account of the polite British dealings with the timid chiefs of the Greater Liu-Chiu.

There were no weapons among this amiable people, and the one critical situation that occurred was due to the indelicacy of Commander Maxwell when, on a walk beyond the town, he took with him a fowling-piece and shot several birds. He was visited that evening by several chiefs, who, it could be seen, were agitated and alarmed. When Maxwell asked them what was the trouble, they answered that all of the people had been alarmed by the firing of his gun.

Captain Hall, who for all his delicacy shared the average Englishman's love of the hunt, is satirical in his account of the conversation:

"One of the chiefs gave a very sentimental turn to the subject, by pretending that the natives were grieved to see the little birds shot."

Hall, however, went on to relate that Maxwell, instead of ridiculing the request, expressed his regret, and forbade any member of his expedition to carry a gun during the stay at Liu-Chiu.

Looking sharply along the coast for military weapons, the officers found nothing except fish-spears and blades worn in the sash for common use. Impressed by this unexpected pacifism, Captain Hall mentioned it to Napoleon Bonaparte when he was received by that frustrated conqueror at St. Helena.

"Nothing," Captain Hall narrated, "struck Napoleon so much as their having no arms.

" 'Point d'armies!' he exclaimed, 'c'est-a-dire, point de canons—ils ont des fusials?'

" 'Not even muskets,' I replied.

" 'Eh bien donc-des lances, ou, au moins, ses arcs et des fleches?'

"I told him they had neither one or the other.

" 'Ni poignards?' cried he with increasing vehemence.

" 'No, none.'

" 'Mais!' said Bonaparte, clenching his fist, and raising his voice, 'Mais, sans armes, comment se bat-on?'

"I could only reply that as far as we had been able to discover, they had never had any wars, but remained in a state of internal and external peace.

" 'No wars!' cried he, with a scornful and incredulous expression, as if the existence of any people under the sun without wars was a monstrous anomaly."

The Commodore had grander plans than obtaining the opening of Japanese ports and the protection of American sailors. His search for a Far Eastern coaling station for American warships was extended to a quest for certain islands of the Pacific which lay along the route of future American commerce.

He wanted to raise the Stars and Stripes on strategic ports neglected by Britain and other powers. Finding much-needed coal in Formosa, Perry urged that "the United States alone should take the initiative in this magnificent island."

Charting a route for American steamships, Perry proposed to occupy Great Liu Chiu Island, which neither China or Japan seemed to want, and to seize a harbor in the Bonin Islands, 500 miles south of Japan between Honolulu and Shanghai, which appeared to be unclaimed. When he arrived at the principal harbor he found the British flag flying, but still he recommended that we raise the Stars and Stripes over the Bonins.

Belligerently he told the Administration that it would be necessary to resort to strong measures to counteract the schemes of powers less scrupulous than ourselves. Acting on these convictions, he took over Bailey's Islands, so named in 1827 by Captain Beechey of the British navy, and rechristened them the Coffin Islands after Captain Coffin, the Yankee whaleman who had visited them four years before Beechey. For Perry, and for the air clippers that in our day are affirming American claims to dots of land in the Pacific, the logs of early American whalers are invaluable evidence.

Perry's designs on islands near Japan came to nothing. When Japan met his demands on his second visit in 1854, such proposals were forgotten, and Japan herself without opposition took title to the Bonins and Liu-Chius.

Reading now of Perry's explorations in the light of Pearl Harbor, we find that he truly foresaw the need of founding American settlements in the Pacific and in Asia, "offshoots from us rather than, strictly speaking, colonies . . . vitally necessary to the continued success of our commerce in those regions . . . and "as a measure of positive necessity to the sustaining of our maritime rights in the East."

After his return to the United States, Perry said: "The duty of protecting our vast and rapidly growing commerce will make it not only a measure of wisdom, but of necessity, to provide timely preparation for events which must, in the ordinary course of things, transpire in the East. In the development of the future, the destinies of our nation must assume conspicuous attitude; we can not expect to be free from the ambitious longings of increased national success and power, which are the natural concomitant."

For one particular project, however, destiny said no. He thought that some occupation of Chinese soil was necessary to protect America's growing interest in that empire. To put it in our own imaginative terms, the lone American eagle, seeing the birds of prey gathering over China, must drop down in their midst.

With the opening of the American Civil War, Perry's imperialism was forgotten, but it revived in a loud demand when the Spanish-American War broke out.

This speech about Perry, made by a Japanese captain in San Francisco in 1860, while probably sincere, has an ironical ring as we read it today:

"When Commodore Perry came to Japan, he knocked on the door of the nation, and no one answered. We were asleep—we could not see. He knocked again, and we awoke and let him in. When fully awake we saw the light, we answered the summons, and let him into our confidence. We have seen the light and have followed to the best of our ability. We hope to follow it further, as we see it is a good light."

CHAPTER XXVI

Anson Burlingame Brings China to the World

THE NEXT DIPLOMATIC pilgrim is a character in whom is mixed the elements of Barnum, Bryan, and Beecher. He is an example of how American democracy elevates a fervent speaker into an influential place.

When we learn that Anson Burlingame was the son of an ambitious but impractical Ohio farmer—a devout Methodist given to fiery exhortations at prayer-meetings, and that Anson shone in lyceum debates and was brilliant at stump oratory after he was graduated from Harvard Law School, we have a key to his amazing career as creator of a mission from the Chinese imperial court to foreign powers.

Burlingame, Congressman from Massachusetts during the Buchanan administration, failed to be re-elected in 1860 along with the Lincoln ticket, and promptly accepted the post of American minister to China. The appointment carried him into a hotbed of trouble, for the long-continued Taiping Insurrection was threatening to oust the ruling Manchu dynasty.

Two months before Burlingame's arrival at Macao—by steamer through the Suez Canal—the dynasty had obtained a firmer grip on things though the death of the dissolute and cowardly Emperor and the rise of Prince Kung, his brother, as coregent. Kung's policy was to conciliate foreign powers so that the dynasty, already warring with rebels who controlled half of the provinces of China, would not be weakened by new wars with Britain and France.

The Prince was tall and handsome in a Tartar way, but was unimpressive in foreign relations. He had been wise enough to depend on the progressive Wen-siang, Minister of Foreign Affairs. The coming of the distinterested and idealistic Burlingame was an unexpected blessing to the regency.

Arriving at Peking in July, 1862, Burlingame found himself among the foreign embassies whose governments had recently forced a way into Peking, and he made friends with Sir Frederick Bruce, the British minister, who also had decided to support the Manchu rulers.

Burlingame was a man of good manners, a quality appreciated by the affable and ceremonious Chinese. The fact that his country had not forced China to recognize it as a mighty power was in his favor.

Wishing to view the long-forbidden city, Burlingame discovered that there was no street through it—that one must walk on the broad city-wall. From that elevation he looked down on a thousand watch-towers and ramparts that seemed to symbolize the closed mind of the Manchu dynasty—which he had come to open. Seen against the snow-hooded mountains in the west, the city had an aspect of austere majesty.

From this city wall, the interior "prohibited" city where the Emperor lived could be glimpsed, the yellow tiled roofs of the royal palaces glinting among their settings of green shrubbery.

Estimating the number of foreign residents—diplomatic ministers, *attachés,* missionary-interpreters, clerks, and servants—Burlingame found that they amounted to two hundred, a small company if called upon to defend itself against that always likely happening, an attack by an infuriated mob of natives.

At the moment, however, the people were respectful or cowed and made way for the foreign diplomats as they rode in sedan-chairs, whose green colors denoted the highest rank, to the foreign office, where the five chief ministers of state transacted the Emperor's business.

The American minister went with keen curiosity to call on the Yamen, or council. The foreign office was a low structure of the usual Chinese architecture. In the middle of the room stood a massive carved table, eight feet long. Around it were placed broad, comfortable stools.

The five chief ministers of state, venerable men of grave aspect, received Burlingame and saluted him in the Chinese fashion, by bringing their hands palm to palm and bowing; then they shook hands in the American way. Then, in the order of their seniority, they took their seats at the upper end of the table, while the ambassador and his secretary sat next to their group.

After a train of servants had brought in porcelain dishes filled with bonbons and dried fruits, the conversations began.

The American representative was greatly encouraged by the knowledge the presiding minister, the progressive foreign minister Wen-siang, had of American affairs. He showed that he was interested in a free exchange of ideas between the United States and China and promised that Burlingame should meet Prince Kung.

The meeting with the Prince occurred soon afterwards, and thereafter Burlingame was liked and trusted by Kung and Wensiang.

The minister found that his chief duty was to defend the American consuls located at the treaty ports from the attacks of local Chinese officials who wished to impress the court with their own acivity in blocking the inroads of the foreigners; yet it was true that lawless foreigners were bringing reproach on their countrymen who were trying to operate within the treaty.

Burlingame did not permit any local mandarin's accusation against a consul to go unchallenged. His letters to the court were brief and plain, and he was shrewd enough to place the officials in the position of being impolite, which led them to seek to remove the reproach.

It was well that the American was getting along with the

British Legation, for an offense by a British subject threatened to undo the good relations the British minister Bruce and Burlingame were forming with Prince Kung, and the American was called on to mend matters.

The trouble occurred after Horatio Nelson Lay, inspector-general of the imperial customs service under the treaty, was allowed by the Chinese government to build a number of gunboats in England as a Chinese coast guard against pirates and smugglers. Under Captain Osborn, a fleet of eight new armed steamers, manned by Britishers, arrived, and Lay, who had exceeded his orders, informed the authorities that the British crews were to serve for four years, only under British commanders, and that payment to them was to pass through his hands.

The Government refused to accept the vessels, and they became a threat to peace on the China coast, since revolters, or rich pirates, or the feudal lords of Japan might purchase them.

Burlingame, as intermediary, suggested that the Chinese thank the British ministers and Captain Osborne for what they had done for the government, and then ask the British minister to send the fleet of steamers back to England, sell the ships there, discharge the crews, and remit the proceeds to the Chinese government.

The British legation and the Chinese agreed to this, and thus the American minister became firmly established in the eyes of the Chinese. Eventually, Lay was replaced as inspector-general of customs by Robert Hart, who became distinguished among European officials in China for his sensible and useful work with the imperial government in harbor improvements and in educating the Chinese about the West.

The American was not long in Peking when he proposed that the represented European powers help put the rebellion down without making war on any considerable body of the Chinese people, and obtained an agreement. This decision gave the backing of the treaty powers to a spectacular foreign legion employed by the Chinese imperial authorities, and linked Burlingame to the American soldier-of-fortune Frederick T. Ward, who, General J. W. Foster said, "reflected extraordinary credit upon American valor and military skill."

General Ward's campaign against the Chinese rebels are beyond the scope of this book, and we give just Burlingame's account of his meeting with him.

"Colonel Ward, now, I believe, a general in the Chinese service, is an American to whom my attention was first called by Admiral Sir James Hope, who wanted to introduce him to me, and who commended him warmly for his courage and skill. He is instructing the Chinese in the use of European weapons, and has about two thousand of them trained, whom he has led in a most desperate manner, successfully, in several recent battles. . . . He says he was born in Salem, Massachusetts, went to sea when a boy, became mate of a ship, and then was a Texas Ranger, California gold-miner, instructor in the Mexican services . . . then he joined the Chinese, among whom he has gradually risen to influence and power. He is now their best officer, and for his recent successes has been recommended by the Chinese and the English for still greater promotion. He says he is a loyal American and, though a Chinese by adoption, he desires above all things that his country shall have its full weight in the affairs of China."

Other Chinese armies resented the haughtiness of Ward's soldiers, and officials worried him about the cost of the upkeep of his force, and the imperial authorities feared his ambitions. Such a leader could eventually seize the throne. Their fears were soon at rest. He was fatally wounded while directing an attack on Tzeki, and the relieved mandarins buried him with state honors.

In a later letter Burlingame reported that he had selected the American-born Colonel Burgevine as Ward's successor. It would have been better for the diplomat's record if he had not chosen Burgevine, especially as he did so against the advice of the English officers. He explained his choice thus naively: "I felt that it was no more than fair that an American should command the foreign-trained Chinese on land, as the English through Osborn would command the same quality of force by sea."

Burgevine, an ex-Confederate officer, assumed command of Ward's "Ever-Victorious Army," but was accused by an agent of the provincial governor Li Hung-chang of stealing public money. Chinese judges condemned him to death, but Burlingame and the foreign envoys saved him from this fate. Then the angry Burgevine deserted to the rebels at Soochow and took with him part of his regiment. While his sponsor Burlingame was supporting the imperial troops, Burgevine fought on the rebel side.

Taken prisoner later by Li Hung-chang, Burgevine died when a boat was upset. It was presumed that he was murdered to avoid further disputes as to his punishment, but Burlingame did not probe the mystery and agreed with Prince Kung, who said, "There need be no further discussion about him."

Effervescing about Chinese affairs, conferring often with Foreign Minister Wen-siang, advocating that the Imperial Government should drop its exclusiveness and join the family of nations, Burlingame at last came to an odd climax of his career in China. It amazed him and astounded his colleagues when he was asked to head a world-girdling mission to present the cause of China to the foreign offices of the United States and Europe. He gave Secretary Seward this account of his selection for this sensational mission:

"I was on the point of proceeding to the treaty ports of China to ascertain what changes our citizens desired to have made in the treaties, provided a revision should be determined upon, after which it was my intention to resign and go home. The knowledge of this intention coming to the Chinese, Prince Kung gave a farewell dinner at which great regret was expressed at my resolution to leave China, and urgent requests made that I would, like Sir Frederick Bruce, state China's difficulties, and inform the treaty powers of their sincere desire to be friendly and progressive. This I cheerfully promised to do. During the conversation, Wensiang, a leading man of the empire, said, 'Why will you not represent us officially?' I repulsed the suggestion playfully, and the conversation passed to other topics."

The world-minded Wen-siang did not drop the subject. "Subsequently," Burlingame went on, "I was informed that the Chinese were most serious. . . . When the oldest nation in the world, containing one-third of the human race, seeks, for the first time, to come into relations with the West and requests the youngest nation, through its representative, to act as the medium of such change, the mission is not to be solicited or rejected."

Burlingame was claiming too much honor for his young country. Two years before, the Chinese authorities had made a similar offer to Sir Robert Hart to go abroad to explain to foreign powers the many internal difficulties the Chinese government would meet in introducing such novelties as railroads and telegraphs, and to bespeak forbearance. When he was consulted by them as to the appointment of Burlingame, he supported the idea, but suggested that a Chinese mission should not go without Chinese officials.

Burlingame was given a suite of thirty persons, which included J. McLeavy Brown, Chinese Secretary of the British Legation as first secretary, the Frenchman Deschamps as second secretary, and two mandarins of the highest rank.

From the child on the Throne had come this paper:

"The envoy Anson Burlingame manages affairs in a friendly and peaceful manner, and is fully acquainted with the general relations between this and other countries; let him, therefore, now be sent to all of the treaty powers as the high minister empowered to attend to every question arising between China and those countries. This from the Emperor."

The mission was acclaimed at all the stopping-places across the United States; but truth to tell, it was because an American heading a Chinese delegation was a curiosity and a sensation.

Unfortunately for the lasting success and popularity of the enterprise, the farther Burlingame proceeded from Peking, the more he misled people as to the aims of the Manchu dynasty. A lawyer by profession, he seemed to think that his interest to his Chinese client could best be served by the florid and not-too-exact rhetoric an attorney uses to sway a jury.

Making a triumphant entry into embattled Washington, the mission raised the yellow flag bearing the imperial Chinese dragon over its headquarters at Brown's Hotel, and Burlingame was received with appropriate honors by President Johnson and Secretary Seward.

Delivering to Johnson a letter from the Emperor, he said that at the expense of what might bear the appearance of egotism, he was bound to say that there were nine official ranks in China, and that he had been appointed to the first rank, and that the accompanying mandarins Chih Ta-jen and Sun Ta-jen were of the second rank.

The envoys were given a state dinner and were warmly received on the floor of the House. Concerning the ceremony, a western Congressman wrote to a San Franciscan:

"A few days ago Burlingame and the Chinese were presented. It was a singular sight to see that ancient Asiatic countenance lighted by the conceit and shaded by the tyrannies of 4000 years, led by the smooth-faced Anglo-Saxon, beneath the shadow of the Eagle and the Stars. . . ."

As a matter of fact, the Chinese members of the Mission were distinguished for their urbanity. With gracious manners and ready wit, they charmed and enlightened Americans who had expected to meet barbarians.

It was at a banquet given to the mission by Manhattan men of affairs, with the Governor of New York in the chair, that Burlingame made his most fervent speech in behalf of China.

"China," he said, "comes with no menace on her lips. She comes with the great doctrine of Confucius . . . 'Do not unto others what you would not have others do unto you.' Will you not respond with the more positive doctrine of Christianity? 'We will do unto others what we would have others do unto us.' "

Having awakened an enthusiastic response by this plea founded on ancient wisdom, Burlingame attacked merchants and officials of the West who for their own interests were strongly in China urging their governments to make war on the Manchu dynasty, men who said, "It is the duty of the Western treaty powers to combine for the purpose of coercing China into reforms which they may desire and which she may not desire. . . ."

He went on, "In their coarse language they say, 'Take her by the throat.' Using the tyrant's plea, they say they know better what China wants than China herself does."

Here he was on sound ground, but in his peroration he committed the mistake of interpreting Chinese thoughts in terms of his own occidental mind.

". . . She finds that she must come into relations with this civilization that is pressing up around her, and feeling that, she does not wait but comes out to you and extends her hand. She tells you that she is ready to take upon her ancient civilization. . . . She invites your merchants, she invites your missionaries. She tells the latter to plant the shining cross on every hill and in every valley."

The speech was misrepresentative because it promised, on the part of China, the acceptance and performance of things the Chinese rulers had sent the mission to explain it was difficult to do.

The Editor of the *North China Herald* commented: "The conduct of Mr. Burlingame, the head of this mission, has destroyed our pleasing anticipations. His absurd description of China in a public speech in New York has covered him with ridicule from all who know how widely different is the original picture."

"It is forgotten," commended the English official Sir Robert Hart, "that of the ten or twenty men in China who really think Western appliances valuable, not one is prepared to boldly advocate their free introductions." He went on to say that the speaker and the press have altogether ignored the Chinese message, "Remember our difficulties"; and have replaced it by words that mean, "We are ready for anything or everything: only say the word and it's done."

He added, however, that a redeeming feature of the talk was that Burlingame's main theme was "Leave China alone, and all you wish for will in its own good time follow."

Burlingame's successor, J. Ross Browne, lamely defended the speechmaker by saying that he was "the dupe of his own enthusiasm and of the cunning and duplicity of his employers." The only kind of Western inventions desired by the Chinese authorities, he said, were the gunboats and arsenals that would help them drive out the foreigners.

A month afterwards Burlingame drafted a treaty which added eight articles to the unsatisfactory Tientsin one, and Secretary of State Seward and he signed it. By this treaty the United States acknowledged China as an equal among nations and recognized China's right to unmolested dominion over her own territories, except as relinquished by treaty; and China insured freedom from persecution for foreign religions. Both countries agreed to allow unrestricted migration of Americans to China and Chinese to the United States, and to forbid the coolie trade.

The treaty's provisions struck at the claims of foreign powers that they could attack each other in Chinese waters, and defeated the contention that foreign powers who had been granted concessions at certain ports should have jurisdiction over the Chinese and residents of other foreign nations in those ports.

The agreement left it to China to determine her need of the railroad and telegraph, and offered American engineering skill when she felt the time was right.

European merchants in China objected to the treaty because it halted their pursuit of railroad, steamboat, and mining privileges. It inflamed certain Americans also.

"It invites," the minister explained as to the coolie clause, "free immigration of those sober and industrious people, by whose quiet labor we have been enabled to push the Pacific railroad over the summits of the Sierra Nevada. Woollen mills have been enabled to run on account of their labor with profit, and the crops of California, more valuable than all her gold, have been gathered by them."

The realities of the situation soon caught up with the ambassador. Every month brought thousands of Chinese to the Pacific Coast, and many of these crossed the Rockies and appeared on the plains. Awakening to the menace of the Asiatic swarms robbing the Americans of jobs and subjecting them to low pay, the people blamed Seward and Burlingame.

The fact is that the Burlingame treaty was a superfluous document, its main privileges as to trade and religion having been granted in the treaty of 1858. There are good grounds for belief that in negotiating and signing it the author wished to show the powers of Europe that he was an ambassador who indeed bore the fullest powers, and wished also to have an instrument with which he could work in Great Britain and on the continent in the interest of his client.

Proceeding to England, the Mission was surprisingly well received. Lord Clarendon, head of the Foreign Office, as a result of a talk with Burlingame, changed his policy of forcing China to do things to one of frank intercourse between the Government of Peking and the British crown.

The envoys were cordially received by the monarchs of Sweden, Denmark, and the Netherlands, and historian George Bancroft, the American minister to Prussia, brought about an agreeable meeting between Count Bismarck and the American mandarin. Even the aloof Czar of Russia was gracious and encouraging.

Fate took a hand while the envoys were in Russia, and the mission was shown to be ephemeral and of secondary importance by the blunt fact of Burlingame's death. Having overtaxed his strength, the enthusiast succumbed to pneumonia. However, the work he had set out to do was done, and the Emperor of China and his minister conferred an honorary title of the first rank on the dead ambassador and publicly stated their appreciation of his ability, integrity, and fair play.

Violent events which followed the death of Burlingame showed that the Chinese people were not as kindly disposed to foreign persons and inventions as Burlingame had claimed. The Boxer madness, with its massacres of missionaries and native Christians, was beginning to brew, excited by the very mother of the young Emperor for whom Burlingame thought he was speaking when he said of China in New York: "She invites your merchants. She invites your missionaries."

For all his vapidness, there was a residue of significant truth for Americans of today in the speeches of Anson Burlingame. Perhaps in some vital aspects he was just another prophet who uttered wisdom before the time was ripe to follow it.

Pleading that China's first need was for a feeling of security, Burlingame said: "China, seeing another civilization approaching on every side, is ready for it. She sees Russia on the north, Europe on the west, America on the east. . . . Let her alone; let her have independence; let her develop herself in her own time. She has no hostility to you. Let her do this, and she will initiate a movement that will be felt in every workshop of the civilized world. . . . The imagination kindles at the future which may be, and which will be, if you will be fair and just to China."

This Burlingame plea might be appropriately spoken today by any champion of the Chinese people.

And what of the Chinese commissioners Chih Ta-jen and Sun Ta-jen, whom the death of Burlingame left stranded in Russia? The Seward party, visiting Shanghai, in 1870, watched from the gateway of the "Concession" their triumphant return. The world travelers, used to quiet American and European ceremonies, were welcomed home in a manner gaudily Chinese.

A band of musicians led the procession, making hideous noises with gongs, sticks, and drums; then came a company arrayed in flaring garments, marching under a glowing cloud of banners and flags. Then, borne by coolies, came two resplendent sedan chairs protected from the sun's heat by scarlet canopies, and after these came followers in all degrees of vivid dress and decoration.

Secretary Seward, comparing the modesty of the ministers when they had called on him at Auburn with this flaunting pageantry, said that the pageant was evidence of the decay of the empire, which, weak as it was, insisted on displays of glory.

CHAPTER XXVII

Secretary Seward Visits a Mandarin of Vision

SECRETARY WILLIAM E. SEWARD, who had predicted that the Atlantic would lose importance for the United States, and that "the Pacific, its shores, its islands and its vast regions beyond" would be the "chief theater of events in the world's great hereafter," crowned his career as a statesman by a visit to the Far East in 1870.

Forcefully supporting the wise foreign policy of Daniel Webster, he crystallized the American program in the Far East, varying it, however, by joining with other powers when he felt it necessary to obtain the submission of China, Japan, or Korea to the Western ideas of what was right.

Shortly after the death of Burlingame, Seward sailed on a world tour and made his way by boat and sedan chair to Peking.

The advance guard of the party were twelve Chinese infantrymen who wore metal helmets fastened by long yellow tassels, and blue nankeen tunics and trousers. The Government, believing that words were equal to deeds, had inscribed on the tunic-backs the word "Valor." Then came twelve United States Marines, then the honored visitors and chair bearers; after them American musicians and sailors mounted on donkeys.

The Chinese crowds knew nothing of the statesmanship of Seward, but when they saw the gray hair under his black Thibetan cap and watched his sturdy movements in the white Thibetan greatcoat as he advanced into the cold climate of Peking, they saluted him with veneration.

He was traveling in company with Admiral John Rodgers of the U. S. warship *Colorado,* and as they came nearer to Peking, the two kept their chairs side by side in the rough narrow road. If the Chinese people who saluted the venerable American visitors had understood the conversation that flowed between the chairs, they might have been a little less reverent in their salutes.

"Admiral Rogers," said Seward, "did you ever hear of the interview of Daniel Webster with John Adams, the day before Adams died?"

"No, Mr. Seward."

"Webster said: 'How do you do this morning, Mr. Adams?' 'Not very well!' he replied. 'I am living in a very old house, Mr. Webster, and from all that I can learn, the landlord does not intend to repair.' "So," continued Seward, "this road gives me a more painful impression than anything else I have seen in China —it shows that the Government has no intention to repair!"

At last the party reached the suburbs of Peking, where the rough road they followed dipped fifteen feet below the street level and could scarcely be found because it was knee-deep in mud. Up rose, however, the great eastern entrance to Peking, and led by a red-capped Chinese horseman, they passed under the curiously-carved gate and zigzagged through narrow obstructed lanes, splashing mud on unresentful foot travelers.

At last the guide turned at a high wall and entered a gateway, and there before the weary pilgrims was a spacious open court marked by a flagpole flying the Stars and Stripes. It was the American Legation, the large and comfortable dwelling that had been built by S. Wells Williams. Burlingame had stayed there, and it was now the home of Minister Low; but the parsimonious United States had not appropriated the money to buy it.

The band of music from the ship *Colorado*—the first foreign band permitted to play in Peking—saluted every foreign minister who came to welcome Seward.

It was statesman Wei-sang, institutor of the Burlingame mission, who greeted Seward for China. He arrived at the Legation in a green sedan-chair, with two mounted attendants and four footmen. Ceremoniously arrayed in a rich robe of silks and furs, and a mandarin's hat with a peacock's feather and a coral ball on the top, he welcomed Seward with sincere cordiality.

"Mr. Burlingame's letters and conversations," Seward began after the exchange of courtesies, "made me well acquainted with your character and your sagacious and effective statesmanship."

"We deplore the death of Mr. Burlingame," Wei-sang said. "It is a loss to China that he died before accomplishing his mission.

"And yet Mr. Burlingame's mission was a success. He brought China and the West into relations of mutual friendship and accord. In this view his death was not premature."

"I think," Seward answered, "that China ought to reciprocate with the Western nations by sending them permanent resident ministers and consuls who should be of equal rank with those which the foreign nations accredit here. They ought in all cases to be native Chinese."

"We shall send such agents as soon as they can be educated here in the Western sciences and languages, so as to be qualified for their trusts."

"Better they go unqualified than wait too long," Seward advised, pointing out that the coolies in America needed an official representative. "Chinese experts," he went on, "will learn Western sciences, languages, laws and customs in the United States or in Europe much faster than they can acquire them here . . . China is now regarded by all the Western nations as not merely unsocial, but hostile, because she neglects the exchange of international courtesies aboard as well as at home."

"These are my own opinions," said Wei-sang.

"There is another point," Seward said, "upon which I would

like to speak freely if I should not be accused of speaking in an unfriendly way. Chinese ministers are accorded a personal reception by the sovereigns of the nations, but a minister from the United States, England, or Russia, on arriving here, learns that the Emperor of China is too sacred a person to be looked upon. This, to be sure, is only a question of ceremony and etiquette; but, my dear sir, questions of ceremony and etiquette between nations often become the most serious and dangerous of all international complications."

Seward had used strong words, but he did not break through the Chinese wall. Wei-sang undoubtedly agreed with him, but could do nothing but bow courteously. The Emperor, to the general Chinese mind, was still the unapproachable Son of Heaven.

Interested in Wei-sang's ambition to develop China's foreign relations, Seward encouraged him to pursue his efforts despite popular opinion, stating out of his experience that every wise minister at some time falls under temporary reproach and unjust suspicion.

Wei-sang's answer revealed great wisdom:

"A statesman stands on a hill. He looks farther in all directions than the people, who are standing at the base. When he points out the course they ought to take for safety, they are suspicious that he is misdirecting them. When they have at last gained the summit, they then correct their misjudgment. But this, although it may be sufficient for them, comes too late for the statesman."

With this memorable warning that heartbreak is the cost of true leadership, Wei-sang went away.

Seward departed with great admiration for Wei-sang—a modern-minded statesman who battled with little encouragement against the superstitions and traditions of the Chinese. He had recently attempted to found an imperial college in which modern sciences and languages would be taught by foreign professors, but the effort had failed, and the crowd accused him of playing into the hands of foreign nations.

There were other far-seeing mandarins in the times of Wei-sang:

Under the influence of Dr. Abeel, the Mandarin Seu Ki-yu, who became afterwards governor of the province of Ku-kien, studied the English language and published, in 1848, a quaint ten-volume survey of Maritime Countries which included an account of the War of Independence. The character of George Washington especially impressed him, and he published such praise of this hero that he offended the Manchu Court, which while it knew that there were many good people and things in the West, did not wish the Chinese people to be so informed. Under the Regency of Prince Kung, Seu Ki-yu was honored for his knowledge of the West, and was placed, at seventy, at the head of Wei-sang's institution at Peking: the Institution for Giving Instruction in the Arts and Sciences of the West. When Minister Anson Burlingame went to Peking, he brought the venerable Seu Ki-yu, as a gift from the President of the United States, a portrait of Washington.

Expansionist Seward, in an informal talk with an American commissioner in China, indicated what the United States' policy towards China should be.

Seward sailed up the Yangtze on the *Kin-San* and at the port of Ku-Kiang conversed with two Americans, Mr. Rose, agent for Russell and Company, and Mr. Drew, who served as deputy Chinese revenue commissioner under a British official, Inspector-General Hart.

Drew lamented to Seward that British prestige in China overwhelmed that of the United States. Seward asked why. Drew replied: "Great Britain as well as France, maintains a policy of demonstration and menace; the United States has forbearance and conciliation."

Seward answered him by a series of questions.

"You have been here many years. Do you know of any outrage, or injury, or wrong, that the United States ever complained of, that the Chinese government has left unredressed?"

"I know of none."

"Has Great Britain or France secured to herself in China any political or commercial benefit or advantage which the Chinese Government has not equally extended, by treaty, to the United States?"

"No."

Seward had previously observed that most of the Americans living in China were missionaries, and that there were not as many Americans in China as were in the diplomatic and military service of Great Britain, France, or Russia, stationed there.

"Do you think," Seward concluded, "that the United States ought to provoke China by any act of injustice or wrong? Do you think that it would be wise for the United States, without provocation, to resort to any policy of menace or intimidation?"

Mr. Drew again said no.

"Well," Seward summed up, "I think we are obliged to conclude that a policy of justice, moderation, and friendship, is the only one we have had a choice to pursue, and that it has been as wise as it has been unavoidable. . . . Of the 39 millions which constitute the American people, less than 10,000 dwell in foreign countries, and a smaller proportion in China than in many other countries. The United States cannot be an aggressive nation—least of all can it be aggressive against China."

On this visit to Peking, Seward saw that the influence of the United States was far less distinguishable than that of Great Britain or Russia.

Russia, mystery today, was a mystery then. The Chinese throne feared their near and colossal neighbor, coming ever closer by railroads, telegraph, and diligence-lines. The Chinese statesmen recognized that the Russians on their border could be valuable friends, but that they might also be overwhelming enemies.

Seward, visiting Japan in Perry's wake, was not late enough on the scene fully to grasp the purposes of Japan as to China, but not long after his visit her aggressive aims were partially revealed. It was ex-President Grant who first saw the flashing temper of the Japanese expansionists.

While China and Japan were engaged in a bitter controversy over the island of Liu Chiu (Okinawa), a tribute-payer to China, Grant was making his tour of the world and came to Peking. The Chinese government turned to him as her mediator. He conferred with John A. Bingham, the American minister at Tokyo, who sympathized with the natives of Liu Chiu. In 1879, regardless of Grant's mediation, Japan deposed the king of Liu Chiu and annexed it.

For one who is disposed to think that the matter of change of possession of an insignificant island or a weak state is of little consequence, this Oriental appeal by an envoy of Liu Chiu, made at the Peking court, is worth pondering.

"When the master is worried, the servants ought to feel ashamed; when the master is humiliated, the servants ought to sacrifice their lives! What right have we to exist any longer in this world? When living, we shall not be Japanese subjects! When dead, we shall not be Japanese ghosts! We care not even if our bodies are ground and our skulls powdered. We pondered and pondered during our days of waiting in Foochow. We would shave our heads, change our costume, and early proceed north (to Peking) rather than waste time and let the nation perish; we would weep in the Imperial capital in accordance with the Great Principles until we died, rather than swallow disgrace, endure humiliation and live like cowards in Liu Chiu."

Japan's march to India, and the Netherlands East Indies, and to Pearl Harbor had begun. Her next move was to destroy Chinese influence in Korea. When she destroyed what naval power China possessed, she started the aggression that culminated in our times. Professor Shuhsi Hsu, of Peking University, admirably summed up her ambitions:

"Thus Japan disclosed her hand. She had confined herself to the encroachment on weak neighbors long enough; she would now assume the role of dominating the Far East. She was not satisfied with the detachment of Korea together with the destruction of Chinese naval power . . . she would also cripple China financially, kill Chinese industries in their infant stage, and advance upon her both from the south and the north by seizing the Pescadores, Formosa, and the Liaotung peninsula in order that she might finally live upon her like the fabulous birds that feed upon the bodies of their parents."

In this crisis, the helpless Chinese government summoned as counsellor to the peace mission which they were sending to the Emperor of Japan, the American John W. Foster, ex-Secretary of

State, and sometime counsellor to the Chinese Legation at Washington. Foster made this plea to Japan in behalf of China:

"Territory long held by a nation, through many centuries and dynasties, becomes a priceless heritage. Nothing will arouse the indignation of the people of China and create in them a spirit of undying hostility and hatred, as to wrest from their country important portions of territory."

As to coveted Liaotung, Foster went on:

"This will be especially the case with that portion of the territory . . . because it gives Japan a foothold and base for military and naval operations within easy reach of and constantly threatening the capital of the empire, and because it takes from the present dynasty of China a portion of its ancient possessions. In this clause China hears Japan saying: 'I am going to be your ever-threatening and undying enemy, with my army and navy ready to pounce down upon your capital when it suits me; and I propose to humiliate your Emperor by taking from him a valuable portion of his ancestor's home!'"

Obtaining Liaotung's harbors as booty from the war with China, Japan was not strong enough to keep it against covetous Russia, France, and Germany; they forcefully persuaded her to give up the commanding peninsula.

Then these very powers began to acquire. The three enforcers, with Great Britain, obtained naval bases on the China coast, and Russia went on to lease the very peninsula from which Japan had been forced to withdraw.

It is of continual importance—the Liaotung peninsula. Its strategical value does not change. With its two important naval bases, it enables an outside power to dominate Korea and northern China, and it can be a base for a conquest of all of China and the control of Manchuria. Japan and Russia both felt that it was worth going to war to control Liaotung.

The Chinese were in the grip of the "White Peril."

"The various powers," said the bitter old Empress-Dowager, "cast upon us looks of tiger-like voracity, hustling each other in their endeavors to be the first to seize our innermost territories."

Prepared to make war on Russia to secure her hold on Korea

and her claims to Manchuria, Japan in 1902 entered into an alliance with Great Britain, counting on the British navy to hold back land-hungry Germany and Russia's ally France. Japan then went to war with Russia and destroyed Russian sea power.

President Theodore Roosevelt, as peace commissioner, brought the negotiators together at Portsmouth. Russia agreed to let Japan have a free hand in Korea; ceded to Japan the southern part of the island of Sakhalin, and transferred to Japan, with the consent of China, the lease of the harbors of Liaotung peninsula— Port Arthur and Talienwan and a connecting railway.

Russia, however, was left in possession of three-quarters of its railroads.

While the battle for ports and for railway and mining concessions was being fought by the powers in China, the United States was involved in her war with Spain.

Victorious, she heard Rudyard Kipling's imperialistic verses urging the Americans to join the British and take up the "White Man's Burden." It was a burden that was to come to Americans without their seeking it.

Annexing the Philippine Islands, the United States found that the expansion had changed her situation as to China, and changed also the ideas of the Orient that the Americans were a disinterested nation.

John Hay, Secretary of State under McKinley and during part of the Theodore Roosevelt administration, appeared at this time to reassure China. Well informed in world affairs, he had studied the career of Anson Burlingame and sympathized with his views about China. A more practical man than Burlingame, he worked to benefit the interests of the United States and to help his friends in the British Foreign Office, while keeping China from being torn apart.

On September 6, 1899, through the American ambassadors at London, Berlin, and St. Petersburg, he asked each of these governments to declare that it would not interfere with any treaty port or vested right within any so-called "sphere of interest" it might have in China; and that all harbor dues and transportation charges would be equal for the ships of all nations engaged in trade with the Chinese. Thus he brought into effect the Open Door principle that became associated with his name.

Announcing that an agreement had been reached, the Secretary of State officially declared that his country's intention was "to preserve the territorial and administrative entity of China."

The United States now stood as the natural protector of China, and looming large in that rôle, excited the envy and antagonism of Japan.

CHAPTER XXVIII

An Annapolis Sword for Li Hung-chang

THERE WERE GRAVE occurrences from time to time in the Far East which the United States officially took no cognizance of. It could not, for instance, be held responsible for the doings of soldiers of fortune from America who found it thrilling to lead a foreign legion for the Manchu emperor or for the rebel chief seeking to dethrone him; and it could not at a later period obstruct or admonish American soldiers or sailors whom minister Li Hung-chang saw fit to employ in preparing the defense of China against the preparing aggressor Japan.

What statesmen could not recognize, however, writers could, and informal but authentic note has been taken of how when Japan in 1894 put into action against China her navy built up by ships purchased in France, Holland, and Great Britain, an Annapolis man, Philo Norton McGiffen, stood out on China's side in the war at sea.

The years have given him the distinction of being the first American naval officer in history to command a warship in a battle against Japan. The war in which he fought has a general significance in that the victory of the Japanese gave them the naval pride that led them to attack Russia and then the United States.

In an attempt to compete with Japan's policy of acquiring warships in the shipyards of Europe, High Commissioner Li Hung-chang had ordered English yards to build four ironclads for the Chinese Navy, and had selected the winning sailor-of-fortune McGiffen to go there and superintend the construction.

The Decatur-like stuff in McGiffen was hidden under the behavior of an inveterate prankster.

There was, for example, the night when he bombarded the interior of an Academy building.

At the head of the stairs stood a pyramid of cannon balls—24-pounders that were relics of the War of 1812. The stairway was big and square, and as it ascended it enclosed a well, or open area. One evening a wild cry startled the guard; then a body hurtled down the well from the top floor. Cadets rushed to the ground floor and circled the fallen figure, while the officer in charge rushed up, crying: "Get back, give him air, make way!" The figure was that of a dummy in a well-worn cadet uniform.

McGiffen, the perpetrator of this hoax, was not discovered, and he felt encouraged to attempt an even more sensational prank. Tempted by the pyramid of 24-pounders, he slipped out of his room one night and sent them bumping down the stairs. Some of them broke through the balustrade and dropped with resounding thuds to the polished floor below.

This time he was detected and sentenced to a term on the prison-ship *Santee*. Even this confinement in the *Santee* did not suppress him. The eve of the Fourth of July came. Obtaining a charge of gunpowder the cadet escaped to the academy grounds, loaded some big guns captured in the Mexican War, and fired a salute that aroused the entire garrison and blew out Annapolis windows.

Graduating in 1882, McGiffen was assigned to duty on the *Hartford,* flagship of the Pacific squadron. Two years later he was examined for the grade of past midshipman, but vacancies were scarce, and since promotions were given only when vacancies occurred, instead of receiving a commission he was honorably discharged with a year's pay.

After knocking around a bit, the news of China's war with France attracted McGiffen in the Far East, and there he applied in person to Minister Li Hung-chang, who gave him a commission in the Chinese Navy. Afterwards, he was appointed professor of seamanship and gunnery at the Naval College at Tientsin, and there taught most of the Chinese officers who were to engage in the coming Chinese-Japanese war over Korea.

Fighting against the Japanese navy, McGiffen served under Admiral Ting Ju-chang, and the American's testimonials to the Chinese admiral contains the story of why the Chinese lost the war.

"Chief among those who have died for their country," McGiffen wrote, "is Admiral Ting Ju-chang, a gallant soldier and true gentleman. Betrayed by his countrymen, fighting against odds, almost his last official act was to stipulate for the lives of his officers and men. His own he scorned to save, well knowing that his ungrateful country would prove less merciful than his honorable foe."

The most important duty of the strong Japanese fleet was to keep the sea route open between Japan and Korea, and to support the landing of armies. The Chinese fleet escorted their transports from Port Arthur to the Yalu River without interference from the enemy.

On September 14, 1894, Admiral Ting sailed with his entire squadron for the Yalu, and landed troops and stores under the guns of his warships and torpedo boats. On the morning of the seventeenth, smoke having been reported, Ting formed his line of battle—his two battleships in the center, the smaller vessels on the flanks, and the gun and torpedo boats under cover of the fleet. McGiffen commanded the torpedo boat *Chen Yuen*.

The Chinese fleet soon met the two Japanese squadrons led by Admiral Ito. Early in the action the Chinese fleet was thrown into disorder and was not able to re-form. The battleships *Chung Yuen* and *Ting Yuen* fought gallantly and followed up the Japanese warships as they drew out of range, but the smaller vessels of the Chinese fleet were disabled, detached, set afire, or sunk. After seven and a half hours' engagement, the Japanese ships steamed out of range, and both fleets went into harbor for repairs.

On January, 1895, ten Japanese torpedo boats succeeded in entering the harbor where the Chinese fleet lay; they sunk a half-dozen vessels, including the battleship Chih-Yuen, which McGiffen brought out from England. On the twelfth, Admiral Ting capitulated to Admiral Ito, and when the Japanese fleet steamed into the harbor and took possession of the remaining Chinese vessels, Ting committed suicide. McGiffen escaped into Port Arthur dreadfully wounded and the doctor aboard the U. S. warship *Monocacy* ministered to him.

McGiffen returned to the United States a nervous wreck. He insisted on living alone in a room in a New York lodging-house, and in his loneliness he wrote to some of his Annapolis mates to visit him.

Park Benjamin, writing in the *Army and Navy Journal* three years after the battle of the Yalu, draws this pathetic picture of him:

"What he wanted most was to talk about the Yalu fight, and to rehearse minutely again and again every detail of it.

"Rising up from his pillow, with his eyes blazing, he told of the fearful fire on the forecastle and the smothering of it under the deadly hail that swept down all but himself; of the frightful moments when he lay disabled under the muzzle of one of his own guns; of the hypodermic syringe of morphine grimly put into his belt before the action 'lest death should wait too long'; of the hideous splashing of him with the blood and mangled flesh of his own men, and of his tumult of joy when his well-aimed shell carried wholesale slaughter upon the deck of the Japanese flagship.

"And, as if words were not realistic enough, he would show the gashes in his wrist and bare his whole left side to exhibit a great wound. And then he would bring forth his uniform, scorched and riddled and covered with old blood, and put it on and act the drama over again; until one forgot the sickening horror of it all in the recognition that this was a Berserker of the nineteenth century chanting a saga as wild and fierce as ever the conquering Norsemen sang from the deck of the Long Serpent in the days of Erik the Red.

"It was pure battle fury. There was no patriotism behind it; no lofty motive; no desire to protect; no self-sacrifice; no flag. For China, he had only contempt. He praised her sailormen for bravery and endurance, but denounced her officials, Admiral Ting always excepted, as traitors, even drawing monthly salaries from the enemy. Yet, inconsistently enough, he zealously insisted on his rank of Commander in the Chinese Navy, which, he claimed, he held by Imperial rescript, although he received no pay, and would not return to China because, as he said, his friends there were 'all dead.' "

Robert M. Thompson, a friend of the American Navy, had McGiffen placed in a comfortable hospital, but there he shot himself.

CHAPTER XXIX

The Air Clipper Carries On

IT IS ALMOST trite to say that what the sailing ship was to historic China run of which we have written, the air-clipper is to the future road to the Orient. The square-rigger passed; the luxurious steam liner succeeded it; and then the pioneer winged clipper rose from the waters of San Francisco harbor and, flying the well-defined course from island to island, maintained the American-Chinese link and expanded it beyond the open ports up the rivers and into the vast interior.

Today the Chinese peasant whose father or grandfather massacred "foreign devils" in the Boxer uprising, hears placidly the hum of the transport overhead, and if it was malignant, curses the Japanese who took it over as a weapon to cow or destroy a people. The Chinese community, before the Japanese invaders made the plane an engine of death, had come to know it as an invention blessed by their gods for the help it brought to victims of flood and famine. If afterwards volunteer airmen from the West banded to fight the Japanese aggressors and oppressors, they also, the peasant considered, were workers of good to the people of China.

The story of the air transport service rendered to China by the United States began with General Mitchell, who eminently belongs in our narrative of voyagers to China. In 1920, Billy Mitchell, as Chief of the Air Service, decided to demonstrate that the

United States could establish an airway to Alaska and Asia. Captain Streett, the actual commander, assisted by the Canadian authorities, took four airplanes from New York to Nome in fifty-four hours. At Nome the airmen could have crossed to Siberia and thereby entered Asia, but at the request of the State Department the airmen were asked not to land on Russian territory, and they resisted the temptation; however, their successful flight showed commercial and transportation companies that there was an inviting, practical airway to the Orient.

In 1924, the United States Air Service was taking the developed China run and was performing an insect-dusting mission in the Philippines. Those good-intentioned pilots had no idea, as they created clouds of arsenic solution over the locust-ravaged fields of the island of Mindanao, that two decades afterwards American military airmen would be doing a more deadly dusting of human ravagers from Japan.

Billy Mitchell was delighted to discover that the Chinese warlords had a sense of humor. He told this story of his first visit to China:

". . . We went up to visit Marshall Chang Tso-Lin, the war lord of Manchuria, at Mukden. I had known him a great many years and he was always an interesting character to me. He had some new French airplanes that were very good and well kept up; also he was building some large new arsenals to manufacture guns and ammunition. I thought, while I was flying one of his new ships, that I might just as well take some photographs of what was going on. So I told my aide to take my camera and photograph all the new military works in that vicinity. I asked him if he knew how to work the camera, and he said he did. After flying around for an hour or so, and using up a couple of rolls of film, we landed. To my great disappointment, I found that he had just been pressing the release on the shutter, instead of setting it and then pressing it; consequently the photographs were all blanks. I told General Chang about it, as I thought it was too good a joke to keep. He laughed heartily and told me it was in return for a joke I told him many years before, when he had invited me to dinner. The flies were very bad and lit on his bald head; so he asked me me how I thought he could get rid of them. I advised him to tattoo a spider's web on his head and then the flies would be scared and stay away! He had never forgotten this."

In 1932 Pan American Airways, having absorbed Alaskan Airways, started to expand to the Orient. The North American Aviation Company already had control of a Chinese transport system which was subsidiary to its Alaska system, and Pan-American acquired this Chinese line, the China National Aviation Corporation, or CNAC. Its competitior was a line backed by German interests, both lines being controlled by the Chinese Government.

On April 21, 1934, the Japanese *Advertiser,* published in English in Tokyo, reported that in the current year United States companies had sold $2,800,000 worth of airplanes to China, including from eighteen to twenty-five Corsair scouting planes and light bombers sold by United Aircraft Corporation to the Government at Nanking, which, with this addition, owned fifty Corsairs of the U. S. Navy type.

At about this time the Curtiss-Wright Company sent Major Doolittle to China to teach Chinese officers the use of pursuit, scout, and battle planes. Though the mission was not then in his dreams, it was a rehearsal for his famous pioneer flight of World War II to bomb Tokyo.

The Japanese press, infuriated by these accounts of American aid to the Chinese, carried the news under headlines like this: "American Air Force Shakes Finger Under Japan's Nose." The Japanese authorities declared that American air transport services were a menace to their empire's security. An undeclared war in the air between Japanese and Chinese-American planes was brewing.

Mr. Amau, spokesman for the Japanese Foreign Office, issued this warning:

"Supplying China with war planes, building aerodromes in China, and detailing military instructors or military advisers to China, would obviously tend to alienate the friendly relations between Japan and China and other countries, and to disturb the peace and order of East Asia. Japan will oppose such projects."

Pan American Airways went ahead with its first passenger flights from the Pacific Coast of the United States to the Philippines and China. On October 14, 1936, the city of San Francisco, often stirred by the western march of Americans, watched the first air passenger clipper glint up in its run of 8000 miles.

With headquarters at Nanking, the Chinese line CNAC by 1937 was flying passengers and freight up the Yangtze River through Nanking. In the north, its fogged air shuttle wove together Canton and Hong Kong.

Japanese leaders complained that the United States "holds absolute sway over Chinese commercial flying, both machines and pilots being American."

In 1938 Japanese fighting planes shot down the Samoan Clipper, flown by Captain E. C. Musiak, killing the commander and his crew. After this attack a Japanese spokesman advised people to travel on the planes of the German-backed company, because, he said, "CNAC planes carried Chinese military leaders upon military missions and transported military supplies."

The dramatic story which follows, issued at the time by Pan American Airways after a flagrant assault on one of its planes, is a curtain-raiser for the exploits of American fighter pilots after Pearl Harbor.

"Among the most heroic sagas of the air are those of the American pilots flying the China National Aviation Corp. commercial planes. Mile by mile, as the Jap war machine rolled westward, CNAC moved a step ahead of the invaders to keep Chiang Kai-shek's capital, wherever it might be, in touch with the essential provinces and with the outside world.

"CNAC schedules its flights between Japanese air raids. The pilots never dare fly in good weather, but must pick out for their schedules conditions which make it too difficult for military aircraft to navigate. They do most of their flying at night, with lights out, at high altitudes, with silent radios, navigating by the stars if they can see them, mostly by instrument, enveloped in the clouds.

"Under such conditions, unarmed, unprotected, unaided, these boys from Kansas, Nevada, New Jersey, California, and Florida—and their Chinese colleagues—have done a heroic job."

Typical of their work was this recent adventure of Capt. H. L. Woods of Salina, Kas., and Capt. Harold Arthur Sweet of Salt Lake City:

"Capt. Woods, en route from Chunking to Chengtu, was picked up by a flight of five Jap bombers. With no clouds to hide him, he dived in and made a landing in the tiny intermediate field at Siufu, rolled the ship to the edge of the trees and got his passengers safely into the dugouts. Scarcely a minute later, five Japs dived on the field. Before they left they had dropped more than 200 bombs on the tiny airport. One of them blew the port wing off the DC3 and the Japs, out of ammunition, pulled up and disappeared. No one was hurt. The field was full of bomb craters. The starboard wing was completely mangled. The force of the exploding bomb had moved the whole ship six feet sideways. It was peppered with machine-gun bullet holes, with ragged nicks from shrapnel, with dents from flying stones. Woods radioed Hong Kong, advising that with a new wing he would be able to get out; that he was putting crews at work 'mounting' a runway; for help to hurry.

"Hong Kong had no spare wing; had no materials to build one. The only thing available was a DC2 wing. Through the night engineers and maintenance men struggled with their problem. They figured; scaled through curves. Could a DC3 be flown with half a DC2 wing?

"They figured that with certain adjustments it could! The mechanical crew went immediately to work to make those adjustments. Next, how to get the spare wing from Hong Kong to Siufu! The distance is 860 miles as the crow flies. The only way to get it there was to fly it. So, to the underside of the standby DC2, the spare wing, with its 'adjusted' sections, was lashed. Specially streamlined knobs were put on both ends of the wing to taper it into the plane's fuselage. The plane was an unwieldy-looking affair.

"Would this contraption fly? Capt. Harold Sweet volunteered to try—and to deliver the wing if he got off the ground. Fingers crossed his colleagues stood watching him. He pushed the DC2 almost to the last yard of runway before he got the wheels off the ground.

"Slowly he climbed—in wide circles to keep out of the range of the occupied territory and the guns of the Japs. Little by little, he gained altitude, made a final circle of the field, carefully dipped a wing and sped off to the north. Safe in China's territory, he radioed back that the ship was flying normally, except for slight longitudinal instability and buffeting, and that all was well! After landing at Kweillin for gas, he got off again safely, turned his plane's nose toward Siufu. Midway, the radio warned that more bombers were heading in his direction, so he and his cargo had to go scouting over the hills and through the clouds to Cahutong to hide out until the Japs had lost his trail. Later that day he made it to Siufu.

"But by the time he got there, things had happened. Fearful that more Jap bombers would return to finish off the damaged Douglas before it could be repaired, Woods and his crew and his coolie helpers had dragged the DC3 off the field and three miles down the road to hide it in a clump of bamboo trees. Within an hour after they had completed their camouflage job, a flight of seven Jap bombers returned and spent nearly an hour looking for the wounded Douglas before giving up and winging away. On the second and third days flights totaling up to 50 bombers scoured the countryside around Siufu, some of them diving to within 200 feet of the boys and the ship huddled under the bamboo without finding a trace of the Douglas.

"That third night the two skippers, Woods and Sweet, and their crews fitted the DC2 wing to the DC3 and put the ship in technical order. Meanwhile the coolies filled in the bomb craters to make a runway. Working desperately against time, just as the first gray light of day came threading through the trees, Woods took the DC3 off with its unbalanced monoplane and Sweet followed him with the DC2. Four hours later both landed safely in Hong Kong.

"Woods' report from Siufu on the bombing totaled eleven words. Operations Manager Sharp's report from Hong Kong—on the wing compromise—took nine words. Descriptions of the two planes returning to Hong Kong took five words. That's the official record. W. L. Bond, lent to the Chinese to manage CNAC, filled in the story when, home on leave, he dropped in at Pan American's offices in New York a few days ago."

Wiley Post and his Australian buddy Harold Gatty . . . Hugh Herndon, Jr. and Clyde Pangborn . . . the Lindberghs . . . Howard Hughes . . . Colonel Jimmy Doolittle . . . Amelia Earhart . . . Major General C. L. Chennault . . . General H. H. Arnold—these and scores of other American pilots were pioneers of the air way to China.

The United States Navy in 1934 took to the air over the track of Commodore Perry when its little squadron made a non-stop flight to fateful Pearl Harbor. A few pages back we spoke of the brewing of an undeclared war between Japan and the United States. It came. That our fliers were more decisive under provocation than American statesmen is indicated by a paragraph of history in the pocket-book A. A. F. Guide:

"Our China-based air force which wears the insignia of the Flying Tiger grew out of the China Air Task Force which in turn originated in the Flying Tigers of the American Volunteer Group. The latter, made up of former A. A. F., Navy, and Marine pilots, had been at war against the Japanese for some five months before the attack on Pearl Harbor."

CHAPTER XXX

American Armada

THE SEAS AND harbors explored by friendly Yankee square-riggers and steamships have in the last few decades been threatened by the Japanese military storm which broke with Pearl Harbor. Studying the fair, defensive American Monroe Doctrine, the military clique of Japan took it as a pattern for a wave of aggression that swept down on China, Indo-China, Thailand, Burma, the Netherland East Indies, and the Straits Settlements. They expressed their folly in the purring phrase: "The Greater East Asia Co-Prosperity Sphere."

American representatives in the Far East informed the United States State Department that the Japanese militarists were on the march, but the United States was watching Hitler and Mussolini, and hoped by diplomatic threats and maneuvers to keep back the Japanese tide. But the Japanese typhoon gathered tremendous force.

Ambassador Grew had repeatedly warned of a "swashbuckling temper" in Japan, and Secretary Cordell Hull in turn had warned Americans that it "would be both a blunder and a crime for civilized peoples to fail much longer to take notice of present dangerous tendencies," and added that the world was threatened with "another period of long night—such as the Dark Ages."

Previously, when Japan had seized several strategic points in South Manchuria, Secretary of State Henry Stimson showed a challenging firmness. He went to work with other nations to restrict the Japanese, who were recruiting labor battalions from every village and house. Taking advantage of an existing evil, the invaders increased the production of opium, heroin, and cocaine to stupefy the people. A street in Peiping that had two opium shops in June 1937, had 147 in 1939.

Stimson and Hull stand out nobly in America's defense of China because they saw the wisdom of President Theodore Roosevelt's policy of keeping Japan in her place. When he sent the White Fleet to the Orient under Commander Robley Evans, announcing at the same time that the policy of his country was to "Speak softly, and carry a big stick," he spoke words for the ages.

In 1937, President Franklin D. Roosevelt made his Quarantine address at Chicago, calling for a concerted effort by peace-loving nations to oppose international anarchy and the contagion of war.

In the same year Japanese aircraft, maddened by the aid unofficial American airmen were giving to assaulted China, bombed the United States gunboat *Panay* and Japan, having shown her fangs, said "So sorry!" She went on to ally herself with the Fascist powers. On October 19, 1939, as a true representative of the spirit of his people, Ambassador Grew spoke sharply before the America-Japan Society of Tokyo:

"It is probable that many of you are not aware of the increasing extent to which the people of the United States resent methods which Japanese armed forces are employing in China and what appear to be their objectives. . . . American people have been profoundly shocked over the widespread bombing in China, not only on the grounds of humanity but also on the grounds of direct menace to American life and property, accompanied by the loss of American life."

Ambassador Grew reported in 1941 that a colleague among the embassies in Japan had reported to the Embassy staff that in case of trouble with the United States, Japan's *Gumbatsu* planned a surprise mass attack on Pearl Harbor.

When Admiral Nomura arrived in Washington in the same year, Secretary Hull asked how those Japanese militarists could possibly expect the United States "to sit absolutely quiet while two or three nations before our very eyes organized naval and military forces and went out and conquered the balance of the earth, including the seven seas and all trade routes and the other four continents."

He asked also what the United States had to gain by remaining complacent in the movement to substitute force and conquest for law and justice.

The Japanese diplomat insisted that the United States should stop the aid it was giving to China, so that Japan could settle "the Chinese affair" in its own way.

On October 10, 1941, according to a Japanese admiral, the Navy of Japan received sealed orders to deploy for war against the United States.

In November, diplomat Salnio Kurusu arrived from Tokyo to assist Admiral Nomura in erecting a screen of words while the militarists prepared to launch the attack on Pearl Harbor.

On December 6, President Roosevelt telegraphed a personal message to the Emperor of Japan, hoping that the two countries could agree on peace in the Pacific.

On Sunday, December 7, the two Japanese diplomats delivered to Secretary Hull a memorandum packed with bitter accusations against the United States Government, ending with a declaration that the Japanese Government could not reach an agreement with it through further negotiations.

Whatever the verdict is as to the American unpreparedness at Washington, Hawaii, and Manila before Japan's attack, it is an unassailable truth that the Nipponese took the treacherous offensive.

Word was brought to Secretary Hull of the treacherous attack on Pearl Harbor, made just before the visit of the envoys. He stormed at them:—

"I have never seen a document more crowded with infamous falsehoods and distortions—infamous falsehoods and distortions on a scale so huge I never imagined until today that any Government on this planet was capable of uttering them."

In the anguish of Pearl Harbor, Americans saw with awful clearness what the nation's course must be.

Then the road to China taken by the old hard-driven square-riggers and the churning paddle-wheelers became a sea-way and sky-way for the mightiest of armadas.

Back of the armada looms the Ship of State that was so uncertain in the last century but is definite now in its objective. It will make Asia a "co-prosperity sphere" indeed, but it will do so with the aid and in the interest of all mankind.

Yankee ships in China seas . . . Yankee clippers over the Pacific and in the skies of Asia. Patrols of peace, and reaffirmers and guardians of the Open Door and the unravished territory. That is the purpose—so may it be.

THE END

ACKNOWLEDGMENTS

THE AUTHOR HAS been especially guided by the excellent bibliographies found in Tyler Dennett's *Americans in Eastern Asia in the Nineteenth Century,* Carl C. Cutler's *Greyhounds of the Sea,* Eldon Griffin's *Clippers and Consuls* (1845-50), and the recent reading list prepared by James Wilbert Snyder, New York University—*Bibliography for the Early China Trade, 1783-1845.*

The author's own research has been mainly confined to hunting for human materials and lively incidents in old logs and memoirs; in exploring the story of the interchange of commerce between America and China; in depicting life in the ports of China and the East Indies; in pursuing investigations in the opium trade; in the paddle-wheelers plying the Pacific and the Yangtze; in the history of the colossal Russell and Company, the East India Company, and the competitive organizations; in Chinese rebellions, customs, and progress. As to facts about clipper ships and foreign relations, he has largely depended upon, and is grateful for, the work of the authorities here listed:

Ships and Shipping: Willis J. Abbot, Robert Greenhalgh Albion, Arthur H. Clark, Carl C. Cutler, Joseph Connolly, Hawthorne Daniel, C. M. Hopkins, Howe & Matthews, Winthrop L. Marvin, Samuel E. Morison, Ralph D. Paine, Charles Oscar Paullin, and the British sea historians E. K. Chatterton, W. S. Lindsay, and Basil Lubbock. The author is also indebted to many a forgotten ship or port scribe for anecdotes and incidents.

Diplomatic and Trade Relations with China: F. M. Bemis, Tyler Dennett, Eldon Griffin, Owen Lattimore, Shuhsi Hsu, of the University of Peking, and the State Department's *Peace and War, U. S. Foreign Policy, 1931-1941.* Valuable indeed in recreating the picture of life in Canton and in telling of relations of the American merchants to the Chinese mandarins and merchants was the out-of-print book *The Canton Chinese,* by the Baltimore traveler,

Osmond Tiffany Jr., and *Personal Reminiscences,* by Robert Bennet Forbes.

These collections of papers in the N. Y. Public Library have been consulted: the Hacket Papers (the Hacket brothers built the frigate *Alliance* and the Shaw ship *Massachusetts*), the Hudson-Rogers Collection, the Essex Institute Historical Collection, the William Edgar Papers, photostats, 1750-87, and the Mercantile Papers, New York Custom House Papers, 1792-75.

The publications of these societies and publishers have been helpful: American Geographical Society, American Council of the Institute of Pacific Relations, Maryland Historical Society, Historical Society of Pennsylvania, Nantucket *Inquirer* and *Register,* Marine Research Society and the Essex Institute of Salem, Pan-American Airways, India House, and the Metropolitan Museum of Art, New York.

To Ernestine Henderson, for editorial aid and wifely encouragement, the author's debt is great.

Persons to whom the author is grateful for cooperation in discovering sources are: John Sloane, of the house of W. & J. Sloane, importers; Herbert S. Wheeler, buyer-resident in China for the Sloane firm; Miss Clara Powell, librarian of the Chamber of Commerce of the State of New York; Henry Clapp Smith of Dutton's Inc.; Donald T. Clark, Asst. Librarian, Baker Library, Harvard University; Edward Dreyer, Editor, Hastings House; the late Carl Crow, and Lieutenant and Mrs. H. Woodward McDowell, Berkeley, Cal.

BIBLIOGRAPHY

THROUGH THESE BOOKS, the author has ranged. Many of them are of interest only to the specialist and are out-of-print. Many, on the other hand are of general interest and are obtainable in public libraries and bookshops.

AAF, *American Air Force Guide,* Pocket Book, 1945.

Abbot, Willis J., *American Merchant Ships and Sailors.*

Abeel, David, *Residence in China* (rare).

Abend, Hallet, *Treaty Ports.*

Albion, Robert Greenhalgh, *Square-Riggers on Schedule.*

Bancroft, Hubert Howe, *The New Pacific.*

Barrett, Walter Clerk (Joseph H. Scoville), *Old Merchants of New York* (4 volumes—rare).

Barrows, Edward M., *The Great Commodore.*

Beach, Harlan P., *Dawn on the Hills of T'ang.*

Bemis, S. F., *The American Secretaries of State and Their Diplomacy.*

—— *A Diplomatic History of the United States.*

Brady, Cyrus Townsend, *Under Tops'ls and Tents.*

Bridgman, Howard A., *New England in the Life of the World.*

Chapelle, H. J., *History of American Sailing Ships.*

Chatterton, E. K., *Old East Indiamen.*

—— *Steamships and Their History.*

Cary, Wm., *Wrecked in the Old Feejees* (log published by Nantucket *Inquirer* and *Mirror*).

Chen, Gideon, *Tsen Kuo-Fan, Pioneer Promoter of Steamships in China* (rare).

Ching, Henry, *The Oriental Policy of the United States.*

Clark, Arthur H., *The Clipper Ship Era.*

Clark, Grover, *Economic Rivalries in China.*

Cleveland, Captain Richard, *Narrative of Voyages and Travels* (rare).

Cleveland, H. W. S., *Voyage of a Merchant Navigator, Captain Richard Cleveland* (rare).

Connolly, James B., *Master Mariner, Life and Voyages of Amasa Delano*.

Cutler, Carl C., *Greyhounds of the Sea*.

Daniel, Hawthorne, *The Clipper Ship*.

Delano, Amasa, *Narrative of Voyages and Travels in the Northern and Southern Hemispheres* (rare).

Delano, Warren (see Robert Bennet Forbes, *Personal Reminiscences*, listed below, and also *Odyssey of an American Family* by Hall Roosevelt and Samuel D. McCoy).

Dennett, Tyler, *Americans in Eastern Asia in the Nineteenth Century*.

Dulles, Foster Rhea, *The Old China Trade*.

Felt, J. B., *Annals of Salem* (rare).

Forbes, Robert Bennet, *Personal Reminiscences* (rare).

Fortune, Robert, *A Journey in the Tea Countries of China* (rare).

Gilman, Wm., *A. Low and Brothers' Fleet of Clipper Ships*.

Goodrich, L. Carrington, *A Short History of the Chinese People*.

Gosse, Philip, *The History of Piracy*.

Gragg, W. F., *Cruise of the* Mississippi *to China and Japan* (rare).

Greenwood, Gordon, *Early American-Australian Relations*.

Griffin, Eldon, *Clippers and Consuls: American Consular and Commercial Relations with Eastern Asia, 1845-1850*.

Gutzlaff, Rev. Chas., *The Life of Taou Kwang* (rare).

Hall, Basil, *Narrative of a Voyage to the Great Loo-Choo Islands* (rare).

Henderson, Daniel, *From the Volga to the Yukon: the Russian March to Alaska and California*.

Henderson, Helen W., *A Loiterer in New England*.

Hill, Captain Samuel, *Journal of the* Ophelia *from Boston to Canton, 1815* (rare).

———— *Journal of the* Packet, *on a Similar Voyage 1817-22*.

Hilliard, Katharine, *My Mother's Journal* (rare).

Hone, Philip, *Diary, 1828-1851* (rare).

Hopkins, C. M., *The American Tea Clippers*.

Hornbeck, Stanley Kohl, *China and the American Foreign Policy*.

Hornell, James, *Edye's Account of Indian and Ceylon Vessels in 1833.*

Howe and Mathews, *American Clipper Ships* (rare).

Howay, F. W., *Early Days in the Maritime Fur Trade on the Northwest Coast* (Canada Historical Review).

Hsü Shuhsi, *China and Her Political Entity.*

Hughes, Ernest P., *Invasion of China by the Western World.*

Huntington, Ellsworth, *West of the Pacific.*

Hutchinson, Paul, *China's Real Revolution.*

Johnston, J. D., *China and Japan: Cruise of the U. S. S.* Powhatan, *1857-60* (rare).

Kimball, Gertrude Selwyn, *The East India Trade of Providence.*

King, T. Butler, *Steam Communications with China, May 4, 1848,* U. S. Naval Affairs Committee Report.

Laing, Alexander, *The Sea Witch.*

Latourette, Kenneth Scott, *Early Relations Between the United States and China.*

——— *The Development of China.*

Lattimore, Owen, *America and Asia.*

———*China Under the Republic.*

Lawton, Launcelot, *Empires of the Far East.*

Lindsay, W. S., *History of Merchant Shipping and Ancient Commerce* (4 volumes).

Low, Chas. R., *Maritime Discovery; Nautical Exploration from Earliest Times.*

Lubbock, Basil, *The China Clippers.*

Maclay, Edgar Stanton, and Philip, Barrett, *Life and Adventures of "Jack" Philip.*

McKay, Richard C., *South Street: a Maritime History of New York.*

———*Some Famous Sailing Ships and Their Builders.*

Mackie, John M., *Life of Tai Ping Wan, Chief of the Insurrection* (rare).

Marvin, Winthrop L., *The American Merchant Marine.*

Merwin, Samuel, *Drugging a Nation.*

Milbank, Jeremiah, *First Century of Flight in America.*

Millard, Thomas F., *The New Far East.*

Morrison, John D., *History of New York Shipyards.*

Morison, Samuel E., *The Maritime History of Massachusetts.*

Morse, H. B., *The Chronicles of the East India Company Trading to China.*

——— and MacNair, H. F., *Far Eastern International Relations.*

Mottram, R. H., *Trader's Dream; the Romance of the East India Company.*

Norman, Commander F. N., *"Martello Tower" in China* (rare).

Owens, Hamilton, *Baltimore on the Chesapeake.*

Paine, Ralph D., *The Old Merchant Marine.*

——— *The Ships and Sailors of Old Salem.*

Parkinson, C. N., *Trade in the Eastern Seas* (rare).

Paullin, Charles Oscar, *Commodore John Rodgers* (rare).

——— *Diplomatic Negotiations of American Naval Officers* (rare).

——— *Early Voyages of American Vessels in the Orient* (rare).

Perry, Mathew Galbraith, *Expedition of an American Squadron to the Chinese Seas and Japan.*

Phillips, James Duncan, *The Life and Times of Richard Derby.*

Putnam, G. P., *Salem's Vessels and Their Voyages.*

Roosevelt, Hall, and McCoy Samuel D., *Odyssey of an American Family.*

Samuels, Captain Samuel, *From the Forecastle to the Cabin.*

Schurz, Wm. Lytle, *The Manila Galleon.*

Seeger, Elizabeth, *The Pageant of Chinese History.*

Seward, W. F., *Travels Around the World,* edited by Olive Risley Seward.

Shaw, Major Samuel, *Journals* (rare).

Spears, John R., *The Story of the American Merchant Marine.*

——— *The History of Our Navy.*

Staunton, Sir George, *An Embassy* (rare).

Steiger, G. N., *A History of the Far East.*

Stevens, George B. and Marwick, Rev. W. Fisher, *The Life of Peter Parker, M. D.* (rare).

Taylor, Bayard, *A Visit to India, China and Japan* (rare).

Tiffany, Osmond, Jr., *The Canton Chinese* (rare).

Treves, Sir Frederick, *The Other Side of the Lantern.*

Trow, Chas. E., *The Old Shipmasters of Salem.*

Ts'ui, Chi, *Short History of Chinese Civilization.*

Weinberg, Albert J., *Manifest Destiny: A Study of National Expansionism in American History.*

White, John, *History of a Voyage to the China Sea* (rare).

Williams, E. W., *Life of S. Wells Williams.*

Williams, S. Wells, *The Middle Kingdom* (rare).

Wyer, H. S., *Spun-Yarn from Old Nantucket.*

INDEX

F

Flying Cloud, clipper, 179
Foochow, tea port, 163
Foote, Com. Andrew Hull, 167
Forbes, Edith, 155
Forbes, John M., 173
Forbes, Paul S., Russell partner, 155, 162
Forbes, Robert Bennet, Russell partner and manager, 147, 148-162, 192
Foreign relations: United States with China, 201-220; U.S. with Europe, 201-212, 226-237, 241-245; with Japan, 220-226
Formosa, Americans in, 215
Foster, John W., diplomat, 243-244
French relations with China, 214, 219-220, 244; naval commanders, 7
Furniture, Chinese, 33
Fur trade, ships in, 61-62, 66-73, 82

G

Germany: interests in China, 244-246
Girard, Stephen, merchant, 21
Glasspole, Richard, prisoner of pirates, 111-116
Grand Turk, ship, 25-32
Grant, President, in China, 243-244
Gray, Robert, skipper, 67-68
Gray, Wm., merchant, 33
Great Britain: administration in China, 16-18, 38, 79-82, 131-132, 137, 156-161, 201, 228-229; East India Co., 3, 16, 28, 38, 41, 45, 52-53, 61, 73, 79, 90, 107-110, 111-112, 131-132; early history in Far East, 53; missionaries, 88, 131; navigation laws, 175-181, opium trade and war, 137-146, 156-160; society in China, 17-18, 38, 92-93; in India, 17, 35-36; Tea Races, 175-181
Great Liu-Chiu Island (Okinawa), 223-226
Green, John, skipper, 3, 8, 15, 16, 33, 163

Green, Richard, British ship-owner, 176-177
Grew, Joseph C., ambassador, 257-258
Griffin, Eldon, historian, 217
Griffith, John Willis, ship architect, 169
Gros, Baron, 219-220
Guano trade, coolie ships in, 184-190
Gutzlaff, Chas., missionary, 207

H

Hacket Brothers, shipbuilders, 41-43
Hall, Captain Basil, author, 223-224
Hall, Samuel, shipbuilder, 155
Hall and Co., Aberdeen shipbuilders, 180
Harris, Townsend, commissioner, 162
Hart, Sir Robert, inspector-general, 229, 232, 234
Harvard University, 154, 202
Hathaway, Francis S., merchant, 216
Hawaii, 62
Hay, John, Secretary of State, 244-246
Hayes, Wm. H., skipper, 170
Heard, Augustine, 147, 154, 164
Hilliard, Katharine, ed., *My Mother's Journal,* 7, 94
Hone, John and Sons, brokers, 150
Hong Kong, 152-153, 164, 201, 254
Hong merchants at Canton (Cohong), 13-15, 18, 31, 139-140, 157-158, 173-174
Hope, Admiral Sir James, 202
Hope, fur ship, 67-68
Houqua, dean of hong merchants, 173-174
Houqua, ship, 173
Howland and Aspinwall, shipowners, 170
Hull, Cordell, Secretary of State, 257
Hurley, Patrick, commissioner, 204

Morris, Robert, financier, 3-4, 19-21, 23, 40
Morrison, missionary ship, 132-133
Morrison, Robert, missionary, 88, 130-133
Muriaviov, Governor-General of Siberia, 212
Musiak, Capt. E. C., air pilot, 253
Mutineers: of the *Bounty,* 103-105; aboard Cleveland ship, 70-72

N

Nanking, port, 201, 210
Nantucket whalers, 102-105
Navy, officers and ships, see under United States
Netherlands East Indies, 243, 256
New Bedford whalers, 102-105
Newburyport, 201
New England ports, 25-27, 31, 105-106, 141, 163, 192, 201
Newspapers, etc., 202, 216, 234, 249
New York, port, 4-5, 23-24, 29, 58, 61, 64-68, 69, 81, 140, 169-176
North American Aviation Co., 252
Nye, Gideon, Jr., merchant and consul, 215-218

O

Olyphant, David W. C., merchant, 130-133
Open Door policy, 201-204, 211-212, 215-218, 219-220, 231-242, 244-246, 256-259
Opium ships: American, 11, 138, 156, 160, 163, 165-167, 204; British, 137, 156, 160, 163, 165-167
Opium trade: Americans in, 24, 111, 138, 146, 154-162, 165, 167, 204; Britons in, 137-140, 157-161, 165, 167; India planters in, 155; smugglers, 195; U.S. Naval patrol, 165-167, 204; war over opium, 156-163
Oriental, champion tea clipper, 176, 180

P

Pacific Mail Steamship Co., 189, 193-195
Pacific Northwest fur trade, 61-62, 66-73, 82
Pacific Ocean, island bases, 224-225
Palmer, Nathaniel, B., skipper, 173-175; Theodore, 176
Pan-American Airways in China, 252-256
Parker, Comdr. Foxhall H., U.S.N., 167, 213
Parker, Daniel, N.Y. merchant, 3
Parker, Dr. Peter, missionary and diplomat, 100-101, 133-136, 159-162, 195, 213
Peabody, Joseph, Salem merchant, 33, 105
Peale, Jonathan, Salem merchant, 53-54
Peking, description of, 227-228; embassies to, 39, 79, 211, 221-229; legations at, 227-228
Pelew Islands, 132
Pepper trade, 34, 53, 120
Perkins and Co., 148
Perry, Comdr. Matthew Calbraith, 205, 220-226; Oliver Hazard, son, 222
Perth Amboy, N.J., tea port, 65
Peru, Chincha Islands, 187
Philadelphia in China trade, 20, 21
Philippine Islands, 56, 245, 251
Philip, Capt. John, U.S.N., 127, 167, 196-198
Pickman, Benjamin, Salem merchant, 33
Pierce, President Franklin, 202, 215
Pirates: American, 5-6; Chinese, 112-115, 117-118, 126; Mistress Ching, pirate queen, 112-115, 117-118; Glasspole's captivity, 112-116; Malay pirates, 6, 118-127
Pitcairn Island, visit to, 103-105
Poetry, 88-89
Polk, President James K., 214
Pottinger, Sir Henry, 165
Porcelain, 33

Sooloo Islands, 74
Speer, Wm., D.D., missionary, 190
Spice trade, 53
Square-riggers, described by Bill Adams, 182-184
Standard Oil Co. ships, 182
Staunton, Sir George, 39, 79
Steamships in China trade, 190-198; built by Chinese, 191-192
Stewart, Wm., skipper, 24
Stimson, Henry, Secretary of War, 257
Sweet, Capt. Harold, air pilot, 254

T

Taiping Rebellion, Americans in, 205-211
Taylor, Chaplain Fitch W., U.S.N., 94-96, 125, 129
Tea races to London, 176-181
Tea trade, 3, 8, 13, 24, 30, 31, 64-66, 82, 163, 176-181
Tiffany, Osmond, Jr., traveler, 9, 155
Treaties with China, 201, 203-204, 214, 234-235
Treaty ports, 201-202, 231, 245
Turkey, Smynna, opium shipments from, 138-139
Typhoons, ships in, 46-49

U

United Aircraft Corp., 252
United States: air force in China, 256, 259; commissioners to China, 99, 118, 201-220; consuls, 158, 163, 187, 197-198; coolie trade, 188-190; expansion in Far East, 205, 220-226, 245; Marines in Korea, 167-168; naval commanders & ships, 107-111, 118, 121, 127, 165-167, 194, 201-203, 211-212, 214-215, 220-226, 247; naval policy & expeditions, 107-111, 165-168, 196-198, 213-215, 218, 220-226, 256; opium patrol, 162, 165; State Dept. policy with

China, 108, 162, 201, 211-220, 226-242, 256-259; treaties with China, 201, 203-204, 214, 234-235; policy toward other powers, 201-220, 256-259; policy towards Japan, 221-226, 256-259
University of Harvard, 154, 202
University of Pennsylvania, 219

V

Valignani, Catholic missionary, 129

W

Ward, General Frederick Townsend, 205, 228-229
Wars: China with Great Britain, 156-163; with Japan, 252, 256-259; Japan with United States, 252, 256-259
Washington, President George, 241
Waterman, Robert, skipper, 101, 170
Webster, Daniel, Secretary of State, 202, 213; and Fletcher, 166
Webster, Harriet, bride of Peter Parker, 100-101
Wei-Sang, Chinese sage, 228, 231, 239-241
West, Nathaniel, skipper, 30
Wetmore Co., merchants, 147, 154, 162
Whalers, voyages of, 82, 102-105; wives of whalemen, 102
Whampoa, Canton anchorage, 10, 12, 72, 152, 217
Wheeler, H. S., importer, 182
Whetten, John, skipper, 24, 62
White, Lieut. John, U.S.N., 86, 118-120
Wilkins, Captain, murder of, 123-126
Williams, S. Wells, missionary and author, 133, 195
Women in the Orient: American, 7, 87-102, 188; British, 95-99; Chinese, 39, 73, 97; Indo-China, 86-87; Malay, 74-79; Netherland

East Indies, 36, 39, 50; wives of
missionaries, 95-96, 100-101
Wyman, Captain T. W., U.S.N.,
124-125

X

Xavier, Francis, Catholic missionary, 128-129

Y

Yale: Chaplain Fitch W. Taylor,
U.S.N., graduate, 129; first Chinese graduate, 192
Yangtse River: Americans on, 165,
196-198, 241; description of, 196;
U.S. naval vessels on, 211; U.S.
steamships on, 190-198